Glimpses of Ancient Indian Poetics

(from Bharata to Jagannātha)

Shri Garib Dass Oriental Series No : 166

Glimpses of Ancient Indian Poetics

(from Bharata to Jagannātha)

Edited by

SUDHAKAR PANDEY
Head
Department of English,
University of Poona

V. N. JHA
Director
Centre of Advanced Study in Sanskrit
University of Poona

Sri Satguru Publications
A division of
Indian Books Centre
Delhi-India

Published by:
SRI SATGURU PUBLICATIONS
Indological & Oriental publishers,
A division of:
Indian Books Centre
40/5, Shakti Nagar,
Delhi-110007
INDIA

First Edition : Delhi, 1993

ISBN 81-7030-360-5

Typeset by:
ABC *for* DTP
6, Rajdhani Enclave, Delhi-34

Printed at:
D.K. Fine Art Press, Delhi

PRINTED IN INDIA

इदमन्धं तमःकृष्णं जायेत भुवनत्रयम् ।
यदि शब्दाह्वयं ज्योतिरासंसारं न दीप्यते ।।

All the three worlds (the Heaven, the Earth, and the Nether World) would have turned into a black dense darkness, had the lamp of language not illumined the entire world!

Kāvyādarsá of Daṇḍin
1.1.

Contents

Preface

The present Volume contains 22 papers on various aspects of Indian Poetics written by prominent specialists in the field. These papers were presented and discussed in the National Seminar on Indian Poetics organized by the Department of English, University of Poona, during 6-8 March, 1986. Of these 22 research articles, some have adopted interdisciplinary approach and have tried to compare and contrast some of the ancient Indian concepts of Poetics with those of the western ones, while some other articles aim at presenting an authentic picture of some of the aspects of *Alaṅkāraśāstra* While some authors have tried to highlight the main issues, others have tried to suggest their relevance to modern literary criticism and some have laid down the actual underlying philosophical frame-work on which the entire edifice of Indian poetics is built. On the one hand there are articles on some of the components such as *guṇa, doṣa,* and *alaṅkāra,* on the other there are papers on theories of poetic communication. While some articles deal with peculiar functions of poetic language like *lakṣaṇā* and *Vyañjana,* others deal with the process of aesthetic experience of Beauty. The development of Indian poetics has made use of the framework of Indian Philosophy and this too has been presented in one article. That an art-experience is neither a perception of actual silver nor an illusion like the perception of silver in a conch-shell, rather it is an experience of the painting of actual silver has also been discussed in one article.

Thus, the Volume contains a variety of issues which, we are sure, will definitely delight the readers.

The very aim of the Seminar was to present glimpses of Indian Poetics in order to create a curiosity in the minds of scholars and students of language and literature who did not have direct access to reading Indian Poetics in original, i.e. in Sanskrit.

We are confident that the present Volume has, at least, partially fulfilled that aim.

We are thankful to the authors of these articles, who include some of the very senior authorities in the field like Prof. Patwardhan, Prof. Krishnamoorthy, Prof. Patankar and others. We are thankful to Dr. Ujjwala Panse, Dr. Nirmala Kulkarni, Dr. Subhash Chandra Dash, Mr. Kashinath Hota and Dr. Sanjay Deodikar for helping us in correcting the proofs. We are also thankful to the Indian Books Centre for having come forward to publish this Volume.

SUDHAKAR PANDEY
V.N. JHA

Impact of Indian Philosophy on Indian Poetics

V.N. Jha

No activity in a Society can remain unaffected by the Philosophy of that Society, be it a literary, or social or cultural or scientific activity. The entire thinking process gets affected or modelled by the philosophy that the society cherishes at a particular time. How can then the Indian Poeticians remain unaffected by Indian Philosopshy? Indeed, they have not remained so. Even a cursory look at the texts of Indian Poetics will bear testimony to this observation. The present paper is an attempt to make this picture clear.

Indian Philosophy

Broadly, Indian Philosophy can be put into three groups: (1) Realistic Philosophy (2) Idealistic Philosophy and (3) Materialistic Philosophy.

Under category (1) comes the Philosophy of the Indian Logicians (Naiyāyikas) and the Indian Semanticists (Mīmāṁsakas) and the Sāṁkhya-Philosophers to some extent; under category (2) can be included Vedānta and Buddhist Philosophy and under (3) will come the later Philosophy of Cārvaka.

The Realistic Philosophy has a fundamental assumption that the world in which we live and with which we consistently behave throughout our life is real; it is knowable and namable. This System of Indian Philosophy further believes that it is through the analysis of our experience that we can establish the reality of this Universe. Thus, an experience is analysable according to them. If so, then how can an art-experience be not analysable? This assumption presupposes a firm belief in cause-and effect relationship.

As against this the Idealistic System of Indian Philosophy holds that there is a limitation to cause-and-effect relationship. According to this system, it is not true that all experience can be analysed. There are some experiences which defy the norm of analysability. For instance, the experience of the Supreme Self. Here Analysis can go to a certain extent; thereafter it is all beyond explanation and, therefore, mystic.

The third category of Indian Philosophy refuses to accept anything which is physically not verifiable. Though this system does not entertain mysticism, it also fails to logically appreciate something which is beyond the range of direct verification. This is the reason that this system could not appeal even to the Realists.

Thus, in brief we can say that there are two main trends of Indian Philosophy: (1) One believes that an experience can be logically analysed, whereas (2) the other believes that all experiences cannot be analysed logically, i.e. some experiences are mystic in character.

The orgin of the second trend lies in the Vedic and Upanisadic Literature where the description of the experience of Self has assumed a mystic form. Although both the trends agree on the point that the Self or Soul is not the body, not the sense organ, not the mind, they vary in holding whether Soul is one or many. Both the trends accept an experience called super-normal (*alaukika*) experience of a *yogin*. However, the realists think the experience of a *yogin* is also analysable. But the idealists believe it is not so.

Indian Poetics

If one looks at the treatments of the Indian Poeticians from Bhāmaha upto Jagannātha, one will feel like drawing the following picture:

Here, too, there seem to be two trends: while (1) one looks at the entire art-experience as inexplicable or explicable to a certain extent and (2) the other aims, at least, at giving a rational account of that experience.

One should note that even Poeticians belonging to the mystic trend feel that they should try to bring rationale as far as possible. Thus, we find the acceptance of a third relationship between an expression and the suggested sense called *vyañjanā*. Once it is realised that a sentence can give rise to its understanding, only two relations such as primary relation (*abhidhā*) and secondary relation (*lakṣaṇā*) were accepted. But when it is realised that the speaker has something totally different to convey through that expression then a third relation is resorted to. Thus, there are two aims in this approach: (1) they want to establish that what is understood as suggested by the speaker is conveyed by the language he use and (2) they want to show that what the connoisseur understands from the speakers's expression is a mystic art experience and it should be left to the connoisseur unanalysed.

For bringing the smell of rationality, the Dhvani theorists have taken resort to Prabhākara's theory of *dīrgha-dīrghatara-iṣu-vyāpāra*which means that the function of an arrow terminates only after hitting the goal. If the goal is near, the arrow will take a shorter journey, but if it is far it will take a longer journey. Similarly, the function of language used by a speaker will terminate only after it has conveyed what is intended to be conveyed by the speaker; if the intended meaning does not involve many steps or complexity it will terminate there only, but if it involves many more steps the function of the sentence will terminate only after that intended sense is understood by the experiencer.

For achieving the second aim, the *Dhvani*-theorists have been helped by the Advaitins and the Buddhists. Both these systems believe that logic has limitation whereas the experience of the Self defies all logic. Therefore, the metaphor of body to the literary art (*Kāvyaśarīra*), of soul to the essence of Poetry (*Kāvyasya ātman*), of ornaments to the figures of speech (*alaṅkāra*) and so on all speak of the conscious extension of the basics of Indian Philosophy to Indian Poetics. As the experience of one's self is a mystic experience so is the art-experience. This is the reason that art-experience is compared with the experience of the Brahman (*brahmāsvādasahodara*).

As against this, the *Anumiti*-school of Indian Poetics aims at a claim that art-experience also is analysable. It further aims at showing that the function of language has its limitation; it conveys the intended meaning through its own function, but the suggested sense is experienced through the process of inference. Thus, the function of language terminates after the intended meaning is understood through its two relationships, primary and secondary, and thereafter it is the field of the operation of other means of knowing, i.e. inference. Thus, the idea of *dīrgha-dīrghatara-iṣu-vyāpāra* is not acceptable to these theorists, because once that is accepted the weaving of mystic net cannot be stopped. This shows the limitation of a language. This also shows that the function of language is well-defined and a human being takes resort to various other means of knowing in order to arrive at an experience. After the function of a language terminates, the function of other means of knowing starts and finally the connoisseur gets the experience. Therefore, there is no point in leaving everything to one means of knowing namely, language, and when it is found that it falls short in generating the intended experience mysticism should not be taken resort to. This is how I look at the *Anumiti-vādins*. Mahimabhaṭṭa's *Vyaktiviveka* can be viewed from this angle.

Conclusion

Indian Poetics has developed in a society which cherished definite and distinct views about an experience. Therefore, it is necessary to develop a proper perspective to understand Indian Poetics. As it is pointed above, the parallelism is so distinct and evident that one cannot afford to neglect this aspect of study.

Indian Poetics and Literary Stylistics: Bharata's Concept of *Lakṣaṇa*

K. Krishnamoorthy

HITOPADESŚA

Sometimes it looks as if Indian poetics has suffered more at the hands of scholar-specialists of the present century than by the traditionist commentators in Sanskrit of the past who did not lay any claims to the modern historico-critical perspective. Unlike Aristotle who has been much studied in the West, Bharata suffered undeserved neglect at the hands of Sanskrit theoreticians as well as modern Indologists, because the attention of one and all is turned to Bharata's central idea of *rasa* to the utter neglect of his over-all vision of the entire gamut of poetry, drama, music and dance as embodied in the almost unknown key-concept of *Lakṣaṇa* which underlies all his other concepts and which constitutes his contribution to aesthetics of all the fine arts as providing a coherent analysis of the very body of art which comes to enshrine *rasa* eventually, only on condition that the body is adequate according to aesthetic norms. The little literature we have on the subject is by the late V. Raghavan who is all the time riddled with text-critical problems and content with accumulating in his compilation all minutiae, without even once turning his eye towards their significance. I believe that, properly understood, it will provide the lost master-key which opens all the locked mansions of *alaṅkāra, guṇa, rīti, vṛtti, chandas, dhvani* and *vakrokti* and *aucitya* which have all been much studied as so many isolated concepts, formulated or developed at different stages in the progressive evolution of Indian poetics. It is my endeavour to indicate, very broadly though, how underneath the surface of thirtysix *lakṣaṇas* defined analytically by Bharata in his *Nāṭyaśāstra* (Ch. XVI), and exposed clearly by that master-aesthetician Abhinavagupta in his *Abhinavabhāratī,* we might find the very roots of Indian aesthetic theorising, which was tacitly accepted by all later writers on the subject, even in the midst of all their multifaceted speculations.

More importantly, we come to realise that the dawn of refined or polished Sanskrit literature is pre-Bharatan, i.e. earlier than 200 A.D. if not 500 B.C. as Dr. Manmohan Ghosh would have it. Since I want to avoid all clash with "chronology specialists who turn all textual evidence of antiquity into controversial issues of chronology or spurious interpolation bringing in authorship problems, I confine myself in this paper to literary illustrations actually cited by Bharata in his own text. It will open our eyes to the fact that the poetic diction and so-called cliche or hackneyed similes and metaphors of Sanskrit verse as well as verbal acrostics like *yamakas* or iterative verbal tricks were all there in full form even before Bharata. It was taken up as a challenging task-this rationale of all creative arts both in form and content. The Indian mind was imbued with the Upaniṣadic distinction between the physical body and the inner spirit activating the body. The disengage meant of the essence from the art medium presented an organic unity of form and meaning in an intellectual way. Bharata adopted the methodology of analysis and simple enumeration. But even when describing the individual parts, he never loses sight of the holistic nature of art. Actually, it is the perfection of parts on the one hand and their appropriate harmony with one another that result in the beauty of the whole. Stylistics is thus the very foundation on which structures are firmly based.

In a short paper, only broad hints can be thrown how *Lakṣaṇa* is all-embracing, and can cover every aspect of stylistics. As in Greek, in Sanskrit also, the word 'kavi' for poet etymologically means a maker; 'poetry is what the poet makes' ('*kaveh karma kāvyam*'); the poetic art is an activity of the poet or '*kavivyāpārā*. Again, this activity has a secular as well as a religious or spiritual dimension. This open admission is of supreme and fundamental importance to the right interpretation of Bharata. All arts are at least in part divinely inspired; the creative activity is made possible by the grace of God. *Kāvya,*

Nāṭya, Śilpa, Citra, etc. as well as Music have a presiding goddess; and the creative act is semi-sacred. It is not wholly profane. This traditional and cardinal faith is a hallmark of Indian culture and it is shared by all our great writers in the past like Kālidāsa and Bhavabhūti among creative authors, and Mammaṭa, Viśvanātha and Jagannātha among literary theoreticians and critics, not to speak of even philosophers like Bhartṛhari and Śaṅkara. Only India believed that literature is efficacious in "*śivetara-kṣati*" or countering inauspiciousness. All poets followed the convention of invocation to a deity at the beginning of their works. Dance-drama was deemed a *yajva* or sacrificial ritual feasting the ears and eyes of gods. The bulk of the opening chapters of Bharata is devoted to bring home this point. Perfectionism as in ceremonial is demanded of the poet in such a set-up; and he has to master perforce all the paraphernalia of his sacred calling. In his own life he must be pure and ethical and cultivate a loving intimacy with all, animate or inanimate. To be blessed with poetic vision, he should practice yogic meditation; and he must practice assiduously the rules of his art, under the guidance of masters. It is thus that his imagination (*pratibhā*) has to be awakened, when he can have a vivid perception inwardly of events, characters and situations transcending time and space. All the myths and legends of the land will become real to his inward eye. His business thereafter is only of seizing and using the linguistic medium which presents itself along with the content to be communicated. If Kālidāsa was invoking the intimately interfused Śiva and Pārvatī for their grace, it was because of the perfectly matched *Vāk* and *Artha* he was seeking to attain in his entire poem. In this he was as much in the company of Bharata as of the *Yajurveda* which speaks of the Cosmic form of the Supreme Lord Virūpākṣa as 'Nīla-lohita' or 'Kṛṣṇa-piṅgala:-

ṛtaṁ satyaṁ paraṁ brahma puruṣaṁ kṛṣṇa-pingalaṁ|
ūrdhvaretaṁ virūpākṣaṁ viśvarūpāya vai namaḥ||

In the absence of this cultural background, the Indian literary concepts lose their real connotation. Formal structuring of a theme or plot involves a conception of essential *sandhis* or parts; similarly their embodiment in language also is conceived in terms of parts, without forgetting their intimate interrelation all the time. They are not only typical but also archetypal so to say. If a poet wants to depict the gay mood and portray what his sweetheart means to him at a moment when the requisite excitants in nature and character have all combined to induce the mood in him, what is the verbal equivalent he would choose to denote the wife? We all know how Kālidāsa, in his *Meghadūta* has put the words *Tanvī* and *śyāmā* in the Yakṣa's description of the perfect beauty of the Yakṣī. None can suspect any conformity to an aesthetic norm in the use of diction in this. Sanskrit is unique in providing hundreds of synonyms, to be coined by the poet as he pleases, if it can reflect the right shade or nuance of feeling to be communicated by him. But Bharata's first instance of Lakṣaṇa is '*(tanvī) śyāmā viśālakṣī* and the second '*matta-mātaṅga-gāminī* according to tradition noted by Abhinavagupta. As if illustrating the hidden simile, Bhāmaha, our first writer on poetics, gives the following: (1) *tanvī śyāmā latā yathā* and (2) *kamalapatrākṣī* and *śaśāṅka-vadanā*(Kāvyālaṅkāra, II 31-32). Bharata's present text itself has the example '*tulyam te śaśinā vaktram*' (XVI. 43), '*viśālākṣīm*' (XVI. 47) and '*mattamātaṅgagamanā* (XVI. 51) under the *alaṅkāra* of simile (*upamā*). These examples are not chosen at random; nor are they arbitrary. The poet's idea will have automatically devised its adequate symbol in a word suggestive of his loving reminiscence of the charms of his beloved. *Tanvī*-suggests her frail build of personality, at once soft and sweet in the memory of the speaker. The poet has dexteroulsy shown his aesthetic sensibility in readily using this word rather than a hundred others he might have utilized to convey the same lexical meaning. Like T.S. Eliot's "objective correlative", it reveals itself when the *kavivyāpāra* is functioning and becomes a primary Lakṣaṇa or characteristic of the poetic mode. Bharata gives it the name *Vibhūṣaṇa* 'natural excellence' to distinguish it from *alaṅkāra* or adornment with a little more conscious design. The damsel is delighting to the eye in all youthful glow is connoted by the two-syllabled word *śyāmā*, while *tanvī* symbolises the implicit simile, viz., *latā yathā* as spelt out by Bhāmaha. Similarly, *viśālakṣī* describes her enchanting looks without need of explicit imagery. However, the image may intrude into the texture of the word itself as we see in *mattamātaṅgagāminī*, where the simile or metaphor has become part and parcel of the word itself, without the need of an additional word even. *Vibhūṣaṇa-lakṣaṇa* thus, is the very concretisation of the artistic sentiment or *rasa* in the very first flash of the creative mind. *Alaṅkāras* like *upamā* and *rūpaka*—which, by the way, are prototypes for all variations of figures of speech called by different names in later texts—are in a way afterthoughts or the poet's explication, as it were, of his hidden intent.

Conscious artistry, however admired by the scholarly few, is less aesthetic according to Bharata and not more. Even if laboured, imagery should seem to be effortless and inspired as Ānandavardhana explicates. Yamaka or verbal chime is illustrated by the following verse in Bharata:

dinakṣayāt-saṁhṛta-raśmi-maṇḍalaṁ
divīva lagnaṁ tapanīyamaṇḍalam/
vibhāti tāmram divi sūryamaṇḍalaṁ
yathā taruṇyāh stangbhāramaṇḍalam//(XVI. 64).

'dyauh' or 'heaven' in Sanskrit is a word in the feminine gender. The setting sun is no doubt a hackneyed subject. But the sun's orb emitting reddish glow of twilight appears to the inner eye of the poet as a beautiful damsel's single breast smeared in red saffron paste. The beauty he envisions is heaven itself appearing in his imagination as a youthful damsel. All this is our prose commentary. But the poet has just exploited to the full the mere gender of the word *dyauh*; and just dropped a hint of it in the simile of the last line which is a prose explanation as it were of what was originally a suggestive flash. The word-unit of 'maṇḍalam' is chiming like a bell at the end of each of the four lines in the stanza; but its beauty lies in its being almost unnoticeable. By no means does it appear contrived.

One more example from Bharata, to illustrate *rūpaka* or metaphor:

padmānanāstāh kumudaprabhāsah
vikośanīlotpala-cāru-netrāh/
vāpīstriyo haṁsakulaih svanadbhih
virejuranyonyamihālapantyah//(XVI. 58).

The poet is describing lakes in the valley as engaged in sweet or genial conversation with each other. Lotuses are their faces. Dark lilies with radiant lustre constitute their bright eyes. The lakes are the lovely women. The cackling swans represent their sweet voice as well as words. The poet has envisioned the lovely lakes as women talking to one another, and the rounded metaphor is only a later working out of his first inspired moment.

In all these apparently trite and commonplace specimens, Bharata shows us an awareness of the creative process whose first moment is called a *lakṣaṇa*, while the metaphor or simile is regarded as a super-added adornment, which the poem could well do even without.

How even this single example of the very first *Lakṣaṇa* can lead to later theories like Ānandavardhana's *dhvani* which emphasizes the *rasavivakṣā-prādhānya* or intent towards the primacy of *rasa* through the suggestive mode as the *sine qua non* of poetry; and Kuntaka's *vakrokti* which pinpoints the 'indirect mode' as the whole and sole criterion for deciding a poem's authenticity, I need not labour here. How the poet's contrived effects in the second moment of his creative work come to form *alaṅkāras*, and how he should strive to make them also as unlaboured and seemingly spontaneous as possible is also indicated. That is why there is no theoretician in Sanskrit who gives the pride of place to artificial figures of speech. Even the so-called *alaṅkāra* theorists in the baseless categorization of modern specialists are seen virtually subordinating its status to either *guṇa* or *rīti* or *vṛtti* in their actual treatment, because they too knew as well as the others, that structural wholeness is more valuable than textual shades of literary beauty. And like Daṇḍin and Vāmana, they may call the entire paraphernalia of poetry as 'alaṅkāra' because, in Sanskrit, the word will then have the most comprehensive significance of 'beauty' and this should not be misinterpreted in the narrow sense of figures of speech. As Bharata said, the absence of negative flaws in poetry should precede if its positive excellences in terms of diction or style can really shine. It is only in Indian poetics that all categories of literary criticism—whether they be *alaṅkāra* or *guṇa* or *doṣa*—all are classified under the dual headings of *śabda* and *artha*. Daṇḍin conceived of *rasa* too in terms of *vasturasa* and *vāgrasa*. The whole *śāstra* or discipline came to be designated "*sāhitya*". It would indeed be most unfair to the concensus of all the Indian theoreticians to pigeonhole them in neat compartments as promulgators of independent theories, as it is being done today in the name of advanced research. My paper would have served its purpose if it makes some at least to give a new look to our enduring heritage, and the essence of which we are yet to assimilate. A commentary in each one of the other thirtyfive *lakṣaṇas*is not possible in the limits of a short paper like this. But I might just indicate that all of them are not exclusive to poetic stylistics as it is often misinterpreted. All the fine arts come under their purview; and only a few select ones have bearings on poetry and drama. But rightly understood, they might yet supply the basic tools for Indian literary criticism. I must be excused for venturing upon what is generally taboo for specialized scholarship. Insightful probing into all the *lakṣaṇas* will bring us to the most revolutionary but inevitable conclusion which Abhinavagupta found, viz.,

"*bandho, gumpho, bhaṇitih, vakroktih, kavivyāpāra iti paryāyāh.*" That realisation will lead us to a proper understanding of the essential unity in the theorisings of even opposed thinkers like Bhaṭṭa Nāyaka, Mahimabhaṭṭa and Ānandavardhana as well as Kuntaka. But as Ānandavardhana put it, there is one important condition:

Yatnatah pratyabhijṇeyau tau śabdārthau mahākaveh An all-out effort must be made to catch the essence behind the word and meaning of one who is really a masterpoet. And it is possible only if we combine a healthy measure of taste or poetic sensibility with the dry bones of scholarship. Instead of strident fireworks, we have to become submissive enough to surrender ourselves to Sarasvatī so that we might be able to catch

all the charm of all the Muses

often flowering in a lonely word.

In this respect, the Sanskrit language defies comparison with others.

---

*Those interested in more particular may read my recent book "Indian Literary Theories - a reappraisal", published by Meharchand Lachhmandas, New Delhi-2.

Some Reflections on the *Rasa* Theory

R.B. Patankar

In my paper entitled 'Is the *Rasa* theory relevant today? (*Philosophy-East and West*, Hawai, 1980). I had suggested that we must first ascertain whether the *Rasa* theory figures at all in the spontaneous responses of our contemporaries to literary works, modern or ancient. As no individual response, however spontaneous it may appear to be, can come into existence except as mediated by the conceptual structure that the community has evolved, the above question becomes a question about the range of responses that the social conceptual framework enables us to make. Do we still retain, as a community, any part of the conceptual structures evolved in ancient India?

We must be cautious here, because we are likely to be misled by two facts: (A) words which sanskritists used are not being used today; but it is likely that the corresponding concepts are still being used, although we are not explicitly conscious of this fact; (B) words which the ancients used continue to be used; but they have lost their original meanings. They are being used so loosely that they are doing positive harm to the present-day criticism. It may also turn out that Sanskritists themselves cannot escape their share of blame for the present state of affairs because of their failure to take certain precautions which they should have taken and also for not emphasizing certain points which they ought to have emphasized.

(A) In the practical criticism in our Language area, i.e. Marathi, words like *Vibhāva, Anubhāva, Sthāyibhāva, Sañcāribhāva* are hardly used today. It might appear that we do not see and evaluate modern literary works from within the Sanskritists' framework; we rather see and evaluate even *Śakuntala* and *Rāmāyaṇa* from within the framework we have imported from the 18th and 19th century Britain.

But from this does it follow that along with these Sanskrit terms, the corresponding concepts have also disappeared from our critical framework? If we scrutinize the framework carefully we shall find that some of these concepts *are* present today. Consider the terms *Vibhāva* (Determinants) and *Anubhāva* (Consequents), We are told that these correspond to the terms Cause and Effect. The latter two are used when we are talking about actual existents; the former two are reserved for the world of Drama or Literature.

What could be the reason for coining/reserving those terms for the world of Drama alone? To see a performance on the stage is, it can be legitimately claimed, a special variety of seeing; which is different from our ordinary seeing, viz. our seeing physical objects around us. No higher claim need be implied, although such claims have been made placing the *rasa* experience almost on par with the Brahman experience. This tendency can be and should be checked by pointing out that if the *Rasa* experience is different from ordinary experiences in some ways, so are the experiences of 'seeing a drama' and 'seeing one's face in a mirror', different from ordinary experience of seeing. And if we do not call the latter two experiences *Brahmāsvādasahodara* experiences, we should think twice before we put forward such a claim on behalf of the *Rasa* experience.

There is, it is often said, a strong reason for making this claim; it consists in the alleged fact that the *Rasa* experience like the Brahman experience is necessarily pleasurable. First of all, let us note that all schools of thought in India have not accepted that the supreme experience is pleasurable in character. I wonder whether the Buddhists would accept this position: perhaps they would regard the experience which has a neutral affective tone as the supreme experience, Secondly, it may be noted, that all exponents of the *Rasa* theory do not claim that it is pleasurable. Ramachandra and Gunachandra can be cited as exponents of the view that all *Rasas* are not pleasurable. And, as we shall see, in some detail in what follows, there is a point in what they say.

The claim to the necessary pleasureableness of the *Rasas* is chiefly based on two grounds;

(a) the psychological assumption that whatever a man does he does for pleasure alone, (b) *Sādhāraṇikaraṇa* transforms an emotional experience, whether pleasurable or otherwise in its original state, into a necessarily pleasureable experience.

It is not accepted by modern thinkers that whatever a man does, he does for pleasure alone, nor that pleasure is the sole object of all human desires. For example, G.E. Moore, the famous cambridge philosopher, has very convincingly shown in his refutation of Hedonism, that the objects of our desires are specific things like food, a glass of water, a book, and not a mental state called pleasure. Secondly, pleasure does not necessarily attend upon the satisfaction of all our desires. At a specific time in the day we desire to have lunch; but every time we have lunch we do not become conscious of the mental state of pleasure; and an unfelt pleasure is a logical impossibility. Further, we know that there are many actions which we do out of a sense of duty or decorum, or out of habit. The question of pleasure does not arise in these cases.

In view of these objections, the above claim can be stated in the following modified form. There are at least some things which we do only for pleasure, e.g. things which have not been enjoined upon us as moral or religions duties or legal obligations. If this is granted, and there is no reason why it should not be granted, a further claim may be made, viz. the act of reading Literature (or seeing a play) belongs to this very category.

This makes it necessary to analyse the concept of pleasure. We may accept the analysis that Kant has given, to start with, while distinguishing among different varieties of pleasure. Kant says, 'this pleasure of the beautiful is also in no way practical, neither resembling that from the pathological ground of agreeableness nor that from the intellectual ground of the represented good. But still it involves an inherent causality, that, namely, of *preserving a continuance*of the state of the representation itself and the active engagement of the cognitive powers without ulterior aim, we *dwell* on the contemplation of the beautiful because this contemplation strengthens and reproduces itself.

The case is analogous (but analogous only) to the way we linger on a charm in the representation of an object which keeps arresting the attention, the mind all the while remaining pussive'. (*Critique of Aesthetic Judgement*, tr. J.C. Mercolith, rp. 1964, p. 64)

If we take pleasure to be a self-presenting, self-reproducing experience, we shall realize that this is of different types, the difference depending on the nature of that which induces it. Kant himself has identified the following types,

(a) pleasure of the beautiful (depending upon the *free* play of cognitive faculties and not tied to the actual existence of the beautiful object),

(b) pleasure of the agreeable (which depends upon the actual existence of the agreeable, but which does not involve the higher faculties of the mind),

(c) pleasure of the good (which depends upon the actual existence of the relevant object and which involves the use of concepts). Along with the pleasure of the good we should also include the practical pleasure of satisfaction of desires. To quote Kant: 'The consciousness of mere formal finality in the play of the cognitive faculties of the subject attending a representation whereby an object is given, is the pleasure itself, because it involves the determining ground of the subject's activity in respect of the quickening of its cognitive powers, and thus an internal causality (which is final) in respect of cognition generally, but without being limited to a definite cognition, and consequently a mere form of the subjective finality of a representation in an aesthetic judgement. This pleasure is also in no way practical, neither resembling that from the pathological ground of agreeableness nor that from the intellectual ground of the represented.' (Ibid, p. 64)

Our next step will be to identify the paradigm or paradigms for determining whether any particular experience can be regarded as an experience of pleasure. We shall have to include the pleasure of the agreeable as one of the paradigms, for it is this with which we are most familiar. This consists of a sensory titillation caused by a sensory stimulus as such; that is, without the mediation of any higher mental faculties. (Paradigm I). The feel of velvet, greenness of a meadow, an isolated sweet sound, taste of something one likes can be cited as examples.

The pleasure that sometimes attends on satisfaction of one's desires should also be included among paradigms of pleasure (Paradigm II) although it often gets fused with the pleasure of the agreeable, as when we are hungry and are given sufficient *quantity* of food which we *like.* The pleasure which accompanies the attainment of good which may be regarded as the third paradigm (Paradigm III), is different from the earlier two, and had better be put in the category of satisfaction or, as Kant suggests, the catagory of regard. The pleasure of the beautiful (Paradigm IV), is, for Kant an austere self-preserving experience which consists of a free (unmediated by concepts) harmony between imagination (the faculty which stands for multiplicity), and understanding (the faculty which stands for unity).

If we use the above paradigms, can we say that the *Rasa* experience is necessarily pleasurable? Although Kant insists on the withdrawal of the ontological claim on behalf the aesthetic object, art experience cannot be completely cut off from ordinary experiences unless it is deconceptualised. So the fourth paradigm that of Kantian Free Beauty has to be set aside in this context of literary experience. Further, unless deconceptualization takes place we need not make any distinction between the actual and the imaginal, in matters of titillation of senses, satisfaction of practical desires (at least up to a point). Whether it is an actual dew-drop on the fresh petals of a flower or its representation which is the cause of an experience will make no difference so far as the pleasure of the agreeable is concerned, *Rasa* experience can be said to induce this variety of pleasure if the object (viz. the play) contains appropriate sensory stimuli. Aristotle mentions some of these. But this will be too meagre to make the whole experience predominantly pleasurable. Velvet covered seats on the stage will induce pleasure in the spectator, but it will be overpowered by an opposite affective tone, if the scene presents an act of a hienous crime.

A dramatic representation of the meteoric rise and success of the hero of a play in the fields of ambition and love might afford the spectator the pleasure of vicarious, but partial, satisfaction of these two particularly strong human impulses, through his act of identification with the hero, on the imaginal plane. If the hero is shown as the champion of the good, vicarous but partial moral satisfaction also can be achieved. These two pleasures (which belong to the practical aspect of human experience) can be had from plays which induce *Rasas* like *Śṛṅgāra* and *Vīra.* (*Hāsya* need not be discussed separately, because it does not give rise to any doubt about its being pleasurable. What it creates is a pleasant, cheerful mood which has been regarded by some as a separate paradigm of pleasure.)

Certain *Rasas* will, however, make it very difficult for us to accept their claim to pleasureableness. The obvious example here is *Vībhatsa.* It cannot be regarded as pleasurable by any stretch of imagination, (Kant also treats the disgusting as an exception when he deals with pleasurable artistic representation of things which are not in themselves pleasurable.)

But the crucial test lies in the case of the tragic experience. A tragedy when presented on the stage may give some sensory pleasure (Paradigm I) if it contains sensory stimulus of the appropriate type. Some tragedies may also provide pleasure or satisfaction of the moral variety if they show the triumph of the good which their chief characters exemplify, although they are ruined on the material plane (Paradigm III). These tragedies have an ennobling effect in so far as they exemplify the superiority of the world of Moral Freedom over the world of Necessity or the triumph of Good over Evil. Some tragedies may be said to satisfy worldly wishes (Paradigm II) of the Id and the super-ego, as the Freudians have maintained in the case of plays like *Oedipus* and *Hamlet.* But surely all tragedies do not belong to the categories mentioned above. *King Lear, Antigone,* the *Rāmāyaṇa,* the *Mahābhārata* can be cited as examples. They do not come close to any of the paradigms as seen above that we have been using so far, except occasionally. As seen above, presence of concepts rules out the possibility of the pleasure of free Beauty in literature (Paradigm IV).

It is here that the theory of *Sādhāraṇīkaraṇa* may be invoked to help us out of the tight corner in which we link ourselves. We are told that our emotions in ordinary life are individual-based, whereas they are universalised in the context of literary experience. Relations between individual egoes are classified into three categories, (a) Individuals belong to the group of our friends, relations, well-wishers, or (b) they belong to the opposite group, or (c) they belong to the group of those who are indifferent to us, and to whom we are indifferent. We feel happy if something good happens to individuals in category (a); we feel unhappy if something good happens to individuals of category (b); and we are indifferent to the fortunes of individuals of category (c). I have shown elsewhere that the conception of human mind underlying this classification is too cynical and simplistic to be acceptable. It is not true that we necessarily feel unhappy if something good happens to individuals of category (b) or that we feel happy if their fortunes are adversely affected. Further, it is not true that we are left unmoved if good or bad fortune visits individuals of category (c). That our relations are always individual-based can be seen in such contexts as the Prime Minister declaring war on a hostile country.

The concept of *Sādhāraṇīkaraṇa* has been traditionally interpreted in two ways; either as a one-way process of ascending from the particular to the universal or as a two-way process (a) ascending from one particular to a universal (b) and a descending process from a universal to another particular. Both the interpretations run into difficulties. The first one would lead to the conclusion that we have before us universals when we watch a play, and that we, the spectators, transcend our ego while watching the performance.

The first conclusion goes against our experience except perhaps in the case of Morality Plays. Secondly, we cannot accept that there is complete ego transcendence, because how can we ever understand a play and enter its world, if we shed our cognitive and valuational structures? To say that we should forget our petty problems is different from saying that we should totally forget everything, including our moral and cognitive concerns. The first can be concealed because preoccupation with our petty concerns constitutes a *Rasa-Vighna*, to concede the second is difficult because it renders the idea of *Ātmānupraveśa* meaningless. Our experience is never that of complete ego-transcendence or complete immersion in the emotional experience induced by the play. The theory of *Savikalpa-Samādhi* will not help us much unless the nature and degree of empirical - self-awareness permissible in the *Rasa* experience is specified. (It may be noted again in passing that *Sādhāraṇīkaraṇa* cannot explain the transformation of a *Sthāyī* into a pleasurable mental state in the context of *Rasas* like the *Vībhatsa.*)

I have suggested another interpretation of *Sādhāraṇīkaraṇa* in a paper of mine, following a hint I got from the Hegelian tradition. I shall try to elaborate on it at this stage. It will be helpful to make a distinction between the notions of universalizable and universal. There are experiences which are universalizable in that they can be sufficiently departicularized so as to become universally shareable or understandable thus making either *Ātmānupraveśa* (i.e. undergoing an emotion) or detached apprehension of it possible. As against these *universalizable* experiences there are *universal* experiences, i.e. experiences which we get as representatives of the human race, i.e. provided we are able to raise ourselves to that level.

In the field of ethics Kant insists that we should choose the maxim of our action as though we were making the choice on behalf of the whole human race. In the same way we can develop a capacity for having experiences as though we were having them on behalf of the whole human race. Great men possess this capacity; if they are literary artists they transmit it through their great literary works; if they are leaders of humanity like Buddha, Christ, Lincoln, Gandhi they can transmit it through their works. Grief caused by the death of a good man is a *universalizable* experience. But grief-charged metaphysical puzzlement caused by that event is a *universal* experience; it has a *universal dimension*. It leads us to ask: Why should Man be at once endowed with the capacity to be morally good and cursed with the inevitability of Death, which is no respecter of goodness or any moral value?

If we take *Sādhāraṇīkṛta* experience to mean experience that we have on condition that we raise ourselves to the position of representatives of the whole human race, this experience will automatically deserve to be placed in a class by itself. But then this experience will not be the characteristic of all and sundry literary works - even of all those which are predominantly emotional. Secondly, *Śadhāraṇīkṛta* experience will not be peculiar to literature alone. For, just as Shakespeare can have it, Gandhiji too can have it; and in their different ways they can make it available to us for sharing or contemplation, that is, if we have the requisite capacity mentioned above. It is a part of human nature to enjoy *Śadhāranīkṛta* experience. It is their privilege as human beings to have these experiences—for the pleasure of it. (This use of pleasure is not covered by any of the four paradigms mentioned above. But a paradigm can be extracted from Kant's discussion of the Sublime.)

Two questions remain to be tackled. The first is how to distinguish *Śadhāranīkṛta* experience in literature from the same variety of experience in other fields? The best way of doing this appears to be to go back to the epistemological and ontological implications of Śaṅkuka's *Citraturagapra-tīti*. He has enphasized what Langer calls the 'virtual', or Wellek and Warren call the 'fictional' nature of the world of Art. Hence the need for terms like *Vibhāva, Anubhāva, Citraturaga-pratīti* and the conceptual structure they imply.

The second question is about the process of *Sādhāraṇīkaraṇa* as we have reinterpreted it. It is not everyman's emotional experience that can be universalized. Only people who have a metaphysical dimension to their way of thinking and life can have it. That this element is present in sanskrit imaginative literature can be shown by producing ample evidence that is available in the *Rāmāyaṇa* and the *Mahābhārata*. But this metaphysical aspect is not taken care of in sanskrit criticism, e.g. in the *Rasa theory*. The theory of *Sādhāraṇīkaraṇa* unless interpreted as we have done it does not provide the necessary critical apparatus for identifying and evaluating literary works. To call *Rasa*-experience *Brahmāsvāda-sahodara* is not to solve the problem, unless one shows how exactly the metaphysical aspect of the experience is to be dealt with. For surely, Sophocles, Shakespeare, Dastoievsky, Becket raise metaphysical issues, without inducing anything like *Brahmāsvāda-sahodara-ānanda* or stillness of the spirit.

Many times the metaphysical issues arise out of man's moral concerns, when Cordelia, a person of great integrity, and Lear, who is more sinned against than sinning, are subjected to ulmost suffering that Kent asks 'Is this the promised end?' Similar questions about the place of Man and his values in the total scheme of the Universe are explicitly asked, or are implicitly present, in great literature. It is not as though Sanskrit literature does not raise such problems or does not show a clash between values as Sophocles or Shakespeare do. This will become clear if we take into account the scheme of the originally three, and later on four, *Puruṣarthas*, as the moral background against which emotional and other responses are to be judged. For example, we cannot understand the greatness of Rāma in choosing to accept exile in the forest, despite the opposition on the part of Lakṣmaṇa and reluctance on the part of Daśaratha and Kauśalyā's entreaty for personal reasons, till Rāma himself tells Bharata about the *Śulka* (bride-price) that Daśaratha had committed himself to when he married the Kaikeya princess. He thought it his duty to honour the pledge given by his father even when it meant a great self-sacrifice. It is interesting to observe that the same *Rāma,* in the same meeting, asked Bharata questions about running of the state, questions which belong to *Arthaśāstra* and *Rāja-dharma*, and they are asked as coolly as Kauṭilya would have asked them (see *Ayodhyā Kāṇḍa*, *Sarga* 115). Whether the *Puruṣārthas* which formed the valuational structure of the society then, are eternally valid is a question we need not enter into here. The more important and relevant point is that emotional content of an experience involves the consideration of impulses (the conative elements) it involves and we cannot talk meaningfully about the conative aspect of human life without taking into account the valuational structure of the society in which these impulses are activated and exercised.

Actually, one reason for placing eight emotional dispositions in a separate class and claiming that they alone can rise to the level of *Rasas,* is their relationship with *Puruṣārthas*. *Rasas* are expected to be *Puruśārthaniṣṭha* The concept of *Rasa* thus contains a valuational element as an essential part. But, although the connection between *Rasas* and *Puruṣārthas* is *mentioned,* there is no provision in Sanskrit Poetics for the discussion of moral problems raised in literary works and the bearing of these problems on the excellence of these literary works as literature, whereas such a provision does exist in the Western critical tradition. What an Aristotelian, or Arnoldian or Marxist critic can legitimately do a Sanskritist critic cannot do.

Let us now turn for a while to the debasement of Sanskrit terms in modern times. Many modern Marathi critics take *Rasa* to mean any emotional experience, and *Āsvāda* to mean undergoing that experience. Whether *contemplative attitude* is compatible with *undergoing* any emotion is a moot point which we shall not enter into. If there is a powerful tradition of Abhinavagupta's followers who insist on undergoing an emotion, there is an equally powerful tradition of Hegelian critics who insist on contemplating an emotion as embodied out there in some sensory medium. There is no reason for doubting the appreciative competence of those who belong to the latter tradition. Therefore leaving it alone, let us focus on the first tradition. If undergoing an emotion is the end of the process of appreciation, how are we going to evaluate, compare and grade different literary works? Evaluation and discrimination become possible only if we evaluate and grade the emotions we are supposed to undergo. This evaluation can only be done by examining them, and particularly their long-term effects on our personality. While undergoing an emotion, one must ask oneself the type of questions that Plato asks, or, if Plato is kept out as too rigid, the questions that Arnold and Richards would ask; the latter has explicitly claimed that the spiritual health of society is one of the primary concerns of a critic.

What we have been discussing has a direct bearing on one type of criticism that has enjoyed vogue for quite some time in Maharashtra: it is called *Āsvādak Samīkṣā* That is supposed to be a reaction against critics who use rigid rules made by unimaginative *Pundits* who had no first-hand experience of any literary work. Whatever might have been the case with the neoclassical critics' way of doing criticism excellently parodied in Polonius's well known speech in *Hamlet* nobody in recent times has done anything like that in Marathi.

So *Āsvādak Samīkṣā* in Marathi was really a protest against nothing. The practitioner of *Vidagdha Samīkṣā* also insists on the spontaneous response on the part of a critic to a literary work which belongs to some literary class or the other, with elastic boundary lines. But he also insists that however spontaneous a response may be, in so far as it is a *human* response, it cannot come into being in the absence of some conceptual valuational structure or the other which is present in the critic. If we attend to this structure we would get at the concepts and criteria with which to analyse and evaluate literary works (and the response they arouse). If we do not attend to it our response will tend to be an irrelevant, idiosyncratic, emotional dribble. If the Sanskrit critics who developed the *Rasa* theory had paid close attention to what we found missing or undeveloped in their theory, things would not have come to this pass. But what they did not do, we can do, if there is the will to do it. *Rasa* theory can be made an active principle in criticism today, not by finding its western correlates, nor by proudly claiming that we had anticipated the modern west, but by living it. The second temptation is difficult to resist; but we must resist it, if we do not want to be jolted out of slunber by being told that Pāṇini is the Pakistan's first grammarian. To live a theory is an arduous but not an impossible task.

The Object-Emotion Relationship In Indian and Western Literary Theories

Krishna Rayan

I

The most authoritative two-sentence description available of the phenomenon of objectification of emotion is, I think, what was offered by Otto Baensch in *Logos* in 1923:

> How can we capture, hold and handle feelings so that their content may be made conceivable and presented to our consciousness in universal form without being understood in the strict sense, i.e., by means of concepts? The answer is: We can do it by creating objects wherein the feelings we seek to hold are so definitely embodied that any subject confronted with these objects, and emphatically disposed toward them, cannot but experience a non-sensuous apperception of the feelings in question.[1]

But two millennia ago Bharata had said the same thing more succinctly if cryptically: *tatra vibhāvānubhāvā-vyabhicāri-saṁyogād rasa-nispattiḥ.* And in 1919, offering a similar but less pregnant *sūtra*, T.S. Eliot had said: "...when the external facts (i.e., a set of objects etc.), which must terminate in sensory experience, are given, the emotion is immediately evoked."[2] Fifty years later, in 1969, explaining the Phenomenological position, Georges Poulet said: "When I read as I ought...any feeling proposed to me is immediately assumed by me... I am freed from my usual sense of incompatibility between my consciousness and its objects."[3]

Unfortunately, all these pronouncements are silent on how exactly an emotion in art is expressed or evoked by its objects, how exactly from its sensuous embodiment an emotion is retranslated by the reader into a non-sensuous state within him. Yet no description or determination of the nature of the aesthetic experience can be attempted without first identifying the nature of the relationship between the object and the emotion. Western aesthetics has therefore kept returning to the problem of objectification of emotion. And in Sanskrit poetics, as we know from *Abhinavabhāratī*, how the *vibhāvas* give rise to the *rasa* was the subject of a debate which wore on from the 8th to the 11th century.

The earliest voice in this controversy is Lollaṭa who describes the relationship between object and emotion as a cause-and-effect relationship; he also locates the effect in the character. By skilful simulation of the character, an actor may succeed in making the audience associate the emotion with him, but its seat nevertheless is essentially in the character. Lollaṭa's notion of objects as causes producing the emotion was demolished on several grounds but most effectively by means of a distinction drawn between causes of emotions in life (*laukika-kāraṇas*) and representations of them in art which act as objects of those emotions (*alaukika-vibhāvas*). Lollaṭa's theory is thus out, but perhaps not wholly, certainly not in actual critical practice. Emotion in a literary work is often perceived as the emotion experienced by a character. T.S. Eliot, for instance, is found identifying the essential emotion of Shakespeare's play *Hamlet* not just as disgust but as the disgust felt by Prince Hamlet. It is equally significant that Eliot describes Hamlet's disgust as occasioned by his mother's guilt. Lollaṭa's fallacy gets exposed here soon enough, because Eliot proceeds to say "... his disgust is occasioned by his mother but his mother is not an adequate equivalent for it."[4] Eliot clearly is mixing up here the causing of an emotion and the expressing of it - mixing up, that is to say, Lollaṭa's view of a *vibhāva* with Abhinavagupta's.

However, the distinction between a *laukika-kāraṇa* and an *alaukika-vibhāva* is not as absolute as one might think. It is not as though by a neat demarcation of territory, objects which cause emotion occur in life and objects which suggest it occur in art. Wimsatt and Beardsley point out in their well-known essay *The Affective Fallacy:*

... it is a well-known but nonetheless important truth that there are two kinds of real objects which have emotive quality, the objects which are the reasons for human emotion, and those which by some kind of association suggest either the reasons or the resulting emotion: the thief, the enemy, or the insult that makes us angry, and the hornet that sounds and stings somewhat like ourselves when angry; the murderer or felon, and the crow that kills small birds and animals or feeds on carrion and is black like the night when crimes are committed by men.

Nevertheless, as Wimsatt and Beardsley proceed to explain, the distinction between these two kinds of real objects is duplicated in the distinction between historical statement and fictitious or poetic statement. In the history of culture and art, the direction of development is from "a mere case of factual reason for intense emotion" to "a specified, figuratively fortified, and permanent object of less intense but far richer emotion."[5] *Kāraṇas* and *vibhāvas* are thus distinct categories, but *vibhāvas* originate by growing out of *kāraṇas* in the course of cultural history.

Śaṅkuka's interpretation of Bharata's *sūtra* is that the emotion, perceived as being experienced by the actor, is inferred from the objects presented by him. To Lollaṭa, the *vibhāva* is a *kāraka-hetu* (the actual cause): to Śaṅkuka, it is a *jñāpaka-hetu* (a premise in a syllogism). The inference theory was rejected on the ground that *vibhāvas* cannot be treated as the middle term (the *sādhana*) from which the major term (the *sādhya*), in this case the *rasa*, can be inferred, because the two are not invariably concomitant. If *vibhāva x* is given, *rasa y* does not necessarily follow. Yet Eliot's well-known dictum is that when the objects are given, the particular emotion is immediately evoked. What Eliot, however, has in mind here is not inference, but reference. In the essay on Andrew Marvell, he contrasts what he describes as "the explicit reference of emotion to object" in Marvell's poem, its "bright, hard precision", with the mistiness and vagueness of William Morris's poem. The concept of reference, of one-to-one correspondence is obviously different from the concept of inference but has this in common with it that there is a specific conceptual linkage between a given set of objects and the relative emotion. The emotion may not be syllogistically deducible from it but should be derivable from it not indeed with the absoluteness that marks denotative reference but certainly with an optimum degree of precision ensuring that there is no indistinctness.

To Bhaṭṭanāyaka, *vibhāvas* (and the *sthāyin*) assist in revealing the *rasa*, by being acted upon by *bhāvakatva* which is essentially a process of universalization. *Bhāvakatva* is defined as a function of language, distinct from *abhidhā* (referential meaning), as distinct from it as Ānandavardhana had declared *vyañjanā* to be. According to Abhinavagupta's explanation of the concept of *bhāvakatva* as formulated by Bhaṭṭanāyaka, it operates in poetry through figuration and properties of poetic expression and in performed drama through speech, gestures, expression of emotion, and (although *bhāvakatva* is a function of language) costume and make-up. According to Formalists in our century, the deviant linguistic patterns which constitute literariness make strange the familiar world that we routinely perceive. According to Bhaṭṭanāyaka and Abhinavagupta, they free the *vibhāvas* and the *sthāyin* from the personal, the practical and the particular and invest them with a universality which makes it possible for the spectator or reader (1) to identify and empathize and (2) to reach a state of untroubled emotion not accessible in empirical reality. It is not quite clear how patterns of verbal expression can achieve this result; presumably literariness and stylization create a world of formal 'beauty' and order in which the fevers of the natural world are terminated and even objects of the less pleasurable emotions are able to induce maximal aesthetic satisfaction. Universalization thus conceived is something that takes place within the reader's mind and is not any kind of treatment which an author applies to his material; nor is it, as in certain Western theories, a process which certain kinds of material have already undergone. There is, for instance, the theory of archetypes: essentially universal patterns of experience which recur in literature and are deeply responded to by all competent readers. There are certain themes, images and character types which are specifically identified as archetypal, whereas the *rasas*, although finite in number, are claimed to exhaust emotional experience. There is a second kind of universal literary material, which is accounted for by the theory of cultural stereotypes offered by Structuralism. Characters are perceived as products of cultural stereotypes and conventions which are individualized by the reader by applying his conceptions of real persons, but these conceptions are in their turn traceable to the stereotypes. The particular thus gets dissolved in a general cultural system, as indeed happens in *sādhāraṇīkaraṇa* though in a different way.

Abhinavagupta's interpretation of the *rasa-sūtra* which is in terms of Ānandavardhana's theory of *Dhvani,* amounts to an almost definitive explanation of the whole phenomenon of *rasa* and the nature of the relationship of object and emotion. The emotion in its permanent form is pre-existent in the consciousness of the reader as a latent emotional set, a psychic residue (in a non-Jungian sense) of previous perceptions. The emotion thus is not produced by or inferred from its objects; they only render it manifest. It emerges from them exactly as unstated meaning emerges from stated meaning - by the operation of the function of suggestion inherent in language. The emotion is not named or described but is instead suggested by its sensuous embodiments which are descriptively or discursively presented. The relation between the objects and the emotion is the same as the relation between an utterance and its connotational meaning. The emotion which a poem or a play evokes is in fact its suggested meaning.

The relationship between object and emotion is the same as the relationship between a lamp and the pot or jar which it lights up. This traditional metaphor for manifestation which Ānandavardhana uses in expounding suggested *vis-a-vis* stated meaning will reward close attention, as the lamp-jar situation is a perfect paradigm of the object-emotion situation. The jar was already there, the lamp only illuminated it. (The objects only activate a waiting emotional predisposition. *Rasa* is revealed, not generated.) The light of the lamp does not cease when it has illuminated the jar. (Like stated meaning which is not superseded when suggestion takes place, the objects continue to be present to our minds when the emotion is realized.) The jar is present to our senses only as long as the lamp shines. (The emotion stays in our consciousness only as long as the objects do.) The lamp and the jar are present together but are not inseparable. (The objects and the emotion are not bound to each other by invariable concomitance.)

The version of *rasa* realization that describes it as a case of the *vibhāvādis* awakening a predisposition in the reader's mind amounts to a notion of suggestion which corresponds to the notion of suggestion as evocation in Western criticism - "the calling up of what is already there in the reader's mind," as David Perkins puts it.[7] He distinguishes it from the kind of suggestion which aims at communicating insights and revelations (such as those offered by mystic experience) which have no pre-existing equivalents in the reader's psyche. In this case the state of mind cannot be sensuously embodied in the text, and suggestion can only take the form of inducing in the reader a heightened awareness which can enable him to go to work creatively on the poem and intuit what has not been said. The kind of arcane experience which Wordsworth hints at in *The Prelude* and which will only tolerate the second type of suggestion was not provided for in classical Sanskrit poetry and poetics which were essentially concerned with recognizable emotional states that could be presented through their traditional objective equivalents.

The concept of *vibhāva* as a suggestive device comes closer than anything else in Sanskrit poetics to the principle of symbol. A *vibhāva* shares the principal characteristics of the symbol - it is 'an outward device for presenting an inward state'[8], a verbal equivalent for something unstated, at once a sensuous embodiment and a means of evocation of a state of consciousness, and above all, a source of rich complex meaning. Susanne Langer regarded *rasa* as a product of the operation of symbol, although in saying so she added: "The supernatural status attributed to its perception shows the mystification that beset the ancient theorists when they were confronted with the power of a symbol which they did not recognize as such."[9] This is not true. The *rasa* experience was described as *lokottara* on sound philosophic grounds, and the word was certainly not an expression of ignorant wonder.

II

As was pointed out at the beginning of the essay, objectification of emotion has been a long-standing interest in Western aesthetics. To go no further back than Hegel, objectification can be viewed as a means of mitigation: in art, says Hegel (1835), "...man contemplates his impulses and instincts: and whereas formerly they hurried him along without reflection, he now sees them externalized, and begins, so soon as they are presented to him as objects, to achieve freedom of them."[10] With this difference that intuition replaces reason, Croce's formulation of objectification (1902) has the same emphasis on contemplation and calming. Croce speaks of 'feelings objectified, intuited, expressed', 'assuaged and calmed', 'contemplated and therefore resolved and transcended', so that 'they do not trouble and afflict us as passionately as those of real life'.[11]

T.S. Eliot's exposition of the concept of the objective correlative (1919) can be regarded as being in one sense a manifesto of modernism, as an oblique plea for poetry and poetic drama shifting their weight from discursiveness to the language of the image - the concrete, specific, distinct object. Although in the essay on *Hamlet* Eliot's example of the objective correlative is a character, the modernist trend in literature which he among others originated was known for its having exchanged one set of objects - plot and character - for another set - image and myth. But his view of the objective correlative as an external equivalent of a particular emotion is traditional enough - so traditional that it could well have come out of *Dhvanyāloka*. In fact, replying to an Indian correspondent in 1955, he spoke of "the author of *Vibhāva* (*sic.*) which I have not read." It would, however, be simplistic to decide that the theory of the objective correlative and the theory of *rasa* are identical. The essay on *Hamlet* clubs the play with the overtly autobiographical sonnets and describes it as "full of some stuff which the author could not drag to lights, contemplate, or manipulate into art."[12] It is possible that when Eliot speaks of emotion he means the poet's emotion and that he regards objectification as a means of depersonalization of the poet's emotion. *Rasa*, on the other hand, is emotion realized within the reader. The point, however, is that whether it be the poet's emotion or the reader's, the nature of the objective correlative would be the same.

Susanne Langer, writing in the 1940s and 50s, argued the case against objectification. The concept of 'symbolic form' which she took over from Cassirer and further developed implies that an emotion or feeling is presented, as she says, "not by recalling objects which would elicit the feeling, but by 'articulating' the feeling, viz. weaving a pattern of words - words charged with meaning, and coloured by literary associations - akin to the dynamic pattern of the feeling..."[13] On the other hand, the late 1940s also witnessed the appearance of the influential essay 'The Affective Fallacy' by Wimsatt and Beardsley which offers what is perhaps the best available analysis of the relationship between objects and emotions. Reiterating the traditional view that emotions are "presented in their objects and contemplated as a pattern of knowledge",[14] they make the point that poetry fixes emotions by ensuring constancy for objects of emotion through cultural change. As noted earlier in this papr, they also indicate how there is a process of evolution involved here - from reasons for emotions to objects of emotions, from history to poetry, from fact to quality.

These are valuable insights, and they as well as the whole relationship of object and emotion become very much more comprehensible when studied in terms of semiotics. The object is clearly a cultural item which conveys a shared meaning (that is to say, suggests a common emotion) to members of the group. That objects are culture-bound is evident from the fact that if the *uddīpana-vibhāvas* of *śṛṅgāra* had been listed not by Bharata but by Aristotle, he would not have given unguents and garlands the importance which Bharata gave them. Once we see the object as the signifier and the emotion as the signified, it becomes clear that the relationship between the two which is a natural relationship in life, based either on analogy or on causation, is altered in literature into a conventional bond. In literary development, an emotion in course of time can get fixed in certain objects, and then the relationship thus fixed by convention becomes permanent and will persist when social change alters the objects of the emotion in real life. Thus although in actuality lipstick and eye shadow rather than flowers are beautifying agents today, yet flowers largely continue in literture to be evocative sensuous equivalents of the erotic emotion.

To apply semiotic theory thus is to see objects in literature as public, conventional, constant. While this is the way literary theory in our century points, in literary practice modernism has been pursuing a contrary direction and opting for symbols tnat are personal, private, ad hoc. The modernist writer does this with a view to obscurity as a means to suggestiveness and more importantly with a view to accurate rendering of the emotions that are integral with his vision. To the Structuralists, however, the author's vision is not a relevant factor, as they regard the text as no more than a precipitate of the conventions of the literary system to which the author belongs, so that his mind is just a 'space' in which this impersonal activity takes place. On the one hand, emotions - the author's emotions - are of no interest to the Structuralist School: on the other, the objects in a text - characters, situations, imagery, style etc. - are regarded by them as expectations which the reader brings to his reading of the text, having formed them from the conventions and codes of the literary system which have become known to him through his reading of other texts in the system - expectations which the text may fulfil, frustrate, delay or modify.

While Structuralism thus devalues or dissolves emotions and objects, the Critics of Consciousness (i.e., the Geneva School) and the Reader-Response critics associated with Wolfgang Iser regard the text as a product of the author's interior mode of consciousness which they view as the subjective correlative of the objects in the work. The objects can therefore be studied by readers as a means of access to the author's inner life and emotions. On the other hand, Reader-Response critics and Reception-Theory critics who share with Structuralists the notion of readers' expectations would tend to study the objects in the text in relation to this factor. Reception-Theory, for instance, defines the reader's response as what results from a combination of the expectations which the reader brings to a text and the confirmations and frustrations that follow when the expectations are 'challenged' by the objects in the text.

Having been partly explained away with reference to the operations involved in reading and having been assimilated into an impersonal system, objects, which had in the past been studied as relatively stable representational contents signifying emotion, have now lost some of their solidity. As for the emotions which they were viewed as evoking in the reader, the reader is no doubt very much at the centre in contemporary theories, as they are all, in one way or another, theories of reading. But they do not regard the reader's response as exclusively or necessarily affective, and they are more interested in analysing the mostly cognitive processes involved in the activity of reading. Apart from their status as embodiments of emotion, objects have always received attention as the formal constituents of a literary work. And those contemporary theories which are formalistic and study literature as artifice do interest themselves in the functioning of objects as the principal internal elements in a work.

NOTES

1. Quoted in S.K. Langer, *Feeling and Form* (London 1952) p. 21
2. T.S. Eliot, *Selected Essays* (London 1932) p. 145
3. G. Poulet, *Phenomenology of Reading* (1969)
4. T.S. Eliot, op. cit., p. 145
5. W.K. Wimsatt Jr., *The verbal Icon*(New York 1954) p. 37
6. T.S. Eliot, op. cit., p. 299
7. D. Perkins, *Wordsworth and the Poetry of Sincerity* (Cambridge, Mass. 1964) p. 100
8. W.Y. Tindall, *The Literary Symbol* (Bloomington 1955)
9. S.K. Langer, op. cit., p. 323
10. Quoted in E.F. Carritt, *Philosophies of Beauty* (Oxford 1931) p. 163
11. Quoted in W.K. Wimsatt Jr. and C. Brooks, *Literary Criticism: a Short History* (New York 1957) pp. 509-511
12. T.S. Eliot, op. cit., p. 144
13. S.K. Langer, op. cit., p. 230
14. W.K. Wimsatt Jr., op. cit., p. 38

The *Rasa* Theory and the *Khyātis*

K.S. Arjunwadkar

The *Rasa* theory of Bharata, the *Rasa-sūtra* forming the central part thereof, and the various attempts to interpret the *Sūtra* made by Lollaṭa and others are too wellknown to the world of Sanskrit literary criticism to be detailed here. Tradition, as reflected in Jhalakikar's commentary, *Bālabodhinī,* on Mammaṭa's *Kāvyaprakāśa*, relates the exponents of the *Sūtra* to various philosophical systems. Thus, Lollaṭa is supposed to be a Mīmāṁsaka, Śaṅkuka, a Naiyāyika, Bhaṭṭa Nāyaka, a Sāṅkhya. Abhinavagupta, noted as an Ālaṁkārika in the source mentioned above, is considered to be a Vedāntin by others. One line of thinking is to take the tradition as authentic and read peculiar tenets of the said philosophical systems in the interpretations by Lollaṭa and others. This is the line taken up by Mahāmahopādhyāya Kasturé, a representative of the old tradition, and Dr. Sunil Subhedar, a representative of modern scholars in this area. I have dealt with Subhedar's arguments in another article[2]. I intend to deal with Kasturé's arguments here.

Mm. Yajñeshvar Shāstrī Kasturé, in his booklet in Marathi entitled '*Rasavicāra āṇi Prācīna Darśanakāra* - i.e. The *Rasa* theory and the Ancient Philosophers - (Hyderabad, 1957), attempts to show how the various interpretations of Bharata's *Rasasūtra* involve elements characteristic of the *Darśanas* to which the interpreters are held to belong (Page 6, 13). The new point Kasturé ushers in is the typical views of the *Darśanas* regarding what happens when X is cognized as Y,—a situation called *Bhrama* and technically termed '*Khyāti*' (page 13). Lollaṭa is a Mīmāṁsaka, for he explains the *Rasa* phenomenon on the basis of the *Akhyāti* (also, '*Ākhyāti*', - a term which Kasturé uses alternatively but which I have not been able to trace to an authentic Mīmāṁsā text) view of the Mīmāṁsakas. Śaṅkuka is a Naiyāyika, for he explains the *Rasa* phenomenon on the basis of the *Anyathākhyāti* view of the Naiyāyikas, - contends Kasturé. There he stops. He does not bother to show how Bhaṭṭa Nāyaka's view of the *Rasa* phenomenon is based on the *Satkhyāti* of the Sāṁkhyas; and, since he does not subscribe to the traditional view that Abhinavagupta was an Advaita-Vedāntin, he does not consider it his duty to show that Abhinava's view of *Rasa* is based on the *Anirvacanīya-khyāti* of the Advaita-Vedāntins. Thus, the test of *Khyātis* as links between the interpreters of the *Rasasūtra* on the one hand and the *Darśanas* on the other applies, according to his own discussion, to only two of the four interpreters of the *sūtra*. He offers no explanation for the reference to the *Brahmāsvāda* of the Vedāntins by a Sāṁkhya, as Kasturé believes, like Bhaṭṭa Nāyaka. This makes credentials of Bhaṭṭa Nāyaka as a Sāṁkhya doubtful.

Although the *Khyāti* terminology did not presumably exist at the time the said interpretations of the *Sūtra* were offered,[3] it may be conceded that the various *Darśanas* did have their own explanations to offer for cases of mistaken cognitions or false knowledge. It now remains to be seen if explanations of the *Sūtra* by Lollaṭa and Śaṅkuka involve words or phrases that would justify their identification as Mīmāṁsaka and Naiyāyika respectively. A scrutiny of what Lollaṭa and Śaṅkuka categorically say, as quoted in Abhinava's commentary on the *Nāṭyaśāstra*,[4] does not reveal that such a conclusion is tenable. The occurrence of the word *liṅga* in Śaṅkuka's interpretation is not enough to associate him with the Nyāya system. No knowledge of the Nyāya system is necessary to infer an unknown entity from a known sign or to make a statement thereabout. Men inferred things from known facts long before logic as a system came into being.

What is particularly objectionable in Kasturé's theory is his stand that all interpreters of the *Sūtra* agree that the experience of *Rasa* is a *bhrama*. Far from that. All those, including Śaṅkuka,[5] who have gone deep into the epistemological evaluation of the experience have taken pains to show that the experience does not fit in any of the known categories of cognition, including false cognition. Śaṅkuka observes that the experience of *Rasa* is a cognition different from such cognitions as the right knowledge, false knowledge, doubt and resemblance. hence it is separately classed as *alaukika*. How can one in his senses pronounce in the same breath that *Rasa-pratīti* is a *bhrama* which is a *laukika* category?

The passage under reference not found in the manuscript of Abhinava's commentary on the *Nāṭyaśāstra*, is inserted here by the editor in the edition thereof published in the Gaekward Oriental Series on the authority of Mammaṭa (*Kāvyaprakāśa*)[6] and Hemacandra (*Kāvyānuśāsana*) A more difficult hurdle is presented by a remark[7] which forms part of Śaṅkukaś interpretation even according to the manuscript. This remark is taken by Hemacandra to allude to a passage by the Buddhist philosopher, Dharmakīrti.[8] This passage intends to prove that even false knowledge may lead to a real achievement,—a situation technically called *Saṁvādi-bhrama*. This allusion, along with its refutation by Bhaṭṭa Tota that follows, points to the view of Śaṅkuka that the experience of *Nāṭya* is a false cognition, a *bhrama*. This strengthens the view taken by Kasturé who may not take upon himself the responsibility of reconciling this part of the interpretation of Śaṅkuka (See Notes 7,8) with that in which he seems to suggest that the *Rasa* experience is *alaukika* (See Note 6). Do I have a reply?

Yes, I have. In the first place, we have to note that *Saṁvādi-bhrama*, being of the nature of a coincidence, cannot be taken as a basis for the explanation of a universal experience. It brings out '*what may happen some times;*' it does not bring out '*what generally happens*'. It may explain, in the present context, what may happen to *a* spectator; it cannot explain what happens to *the* spectators. Like the proverbial *kākatālīya*, it just makes us aware that there can be coincidences. How can a Naiyāyika worth the name base his theory on a coincidence? Naiyāyikas and Buddhists are sworn rivals. It is funny that a Naiyāyika should look up to his rival for support of his theory. If Śaṅkuka does this, the inevitable conclusion is that he is not a Naiyāyika but a free-lance interpreter of the *Rasasūtra* who relies more on his common sense than on any rigorous philosophical discipline.

If the experience of *Nāṭya* is thus not a *bhrama* according to Sanskrit theorists, what is it? Lollaṭa says little about it. But interpreters beginning from Śaṅkuka take pains to point out that it is a cognition distinct from 'knowing' and closer to 'experiencing.' It is hence that Bhaṭṭa Nāyaka, discarding all current terms for knowledge, uses his own newly coined term *bhogīkaraṇa*—'inspiritation.' To experience is different from to know. *Rati* is a word that *names* the sentiment of love: the word does not inspirit love in the reader/spectator. It is the correlatives of a sentiment, presented through words and/or acting, that inspirit it in the reader/spectator. We see Rāma weeping for Sītā before us. Does this cognition partake of doubt? —No. Is it, then, the right knowledge? - No. False knowledge, then? - No. It must be'no knowledge' then. - No. You cannot deny your own experience. Hence, it is *alaukika*, i.e. different from the known categories of worldly cognition as noted above. It is interesting to note the range of new terms used by the critics to convey this idea.[9] This range reflects the hard struggle the critics have been put to in conveying thir idea of art experience. It is, briefly, a mental visualization, - *mānasaḥ adhyavasāyaḥ*

This term at once distinguishes art experience from experience in actual life as well as the field of knowledge. What the real Rāma felt for Sītā is a *bhāva*, never a *Rasa*. What the spectators/readers experience while witnessing the presentation of a play or reading a poem on Rāma is a *Rasa*[10] which develops when their own *bhāva* is generalized - *sādhāraṇīkṛta* - so as to include even that of Rāma. It is interesting to note that corroboration for the distinction of art experience from the field of knowledge comes from an unexpected quarter. Śaṁkara is discussing if knowledge is a mental action/conation; and his view is that it is not. Why? An action, he maintains, is a thing that rests on the will of the doer, - it is *puruṣatantra* To go, for instance, is an action. One may go on a horse, or on foot, or by some other means; or may not at all go. To know is not an action; for it is *vastutantra*.[11] If conditions of knowledge are intact, it is not given to the person concerned to know or not to know. It is not, likewise, the will of the knower that decides whether the object before him should appear as X or Y. If the object is a book, no amount of will of the knower can make it bread. But what when we identify a man with a lion, - *siṁho māṇavakaḥ*? It is not knowledge but an action, mental action, *gauṇaḥ pratyayaḥ*, answers Śaṁkara. Firstly because it is *puruṣatantra*, - one is free to regard or not to regard a man as a lion, or to regard him as something else. Secondly, the person who regards a man as a lion is aware of the separate identities of a man and a lion, even while identifying the former with the latter. Where this awareness is not present, the cognition is not a mental action but false knowledge, *bhrama*, as in the case of a pillar in dim light being mistaken as a man.[12] The concept of *gauṇa pratyāya* as expounded by Śaṁkara is found in Nyāya works by a different name, *āhārya jñana*, which is treated as a variety of *āropa*, i.e. superimposition. An *āropa* is explained to be either *āhārya* or *anāhārya*. It is *āhārya* when intentional,-e.g. identification of X with Y when one is fully aware that X is not Y.

(It is *anāhārya* when the identification is not intentional, i.e., when X is mistaken as Y.)[13] This terminology, already current in the field of dramaturgy since Bharata,[14] seems to have found its way to philosophical works at a much later date on the basis of an analogy, and from there to the Alaṁkāra literature[15] to a limited extent. The Alaṁkāra works treat this topic under the concept of *lakṣaṇā*, using a different terminology which came in vogue since Mukulabhaṭṭa (10th c.A.D.), the author of *Abhidhā-vṛtti-mātṛkā*. *Āhārya jñāna*, according to this terminology, is *sāropā lakṣaṇā*.

When we apply the criterion of Śaṁkara to the field of poetry or drama, the nature of art experience becomes clear. Be it the cognition of a face as a lotus or of the actor as the character enacted, it is a case in which the will of the reader/spectator is actively engaged as the deciding factor. It is a mental action,—mental visualization, *mānasaḥ adhyavasāyaḥ*, in which the visualizer is aware of the separate identities of the face and the lotus, or the actor and the character enacted as the case may be,—only that this awareness is not allowed to interfere beyond a certain limit. It is this that makes art experience possible. Art experience can never be explained on the hypothesis that it is a *bhrama*.

It must, however, be noted that a doyen of Sanskrit scholarship like Jagannātha Paṇḍita treats of this subject in such a way as to make the impression that he has both a Vedāntic basis and an outlook that *Rasa* experience is a *bhrama* While defining and explaining the concept of *Rasa*, he not only uses typically Vedāntic phraseology but also takes for granted Vedāntic concepts and theory of knowledge.[16] It will not be profitable here to go into the details of the Vedāntic concepts, but Jagannātha's treatment of *Rasa* experience as on a par with a dream object or the cognition of tin as silver makes it clear that he regards the experience as *bhrama* He has, no doubt, used the term *alaukika*, but with reference to both the experience as well as the process of *vyañjanā* which brings about this experience.[17] It should be noted that, while he sorts out *Rasa* experience from worldly experiences on the Vedāntic grounds,[18] he also categorically differentiates the experience from *Brahmāsvāda*[19] Jagannātha is perhaps the only author on whom Kasturé could have, but has not, counted for his theory.

Kasturé's attempt, therefore, to relate interpretations of the *Rasasūtra* to various philosophical systems in general (as his predecessors like Jhalakikar have done)and to *Khyāti* theories in particular (for which he alone is responsible) is not only not warranted by the text but also goes against the epistemological position which Śaṅkuka and others assume in their outlook regarding the *Rasa* experience. Kasturé's booklet on this subject is, therefore, a contribution not to a better understanding, but to a further misunderstanding, if not confusion, of the much-debated *Rasa* theory.

NOTES

1. Published by the Bhandarkar Oriental Research Institute, Poona; 1950 edn., p. 87. (Hereafter referred to as Kp/Jhal. followed by page numbers.) To make matters worse, some old and many modern writers on this subject have, on flimsy grounds, assigned the interpreters to a variety of systems. A Summary of all such attempts may be viewed at a glance as an intellectual exercise:

   Lollaṭa: Śaiva, Vedāntin, Mīmāṁsaka, Bhāṭṭa Mīmāṁsaka.
   Śaṅkuka: Bauddha Naiyāyika, Naiyāiyka.

Bhaṭṭa Nāyaka: Sāṁkhya, Mīmāṁsaka, Vedāntin, Śaiva, Mīmāṁsaka and Sāṁkhya, Vedāntin and Sāṁkhya, Mīmāṁsaka and Śaiva, Mīmāṁsaka and Sāṁkhya and Vedāntin.
(Vide: *Saṁskṛta Kāvyaśāstra para Bhāratīya Darśana kā Prabhāva* (Hindi)/Amarjeet Kaur, Delhi, 1979, Pp. 35...)

2. 'The *Rasa* Theory and the *Darśanas*' (Annals of the BORI, 1984 issue).
3. The oldest work to which I have been able to trace the *Khyāti* terminology is Jayantabhaṭṭaś *Nyāya-mañjarī*(880 A.D.), Benares, 1936, Pp. I.161 ff.
4. ...tena sthāyy eva vibhāvānubhāvādibhir upacito rasaḥ ।। sthāyī tv anupacitaḥ । sa cobhayo 'py anukārye । anukartary api cānusaṁdhānabalad iti । ...tasmād (d) hetubhir vibhāvākhyaiḥ ...anukartṛsthatven liṅgabalataḥ pratīyamānaḥ sthāyī bhāvo mukhyarāmādigatasthāyyanukaraṇarūpo 'nukaraṇatvād eva ca nāmāntareṇa vyapadiṣṭo rasaḥ

   *Rasa-bhāva-vicāra*by R.P. Kangle (hereafter referred to as 'Kang' followed by page numbers), Bombay, 1973, Pp. 124, 129.

5. samyaṅmithyāsaṁśayasādṛśyapratītibhyo vilakṣaṇā । Kang. 134.
6. KP/Jhal.88. This passage seems to be the paraphrase of a statement by Śaṅkuka contained in a couple of verses quoted in Abhinava's commentary. The verses run as follows:

   pratibhāti na saṁdeho na satyaṁ na viparyayaḥ ।
   dhīr asāvayam ity asti nāsāv evāyam ity api ।।
   viruddhabuddhyasaṁbhedad avivecitaviplava ।
   yuktyā paryanuyujyeta sphurann anubhavaḥ kayā ।। Kang. 130

7. arthakriyāpi mithyājṇānād dṛṣṭā । Kang. 130
8. maṇipradīpaprabhayor maṇibuddhyā 'bhidhāvatoḥ ।
   mithyājñānāviśeṣe 'pi viśeṣo ' rthakriyām prati ।।
   *Pramāṇa-vārttika*2.57/Kang. 133

9. avagamanam, abhinayanam, mānasī sākṣātkārātmikā pratītiḥ, sākṣātkārāyamāṇatvam (paraphrased by Jhalakikar as

Kavivivakṣitārthasya sākṣādiva karaṇam Kp/Jhal. 89), avighnā saṁvit, camatkāraḥ, mānasādhyavasāyaḥ, nirveśaḥ, rasanam, āsvādanam, bhogaḥ, samāpattiḥ, layaḥ, viśrāntiḥ, carvaṇā. Vide Kang. 130 ff.

10. tena nāṭye eva rasā na loke ity arthaḥ ı kāvyaṁ ca nāṭyam eva ı Kāvye 'pi nāṭyāyamāne eva rasaḥ ı Kang. 195

11. kartum akartum anyathā vā kartuṁ śakyaṁ ı vaidikam laukikaṁ ca karma ı yathā aśvena gacchati, padbhyām, anyathā vā, na vā gacchatīti ı ..... na tu vastv evaṁ naivam asti nāstīti vā vikalpyate vikalpanās tu puruṣabuddhyapekṣāḥ, na vastuyāthātmyajñānaṁ puruṣabuddhyapekṣam ı kiṁ tarhi? vastutantram eva tat ı na hi sthāṇāv ekasmin sthāṇur vā puruṣo 'nyo veti tattvajñānaṁ bhavati ı tatra puruṣo 'nyo veti mithyājñānam, sthāṇur eveti tattvajñānam ı vastutantratvāt ı *Sāṁkara-Bhāṣya*on *Brahmasūtra* 1.1.2.
Also, see: nanu jñānaṁ nāma mānasī kriyā ı na ı vailakṣaṇyāt ı kriyā hi nāma sā yātra (= yā + atra; my emendation for the printed word yatra) vastusvarūpanirapekṣaiva codyate puruṣacittavyāpārādhīnā ca ..... dhyānaṁ cintanaṁ yady api mānasaṁ tathāpi puruṣeṇa kartum akartum anyathā vā kartum śakyam, puruṣatantratvāt ı jñānaṁ tu pramāṇajanyam ı pramāṇaṁ ca yathābhūtavastusvarūpaviṣayam ı ato jñānaṁ kartum akartum anyathā vā kartum aśakyam ı kevalaṁ vastutantram eva tat ı tasmān mānasatve 'pi jñānasya mahad vailakṣaṇyam ı Ibid. 1.1.4.

12. yasya hi prasiddho vastubhedaḥ, - yathā kesarādimān ākṛtiviśeṣaḥ siṁhaśabda-pratyayabhāg anyaḥ prasiddhaḥ, tataś cānyaḥ puruṣaḥ prāyikaiḥ krauryaśauryādibhiḥ siṁhaguṇaiḥ saṁpannaḥ siddhaḥ, - tasya puruṣe siṁhaśabda-pratyayau gauṇau bhavataḥ, nāprasiddha-vastubhedasya ı tasya tv anyatrānyaśabdapratyayau bhrāntinimittāv eva bhavataḥ, na gauṇau ı yathā mandāndhakāre sthaṇur ayam ity agṛhyamāṇaviśeṣe puruṣaśabdapratyayau

sthāṇuviṣayau । Ibid. 1.1.4.

13. yatra bādhāniścayasattve 'pi icchayā tathājñānam, sa āhāryaḥ । sa cecchāprayojya eva, itarabuddher bādhaniścayaprati - badhyamānatvāt ।.... yathā mukhaṁ candraḥ । ... tatra hi mukhe condratvābhāvaniścaye 'pi candrābhedena mukhasya bodhanād āhāryatvam । *Vācaspatyam* (Sanskrit Encyclopaedia), under āropa.
14. *āhārya* is a variety of fourfold *abhinaya* and is used to singnify drapery: *āhāryābhinayo nāma jñeyo nepathyajo vidhih Nāṭyaśāstra*, Kashi Edn., 21.2.
15. prakṛtasya upameyasya adhyavasānam āhāryābhedaniścayaḥ, Kp/ Jhal. 628.
16. rasas tāvad abhidhīyate - .... vyaktiś ca bhagnāvaraṇā cit । yathā hi śarāvādinā pihito dīpas tannivṛttau saṁnihitān padārthān prakāsayati, svayaṁ ca prakāsate, evam ātmacaitanyaṁ vibhāvādisaṁvalitānratyādīn । antaḥkaraṇadharmāṇāṁ sākṣibhāsyatvābhyupagateḥ । vibhāvādīnām api svapnaturagādīnām iva raṅgarajatādīnām iva vā sākṣibhāsyatvam aviruddham । ..... *Rasagaṅgādhara*, Athavale's Edn., 1953, pages 54-55. The concept of *sākṣin* as the perceiver of mental faculties and false cognition is typical of the Vedantins. (See *Vedānta-paribhāṣā* of Dharmarāja Adhvarīndra, *Pratyakṣapariccheda*)
17. Vide: alaukikena vyāpāreṇa gocarīkriyamāṇaḥ । Ibid.
18. ānando hy ayaṁ na laukikasukhāntarasādhāraṇaḥ, anantaḥkaraṇavṛttirūpatvāt Ibid. This he has stated as part of the interpretation of the *Rasasūtra* by Abhinava, Mammaṭa and others, and may not be taken as his own view.
19. iyam ca parabrahmāsvādāt samādher vilakṣaṇā । Ibid.

Bhavabhuti's View on Pathetic Sentiment

D.K. Kharwandikar

In the midst of a galaxy of Sanskrit writers Bhavabhūti (Bh.) holds a unique place as a dramatist and stands next only to Kālidāsa in point of literary achievements. Bh. wrote 3 dramas viz. (1) *Mahāvira carita* (MC), (2) *Malatimādhava* (MM) and (3) Uttararāmacarita (UC). Fortunately it is possible unlike so many Sanskrit writers to fix the date of Bh. with a palpable accuracy. He is generally believed to have lived in the first half of the 8th century.[1] Scholars are also agreed upon the chronological sequence of his 3 dramas. Thus MC was Bh's first drama and UC was the last one. These two facts viz. Bh's date and the chronological order of his dramas are of some relevance for the point I am going to stress in the present paper. Bh. was well-versed in various branches of Knowledge including also the science of poetics. In his UC Bh. has propounded a peculiar view in regard to the sentiment of pathos (*Karuna rasa*). The present paper seeks to give a full exposition of this view in the light of various interpretations furnished by different scholars.

Out of the three dramas Bh. has chosen the story of Rāma for two dramas viz. MC and UC, while the plot of MM appears to be original. As regards the treatment of sentiments it can be noticed that in MC the heroic sentiment is principal, in MM erotic sentiment is principal, while in UC pathos is the governing sentiment. It will be interesting to observe the gradual change in Bh's attitude. We are mainly concerned with his view envisaged in UC.

In the third act of UC Bh. expresses the following view through one of the characters, Tamasā: "Pathos is the only sentiment, although due to diverse circumstances it assumes various forms; just as water assumes various forms such as eddies, bubbles and billows although it is all water only"[2]

The verse has been interpreted in various ways by scholars. A few interpretations are noted below:-

(1) P.V. Kane points out that according to Bh. 'the underlying sentiment through out this drama (i.e. UC) is *Karuṇa*'[3] and alternatively also thinks that 'the author hurls down a defiant challenge to some of his fastidious Critics'[4] who held that in a drama the principal sentiment should be either '*śṛṅgāra*' or '*vīra*'.

R.D. Karmarkar has offered mostly similar view.

According to V.V. Mirashi: "What the verse really means is that in the present play *Karuṇa* is the main *rasa*, but it appears in different forms in different characters."[5]

(2) G.K. Bhat opines that the statement does not aim at creating 'a new theory of *Rasa*,' but 'has a particular relevancy only in the context in which it occurs.' But he doubts whether Bh. intended to reveal the tragic basis of human experience.'[6] V. Raghavan has visualized a deeper sense and has suggested a '*Rasa*-synthesis' in this statement. Thus according to Bh. as viewed by him '*Karuṇa* is the *Prakṛti*; the other *Rasas* are its *Vikṛtis*'[7]. V. Raghavan has drawn upon a passage from Vīraraghava's commentary in support of his statement.

In short the question turns out to be whether Bh's statement is to be taken as restricted to the particular context or as a general statement. Prior to finding out any answer to this question it will be adequate to make a few observations on the traditional views about the principal sentiment in a drama.

(1) Bharata's *Nāṭyaśāstra* (NŚ) is the earliest work on dramaturgy. Bharata has sanctioned the use of all the *Rasas* in a drama without any discrimination.[8] He has repeated the expression *'Nānārasa'* in 20.12 in connection with a dramatic composition. However in one place Bharata has described *'Śṛṅgāra'*, '*raudra*', '*vīra*' and '*vībhatsa*' as the basic *rasas* (*utpatti-rasa*) and others as their derivatives.[9] Presumably he has to suggest the dominance of these sentiments in a drama. So far as the

pathetic sentiment is concerned Bharata has not raised it to any higher position. On the contrary, he is inclined towards avoiding the representation of tragic scenes as appears from the long list of forbidden incidents he has given.[10]

(2) The great poet Kalidāsa, perhaps following Bharata, attests to the use of a variety of sentiments[11] in a dramatic composition and also refers to a play *Lakṣmīsvayaṁvara* based on all the eight sentiments (*aṣṭarasāśraya*).[12] The general tendency of most of the sanskrit playwrights appears to give importance to either the erotic sentiment or the heroic sentiment, though they delineated other sentiments also according to the requirements of the dramatic situation. No writer has given prominence to the pathetic sentiment to the extent Bh. has done.

(2) It is further to be noted that no writer on dramaturgy prior to Bh. had specifically formulated that '*Śṛṅgāra*' or '*Vīra*' should be made a principal '*rasa*' in a drama. It was Ānandavardhana (c. 9th Cen.) who made it clear that only one sentiment should be made principal in a composition and other sentiments should be relegated to a subordinate position.[13] It is noteworthy that Ānandavardhana admits the highly pleasing nature of *Śṛṅgāra*, but he also points out that the quality of appealing the hearts par excellence resides in the sentiment of love in separation and the pathetic sentiment.[14]

The literary activity of Ānandavardhana is placed by P.V. Kane between 860 and 890 A.D.[15] and he is thus posterior to Bh. Although he does not quote from any of Bh's works it is possible that Bh. who lived 100 years earlier might have left some influence on him regarding his view on the sentiment of pathos. Another common point shared by both Bh. and Ānandavardhana is that both regard *Karuṇa rasa* as the nucleus of *Rāmāyaṇa* in similar terms.[16] Of course the mutual relation between Bh. and Ānandavardhana cannot be conclusively established at this stage.

Dhanañjaya, the author of *Daśarūpaka* (C. 10th century) and Viśvanātha, the author of *Sāhityadarpaṇa* (C. 14th century) categorically mention that '*Śṛṅgāra*' or '*vīra*' should be made a governing sentiment in a drama.[17] Probably they are reiterating some old tradition in this respect. Bh. should have presumably known this traditional view and he should have also noticed that no dramatist prior to him had given '*Karuṇa rasā* a principal position.

It is possible to surmise the circumstances that goaded Bh. to propound 'pathos' as the principal sentiment. In MC he says: In this drama there is heroic sentiment developed through the principal characters.[18] As the title of the play viz. *Mahāvīra-Carita* would have it, Bh. wanted to give prominence to the heroic sentiment perhaps following the traditional path. But the play miserably failed to gain popularity despite Bh's tall claim of being the 'Master of Speech' (Vaśyavāc). He had to face bitter criticism and while writing his second play MM, he had to declare pointblank that his writings were not meant for the censorious critics.[19] This time, however, he veers the heroic sentiment of his first drama and states that a (dramatic) composition should abound in the subtle presentation of various sentiments.[20] But even now he follows the conventional view and makes '*Śṛṅgārā* as the principal sentiment though sentiments like *Raudra, Vibhatsa, Karuṇa* etc. are also depicted side by side. Still his object of being the topmost dramatist was not translated into reality.

All this has driven Bh. to forsake the traditional path and he has to proclaim through the *sūtradhāra* of UC that people are mostly of fault finding nature and therefore one has to do one's duty regardless of public criticism.[21] Infused with the spirit of indifference towards critics Bh. repeats his claim of being the 'Master of Speech' in his last drama UC.

The statement of Bh. in regard to the principal position of '*Karuṇa rasā* is to be viewed on this background. While dealing with the later part of Ramaś story, as he understands, lies in the pivotal event of the tragic separation of the Krauñca-couple which he has fully narrated in Act II of UC. He has pinpointed the heart-rending agonies of the characters in this play and in particular he has time and again dwelt upon the sufferings of Rāma. According to Bh. Rāma was born as if to experience sufferings throughout his life.[22] Bh. realises that the keynote to the entire life of Rāma is '*Karuṇa rasā* which he has boldly projected in UC in defiance of the traditional supremacy of '*Śṛṅgārā* or '*Vīra*'

A possible objection may be raised as follows:

The end of the Rāmāyaṇa is tragic, but the UC ends in the reunion of Rāma and Sītā. When Bh. is giving so much importance to the '*Karuṇa* rasa' what should have prevented him from making the end of his drama tragic?

According to the canons of Sanskrit dramaturgy as laid down by Bharata etc. a tragic end of dramatic composition is forbidden and as a result we have practically no tragedies in Sanskrit in the strict sense of the term. It is true that Bh. at times deviates from the traditional path and would not have hesitated to make the end of his play tragic just because it was against convention or rules of dramaturgy. In all likelihood Bh. wants to give poetic justice to his characters, viz. Rāma, Sītā etc. and the demands of this poetic justice have made him differ from the great poet Vālmiki. That is why in the last Act of UC Bh. expressly puts the question to Vālmiki: '*eṣa te kāvyārthaḥ*/ (Is this the significance of your poem?) Thus Bh. has clearly suggested the disapproval of the tragic end of *Rāmayaṇa.* Moreover as G.K. Bhat has pointed out in his edition of UC (p.36) how the central theme of the play does not naturally lead to a tragic end and how it is necesary to make a distinction between tragedy and the tragic feeling.

Coming back again to the verse (UC III. 47) under consideration we have to observe that Bh. has confined the sentiment of pathos not merely to the particular context in which the statement is made but wants to make it applicable to the entire gamut of human life. In support of this he cites all illustration from the Vedānta philosophy. Just as water assumes various forms such as eddies, bubbles, ripples etc. so also pathos is the only sentiment in reality and the rest are just the modifications of pathos. The word '*vivarta*' in the verse may have a Vedantic import, viz. 'fallacious appearance attributed to the real substratum'. Bh. has used this term thrice in UC.[23] Bh. it is to be borne in mind, is a self-conscious writer and is in the habit of peeping in the midst of the happenings of his plays off and on.[24] With a train of bitter experiences in his personal life Bh. can reasonably be supposed to pass comments on human life, as it were, through the mouth of Tamasā. It is in this spirit that he rushes to the conclusion: '*Karuṇa* is the only sentiment and all other sentiments are its modifications.' It will thus be more plausible to read a deeper sense in this statement and maintain that Bh. employs '*Karuṇa rasā* as the background for his UC, but also evolves a general proposition that is aptly and universably applicable to human life.

It is worth while to note that with the projection of pathos as the principal sentiment Bh. could win the public encomium and virtually became the 'Master of Pathos' (*Kāruṇyam Bhavabhūtir eva tanute*) Scholars also acknowledged his greatness with the result that the following proverbial expression came into vogue:

'*Uttare rāmacarite Bhavabhūtir viśiṣyate*'(Bhavabhūti is at his best in his *Uttara rāmacarita*)

ABBREVIATIONS

Bh — Bhavabhūti
UC — *Uttararāmacarita*
MM — *Malatīmādhava*
MC — *Mahavīra Carita.*

NOTES

1. 'Bhavabhūtis' literary activity thus lay between A.D. 700 and 730' - Dr. V.V. Mirashi, '*Bhavabhūti*' (p. 11)
2. एको रसः करूण एव निमित्तभेदाद्
   भिन्नः पृथक् पृथगिवाश्रयते विवर्तान् ।
   आवर्तबुद्बुदतरङ्गमयान् विकारा–
   नम्भो यथा सलिलमेव हि तत्समस्त्रम् ।। (4c, III. 47)
3. Edn. of UC, p. 117
4. 10c. cit.
5. *Bhavabhūti*, p. 280
6. Edn. of UC, pp. 34, 35
7. 'The Number of Rasas', p. 163
8. cf. सर्वभावैः सर्वरसैः सर्वकर्मप्रवृत्तिभिः ।
   नानावस्थान्तरोपेतं नाटकं संविघयिते ।। (*NŚ*, 19. 147)

9. *NŚ*, 6-39
10. *NŚ*, 18. 14-17
11. cf. त्रैगुण्योद्भवमत्र लोकचरितं नानारसं दृश्यते ।
Mālavikāgnimitraon, I.4
12. Vide Vikramorvaśīya, II-17
13. cf. प्रसिध्देऽपि प्रबन्धानां नानारसनिबन्धने ।
एको रसो ऽङ्गिकर्तव्यस्तेषामुत्कर्ष मिच्छता ।। (*Dhvanyāloka*, III. 21)
14. शृङ्गार एव मधुरः परः प्रहलाद नो रसः (Opcit II-8) and
शृङ्गारे विप्रलम्भाख्ये करूणे च प्रकर्षवत् ।
माधुर्यमार्द्रतां याति यतस्तत्राधिकं मनः ।। (II. 9)
15. *History of Sanskrit Poetics*, p. 193
16. cf. द्वन्द्ववियक्रौञ्चगोत्थः शोकः श्लोकत्वमागतः । (*Dhvanyāloka* I.S and see commentary on this vesrse.) Also read — रामायणे हि करुणो रसः स्वयमादिकविना सूचितः । (Ibid IV. 5). Bh. who probably follows Kalidāsa's *Raghuvamis'a* (निषादविध्दाण्डजदर्शनोत्थः श्लोकत्वमापद्यत यस्य शोकः) as described the Krauñca episode at length in UC-Act II. In uc - VII.1.12 he describes the *Rāmayaṇa* as having *Karuṇa* and *Adbhuta Rasas.*
17. cf. एको रसोऽङ्गकीर्तव्यो वीरः शृङ्गार एव वा ।
अङ्गमन्ये रसाः सर्वे (*Daśarūpaka*, III. 33-34)
एक एव भवेदङ्गी शृङ्गारो वीर एव वा ।
अङ्गमन्ये रसाः सर्वे (*Sāhityadarpaṇa*, VI-10)
Dhanañjaya and Viśvanātha lived after Bh. and it is not tenable to maintain that Bh. is refuting their view by advocating the supremacy of pathos in UC. Most of the editors quote the above two verses as if to show that Bh. is refuting the view expressed therein.
18. अप्राकृतेषु पात्रेषु यत्र वीरः स्थितो रसः । MC, I.3
19. cf. येनाम केचिदिह नः प्रथयन्त्यवज्ञां
जानन्तु ते किमपि तान् प्रति नैष यत्नः । MM, I-8
20. भूम्ना रसानां गहनाः प्रयोगाः । MM, I-6
21. सर्वथा व्यवहर्तव्यं कुतो ह्यवचनीयता ।
यथा स्त्रीणां तथा वाचां साधुत्वे दुर्जनो जनः ।। UC. I-5
22. दुःखसंवेदनायैव रामे चैतन्यमाहितम् । UC. I-47
Vide also UC III-1 —पुटपाकप्रतीकाशो रामस्य करुणो रसः ।
23. UC-II. 5.8 — शब्दब्रह्मणस्तादृशं विवर्तमितिहासं रामायणं प्रणिनाय ।

UC. VI. 6 — ब्रह्मणीव विवर्तानां क्वापि विप्रलयः कृतः ।

24. cf. अहो सरसरमणीयता संविधानकस्य । (MM. VI.13. 3-4)
अस्ति वा कुतश्चिदेवंभूतमद्भुतं विचित्ररमणीयोज्ज्वलं प्रकरणम् ।
(Ibid, X-23. 17-18)
अहो संविधानकम् । (UC. III-47 - The statement preceding the verse under consideration)

SELECT BIBLIOGRAPHY

1. *Uttararāmacarita* Editions by (i) P.V. Kane, (ii) R.D. Karmarkar, (iii) S.K. Belvalkar and (iv) G.K. Bhat.
2. V.V. Mirashi - *Bhavabhuti*
3. P.V. Kane - *History of Sanskrit Poetics*.
4. V. Raghavan - *The Number of Rasas.*
5. G.K. Bhat - *Tragedy and Sanskrit Drama*
6. G.K. Bhat - *Bharata Nāṭya Mañjarī*

Dhvanyāloka and Linguistic Approach to Literature

R. V. Dhongde

Scope, Limits and Goals

I am going to consider the first chapter (*uddyota*) of Ānandavardhana's *Dhvanyaloka*

It seems that there is a tradition of reading Ānandavardhana's *Dhvanyāloka* in the light of Abhinavagupta's commentary (*locana*) on it. I shall consider them separately.

I am not going to consider the philosophical, aesthetic, and historical aspects of the text. I shall consider them from a linguistic point of view which include formal, semantic and stylistic considerations.

I am sure the analysis of this type of all the chapters of the text would yield interesting areas of comparison between Western stylistics and *Dhvanyāloka* and revive some forgotten points of reference for modern Indian poetics. But the present attempt is obviously a partial one.

As I am not going to take into account the whole of the *Dhvannyaloka*, some of the observations that I make may ultimately need modification or re-evaluation. Unless the total framework of the theory is taken into account, it would be difficult to identify which observations are relevant and which are not.

There is a risk in reading and interpreting *Dhvanyāloka* with the help of *Locana* Though *Locana* is helpful many times, there are places where one feels that the *Locana* defence of *Dhvanyāloka* is unnecessary and where one doubts whether *Dhvanyāloka* really meant what the *Locana* says. For example, in Chapter 2 under verse 1, when Ānandavardhana gives an example from Vālmīki's (*ādikavi*) *Rāmāyaṇa*, Abhinavagupta comments that the word *ādikavi* suggests that the concept of *dhvani* also is an ancient (*ādi*) one. In Chapter 2, Ānandavardhana states that *vācya* and *pratīyamāna* are two parts of meaning. Abhinavagupta's comment that Ānandavardhana wants to show the multi-purposes of *vācya* 'meaning' is his own addition; it is doubtful whether Anandavardhan had that in his mind. The interpretation of Ānandavardhana's text thus needs a fresh considertion.

In both, *Dhvanyāloka* and *Locana*, Sanskrit verses are quoted to illustrate the points. In spite of our beliefs and hard efforts, one cannot deny the fact that Sanskrit is a second language for us. This brings stringent limitations on verifying the illustration or even refuting the arguments on the basis of the examples given. Finding out parallel examples in one's mother-tongue, literature is not a solution. It is because that also implies that one has fully understood the Sanskrit examples. It is needless to state that understanding the Sanskrit verses does not simply mean understanding the literal meaning of them; for *dhvani* implies the context which is a part of a non-recoverable culture.

The only choice left to us is to accept the interpretations offered and to seek modern concepts with utmost care.

Our goal is therefore not to evaluate *Dhvanyāloka* but to elicit information from it in the light of the Western linguistic approach to literature.

We will treat *Dhvanāloka* and *Locana* separately though quite often *Locana* helps in a better understanding of *Dhvanyāloka*. *Dhvanyāloka* contains verses (*kārikā*) and some explanation (*vritti*); *Locana* is a commentary on both.

We are not assuming that the modern approach has tackled all the problems that *Dhvanyāloka* tackles; we are not considering *Dhvanyāloka* as a primitive text. There may be issues discussed in *Dhvanyāloka* which are not considered or which are not satisfactorily death with in the modern linguistic approach. The comparision, in short, has no evaluative goal; its goal is mainly to enrich our overall understanding.

Dhvanyāloka (Chapter 1)

The following is the summary of the main arguments:

(a) *Dhvani* is the soul of poetry.

(b) There are three objections to this proposition.

(i) *Dhvani* does not exist.

(ii) *Dhvani* is nothing but *bhākta artha.*

(iii) *Dhvani* cannot be described.

Objection (b.i): *Dhvani* cannot be something which is not *śabda* and *artha*, or *vṛutti* and *ṛīti.* Poetry consists in words (*śabda*) and their meanings (*artha*). How can *Dhvani* be different from these?

Most probably *Dhvani* is some part of *guṇa* or *alaṁkāra* If poetry is defined as *Dhvani* which is none of these elements, then that definition makes no sense.

(c) Before we define what *Dhvani* is, we should know that *Dhvani* has two parts (*bheda*): the literal meaning (*vācya*) and the experiential meaning (*pratīyamāna*). In figures of speech (*alaṁkāra*) such as simile (*upamā*), we deal with *vācya artha*, it is concrete like the limbs. *Pratīyamāna artha* is like the lustre (*lāvaṇya*) of the body; its liveliness.

(d) *Vastu* (word-based meaning), *alaṁkāra* (figures-of speech), and *rasa* all suggest/create the *pratīyamana* meaning. Examples are given to show the differences between the two parts of meanings.

(e) Out of these three, the experiential meaning based on *rasa* is the dominant meaning in poetry. *Ramāyaṇa* is an example of *dhvani* based on the *śoka* (sorrow) *rasa.*

(f) *Pratīyamāna artha* cannot be captured or understood solely with the help of grammar (*śabda-śāsana*) and lexicon (arthaśāsana). It requires poetic sensibility.

(g) Thus *vācyārtha (literal meaning) is different from pratīyamānārtha* (experiential meaning) or *vyaṅgyārtha* The word carrying *pratīyamāna artha* is rare; one who aspires to be a great poet should have the practice in detecting such words.

A great poet uses *vyañjaka śabda* (words having *vyaṅgyārtha*) that give *vyaṅgyārtha*, not *vācak śabda* that give *vācyārtha*.

(h) However *pratīyamāna artha* is not independent of *vācyārtha*, it is experiential with the help of *vācyārtha*. Just as a person uses a lamp to see the objects in darkness, a poet uses *vācyārtha* to lead to the *vyaṅgyārtha*.

(i) Dependence does not reduce the primacy of *pratīyamāna artha*. Just as though the meaning of a sentence is the sum of the meanings of the words in it and yet the sentence meaning is above word-meanings; similarly, though *pratīyamāna artha* is experienced on the basis of *vācyārtha*, it is something more than and above mere *vācyārtha*. It is experienced by the reader in a flash.

(j) We get *Dhvani* when *vācyārtha* lies low and suggests *vyaṅgyārtha*.

(k) *Alaṁkāra* (figures-of-speech) are concerned either with the form of words or with their literal meaning. In them *vācyārtha* is primary. Examples are given. We get Dhvani only when *vācyārtha* becomes subordinate to *vyaṅgyārtha*. Poetry without *Dhvani* is *citra Kāvya*.

(l) The objection that *Dhvani* does not exist (b.i) is ridiculous. And to say that as it was not defined earlier because it did not exist is illogical.

(m) *Dhvani* has two types: *avivakśita-vācya:* here the *vācyārtha* is improbable and therefore to be rejected. *Vivakṣitānyapara-vācya* here *vācyārtha* is probable but its aim is to suggest *vyaṅgyārtha*. Examples are given.

(n) The objection (b.ii) that *Dhvani* is *bhākta artha* also is wrong. One can find examples where there is *Dhvani* but no *bhakti* or where there is *bhakti* without the existence of *Dhvani*. Examples are given.

(o) The objection (b.iii) that *Dhvani* cannot be described will be refuted by us by offering clear definitions of *Dhvani*.

Analysis

The whole approach seems to be deductive. *Dhvani* is considered to be the soul of poetry; it is said to be in all excellent poetry; it is also said to be beyond the concepts postulated and discussed by other critics. The statement of the hypothesis is followed by citation of evidence and by descriptive statements about the hypothecised phenomenon.

In the first chapter a negative approach is used as a strategy. The objections to the hypothecised *Dhvani* are refuted to establish the validity of the main proposition: *Dhvani* is the soul of poetry.

It is interesting to note that the postulated *Dhvani* is defined by postulating *pratīyamāna artha* which is metaphorically described as *lāvaṇya* and some examples are given. Thus right from the beginning any attempt to define *Dhvani* in terms of linguistic forms or elements (i.e., any formal definition of *Dhvani*) is discouraged.

In order to show the difference between *vācyārtha* and *pratīyamāna artha* (of. 2.1 d) four examples are cited:

(i) A woman tells a stranger to move about fearlessly near the river-bank (where she often meets her lover) as the stranger need not be afraid of the dog there — the dog has been killed by a wild lion hiding behind the bushes.

The verse contains an Imperative 'you may wander fearlessly'. This is *vācyārtha* - the apparent meaning of the words used by the woman. But she is hinting that the stranger may be attacked now by the lion. The implication therefore is a negative Imperative: 'Don't wander over there'. The verse suggests how the woman is keen on protecting her rendezvous from intrusion. The Dhvanyāloka gives four different examples to prove its point:

	Vācyārtha	Vyaṅgyārtha
1.	Non-neg. Imp (*vidhi*)	Neg Imp (*ṇishedha*)
2.	Neg Imp	Non-neg Imp
3.	Non-neg Imp	Neither Non-neg Imp nor Neg Imp
4.	Neg Imp	Neg Imp

The fourth example is worth considering along with the first. In the verse a lover criticises a courtesan by saying that she has brought light to the darkness. The result is that other courtesans cannot move about freely. He asks her not to go ahead.

Here the Neg-Imperative is *vācya* But the suggested meaning may change according to the context:

	Context	Suggested meaning or *pratīyamāna* artha
1.	Her own lover persuading her to stay with him.	He praises her beauty and requests her not to go away.
2.	Her friend teases her.	The friend admires her beauty but teases her about her passionate surrender to her lover.
3.	The lover meets her on the way.	He wants her to go with him. He praises her beauty in an indirect way.
4.	A third person is speaking to the courtesan	He is paying a tribute to her beauty.

In all these tribute is paid to the courtesan's beauty but the Neg-Imp. suggests four different things according to the context. The four contexts are different according to the kind of addresser and his/her relation to the addressee. Thus what we get is the following:

	Context	Suggested meaning
	1	1
apparent or literal meaning (*vācyartha*)	2	2
	3	3
	4	4

In modern semantics we talk about word-level semantics, sentence-level semantics and pragmatics. In pragmatics we consider the context of situation which includes the participants, their social relations, the manner of speech, and the nature of the occasion (formal, informal etc.). This verse appears to be an attempt to cover pragmatics under the domain of semantics. However, nowhere does *Dhvanyāloka* discuss the elements of context that lead to a particular interpretation.

In the earlier examples the *vācyārtha* hints the *vyaṅgyārtha.* In *rasa* - the third type of *pratīyamāna artha* - (cf. 2.1.e) - *rasa* accompanies *vācyārtha* Here *rasa* is felt or experienced at the very time of understanding the *vācyārtha Rasa* is considered to be the main type of *pratīyamāna artha.*

One has to differentiate between the suggested meaning and the experiential meaning which is *rasa.* Ānandavardhana is here referring to the emotional impact of poetry. Whether to consider the emotional effect of poetry or any effect of any verbal communication under semantics or not is yet to be decided even in modern semantics. The whole argument centering around the concept of *rasa* is as yet beyond the scope of linguistic approach to poetry.

One of the approaches of modern stylistics is to consider the relations among elements with reference to the effects they produce. Thus identification of stylistic markers is not simply looking for striking linguistic patterns but choosing only those linguistic patterns that are related to the effect.

It seems that as we move from *alaṁkāra-dhvani* to *rasa-dhvani* the elements to be identified become more and more abstract.

That is the reason why *Dhvanyāloka* holds that the *pratīyamāna artha* is beyond grammar and lexicon (cf. 2.1.f). The Sanskrit grammatical tradition as examplified in Pāṇini is mainly a structural tradition. The *kośaśāstra* in Sanskrit is not supposed to tamper with syntax or semantics. The problem of homonymy, polysemy, synonmic distinctions, for example, are not dealt with in a dictionary (*kośa*). Such areas are reserved for *alaṁkāra-śāstra* In Sanskrit the discussion of semantic problems is either left to some philosophical school or to poetics; they are not considered to be the main concerns of a linguist. The view that it requires poetic sensibility to understand *pratīyamāna artha* closes doors for further analysis.

The view that the word expressing *pratīyamāna artha* is rare and a great poet is always in search of it entails that the style of great poetry is a matter of choice. The western view that style is choice of particular alternant from a set of alternants implies the same.

One wonders if the word *śabda* means only the word and not the expression which may be larger than a word. This is because the *Dhvanyāloka* here seems to be giving an undue importance only to the word-meaning.

How do we understand the meaning of a sentence? (cf. 2.1.8) The question raises a linguistic issue. When one understands a sentence, one certainly does that on the basis of the words in it; but when one understands the total meaning of a sentence, one is not aware of the meanings of its parts.

Dhvanyāloka is not aware of the fact that the meaning of a sentence is not merely a total of the meanings of words it contains. Words have structural relations and they also contribute to the meaning. The syntactic structure of a sentence gives grammatical meaning. The sequence is unimportant in the sense that all grammatical relations are not necessarily sequential.

The word-to-sentence analogy is used to illustrate the relation between *vācyārtha* and *pratīyamāna artha*. When one understands the *pratīyamāna artha*, one is not aware of the underlying *vācyārtha*, though *vācyārtha* helps him to get the *pratīyamāna artha*. In fact just as between words and a sentence there are syntactic structures, between *pratīyamāna artha* and *vācyārtha* there must be semantic structures. There is no attempt in *Dhvanyāloka* to explore the structures. Instead an easy explanation of quick (*jhaṭiti*) realization is offered.

In *Dhvani* the *vācyārtha* is either improbable or insignificant.

Dhvani is defined in terms of *vācyārtha* and *vyaṅgyārtha*. When *vyaṅgyārtha* becomes prominent, there is *dhvani*; when it is subordinate there is *arthālaṁkāra* (cf. 2-1)j, k). For example, in a verse the moon and the night are described. The suggested comparison is that between a lover and his beloved. But the primary aim is to describe the night and the moon.

One can however imagine a context where the lover saying this to his beloved will make the suggested meaning primary. *Dhvanyāloka* never clearly states the context of the text or the context of situation for the verses quoted. In 3.2. we saw that by changing the context of situation one can get different interpretations. If the context of situation does not permit the *vyaṅgyārtha* to be primary and the *vācyārtha* to be subordinate a fair question to ask would be: what is there in the text that imposes this restriction? An answer to this question will have to be stated in terms of linguistic elements in the verse.

In short, either the difference between an *arthālaṁkāra* such as *samāsokti* and *dhvani* (where *vyaṅgyārtha* is said to be superior to *vācyārtha*) should be accounted for in terms of pragmatic elements or in terms of the linguistic structure of the verses. *Dhvanyāloka* shows the differences by giving illustrative verses but does not explore the system underlying them.

Bhakti is said to be different from *vyaṅgyārtha* (cf. 2-1.n). In *bhakti* a word is used with a different meaning. For example, 'the bed tells' means 'the bed indicates' as the primary meaning of 'tell' cannot go well with 'bed'. *Bhakti* thus includes: metaphorical meaning, synecdoche, semantic ambiguity and in some cases polysemy. That is the different meaning in *bhakti* stems from these reasons.

Reviewing the examples one feels that *bhakti* is tied to the meaning of individual words; *dhvani* is a larger concept than *bhakti*. The word cannot be replaced when it has *Dhvani*. *Dhvani* thus implies the best choice. Secondly *Dhvani* is an experiential meaning; it is emitted like light, it is emitted in an aesthetic way.

It seems that by making Dhvani an aesthetic object *Dhvanyāloka* is trying to indicate the difference between the ordinary use of language and the special (i.e., poetic) use of language. *Dhvani* thus becomes a necesary condition of poetry.

We will now consider Abhinavagupta's *Locana* *Locana* is basically a commentary on *Dhvanyāloka* It interprets the text by supplying more information, by creating a proper perspective for the arguments, by explaining some concepts, and by adding more details. It is not a critical commentary as it never disagrees with the original text. We will therefore concentrate on certain significant points raised in it.

In discussing the types of *pratīyamāna artha* Abhinavagupta summarizes the various approaches to meaning.

(a) *Abhidhā*. This seems to be the primary meaning of the word. Reference would be a better example of it. The relation between the object in the real world and the sound image of the word is conventional (*sānketika*).

(b) *Tātparya* Words in a sentence have their relations. This seems to be what is called by some linguists the linguistic meaning of a sentence. Thus even sentences such as 'There are ten elephants on my ten fingers' have *tātparya* meaning. The pragmatic oddity has nothing to do with the linguistic meaning. (Chomsky would call it a syntactically well-formed sentence.)

(c) *Lakṣaṇā* When both *abhidhā* and *tātparya* are unable to give a semantic well-formedness; *lakṣaṇā* begins to operate. The sentence 'the boy is a lion' cannot make sense if only *abhidhā* and *tātparya* are taken into account. The word lion indicates the animal's quality of bravery. This meaning becomes prominant only in *lakṣaṇā* When this becomes habitual, there is no beauty in it. In poetry the poet tries to find out new examples of *lakṣaṇā*

(d) *Dhvani* is the next stage. It makes all other meanings subordinate.

In discussing *rasa-dhvani* Abhinavagupta brings in a moral standard. Feeling passion for one's wife is moral - it creates *rasa* or *bhāva*. Feeling passion for a woman who is married to another person is immoral - it creates *ābhāsa* of *rasa* or *bhāva*. Thus one can put it in a tabular form:

	Proper *chittavritti* (moral)	Constancy (long duration)
rasa	ś	ś
bhāva	ś	–
rasābhasa	–	ś
bhāvābhasa	–	–

Quoting his predecessors, Abhinavagupta twice makes a distinction between *śāstra, ākhyāna* and *kāvya*; they are like one's own master, friend, and wife respectively. In *śāstra* the words are important; in *ākhyāna* the meaning is important; in *kāvya* both are subordinate - *Dhvani* is important.

Abhinavagupta later on makes another distinction in *kāvya* and *śāstra*. In *kāvya* one gets *ānanda* through *rasa*, in śāstra one gets practical knowledge (*laukika*). *Rasa* has no cause as such. Moreover *rasa* is related to a particular moment; it has no past or future reference.

Abhinavagupta mentions five types of *lakṣaṇā*

Types of relation	Example
(a) *vācya-vācaka* relation	*dvirepha* (two 'r' sounds)
	= *bhramara*
(b) *sāmīpya* (vicinity)	'in the river'
	= on its bank
(c) *samavāya* (joining)	'stick entered'
	= man with the stick entered'
(d) *vaiparītya* (opposition)	my enemy has obliged me
	= he has harmed me.
(e) *kārya-kāraṇ*	He takes my life
(causal relation)	= he snatches my food.

Comments

Discussing *tātparya* and *abhidhā* together may lead to non-distinction between word meaning and sentence meaning.

Some of the types of *lakṣaṇā* can be explained in the following way:

(a) *vācya-vācaka* relation: onomatopoeic words also will fall under this

(c) *samavāya* synechdoche

(d) *vaiparītya* satire

Only in (b) (*sāmīpya*) and (e) (*kārya-kāraṇ*) we get a different kind of sentence meaning as the conceptual meaning of the word cannot fit in. But again the centre of focus is the word, not the sentence.

Incidently word-meanings such as collocative meaning, stylistic meaning, emotive meaning and sentence-meanings such as thematic meaning, contradiction, syntheticity are not accounted for in this framework.

In the discussion of *rasa* we quite often find a reference to propriety which is based on moral grounds. Ironically, the examples given in the text are about persons not necessarily married to each other.

It seems that in differentiating *śāstra*, *ākhyāna* and *kāvya* sound-image, information, and poetic meaning are distinguised. In modern stylistics distinctions are made among scientific writing, ordinary writing and literature. In scientific writing terms are well-defined and only terms matter. Any *lakṣaṇā* is discouraged. In ordinary use of language both precision of meaning and *lakṣaṇā* are not cultivated. In literature, there are no terms. Novel ways of meaning extension and novel patterns of meaning are discovered.

Conclusions

Dhvanyāloka does not have a structural approach to the study of meaning. It hardly talks about any structural elements and their constructions.

Dhvani is a primitive. It is more of a psychological entity than a formal one. So is *rasa*.

Conventional primary meaning of words (*vācyārtha*), meaning of sentence, types of meaning extension (*lakṣaṇā*), and suggested meaning (*Dhvani*) are the four aspects of meaning identified. But they do not form a system. Poetry is said to contain *dhvani*. One can get *dhvani* directly from *vācyārtha* or via *lakṣaṇā* The distinctions between word-meaning and sentence meaning can be based on some of the concepts in *Dhvanyāloka*

Dhvanyāloka gives examples of pragmatic meaning though it does not analyse it.

Taking into account both *Dhvanyāloka* and Locana, one finds that the concept of *lakṣaṇā* needs to be analysed. *Lakṣaṇā* is a word-meaning, a sentence meaning, and a contextual meaning as well. The following diagram will illustrate this:

(a) Conventional: *abhidhā* onomatopoeic: *kākā*
arbitrary : e.g., *go*

(b) *nirūḍhā lakṣaṇā*
e.g., *kuśala, lāvaṇya dvirepha*

(c) in a sentence

(d) word meaning + grammatical meaning. *vācyārtha*

(e) pragmatic oddity sānipya: *gaṅgāyāṁ ghosh, samavāya* synecduchee.g. *baṭu - sinha*
e.g., *yaṣṭi* ī man with a stick metaphor: *sādharmāya*

(f) in a context

(g) textual *vaiparītya* (opposition) e.g., enemy's praise satire *Kāryakāraṇa bhārae*.g., *Prāṇ-anna.*

(h) situational *vācyārtha.*
(which is *mukhyārtha*) is subordinated in both (g) and (h) and also in the examples of *pratīyamāna* we discussed under 3.2. The distinction between the two is not clear.

The Theory of Communication: An Indian View-Point

A.P. Dikshit

The problem of communication is, in fact, three dimensional relating to (a) the writer, (b) the work or the writing and (c) the audience or the receiver.

However, to immediately grapple with the situation, I would like to mention that communication, with an exception like Benedetto Croee and the like-minded thinkers, of course, has been widely accepted in the West as an essential quality of Art. Abercrombie denies any place to a work amongst Art, if it does not communicate. No communication, no art, is his formula. I.A. Richards talks of the two pillars upon which a theory of criticism must rest, and communication is one of them. What Richards means by the term 'Communication' is, as he says, neither the strict 'transference of experience', nor it is the 'participation in identical experience', but it "takes place when one mind so acts upon its environment that another mind is influenced, and in that other mind an experience occurs which is like the experience in the first mind, and is caused in part by that experience." "For communication defined as strict transference of or participation in identical experiences does not occur."

Tolstoy insists so much upon communication that his 'Infection theory' becomes the subject of indignation for critics and aestheticians like Roger Fry, whom Richards quotes in this respect in his "Principles of Literary Criticism".

It would be interesting to note that Sanskrit poeticians, and poets too, as far as my knowledge goes, hardly ever talk directly about communication and still they have been able to formulate a theory like that of *Rasa* which gives an evidence that they knew about and believed in communication. Scholars who gave the uppermost importance to *Rasa* in poetry and talked about the *Jhaṭiti Pratyaya or Asaṁlakṣyakramavyaṅgyadhvani* cannot be said to be lacking in knowledge about communication. May be that they did not want to increase the burden of the poet already much burdened by acquiring efficiency in different sources of knowledge such as *Śilpa* etc. (न तद्‌ ज्ञानं न तच्छल्पंन सा विद्या न सा कला । जायते यत्न काव्यांगं अहो भारो महान्‌ कवेः ।।), nor did they want to put the poet under any kind of pressure, whose imagination, he believed, surpasses all the laws of the Destiny and who is the sole master, the *Prajāpati* of this vast world of poetry endowed with the capabilities of giving shape to it according to his own wish. They wanted to give him the entire freedom to create things that were never there, but they would take all the care not to allow the poet to indulge in any kind of impropriety lest it might effect the poetry adversely and may cause the *Rasabhaṅga* or may hamper the emotional quality of the poem. Their expectations were rather from the reader that he exercises his capabilities in understanding the poem on the basis of the clues given in a poem. It was his share of burden to prove his competence as a sensible reader of poetry. This tradition came down to the 17th and even 18th century *Vikrami* till the time of poet Ghanānand whose remarkable achievements in the field of poetry won the admiration of his contemporaries as well as that of the later critics who put several conditions before the reader of his poems. Incidentally, Cleanth Brooks appreciates this kind of stand when he passes the remark against the theory of communication saying in his essay on "What Poetry Communicates" as follows:

"The theory of communication throws the burden of proof upon the poet, overwhelmingly and at once. The reader says to the poet: Here I am; it's your job to get it across to me - when he ought to be assuming the burden of proof himself." (*The Well Wrought Urn*).

There is nothing new if his arguments carry him back to the term 'Maker' for the poet in preference to the term 'Communicator' which this theory of communication favours. However, Richards has no intention to show any kind of disregard to the poet, as would be clear from what he states in this matter. According to him "Although it is as a communicator that it is most profitable to consider the artist, it is by no means true that he commonly looks upon himself in this light. In the course of his work he is not as a rule deliberately and consciously engaged in a communicative endeavour. When asked, he is more likely than not to reply that communication is an irrelevant or best a minor issue, and that what he is making is something which is beautiful in itself, or satisfying to him personally, or something expressive, in a more or less vague sense, of his emotions, or of himself, something personal and individual. That other people are going to study it, and to receive experiences from it may seem to him a merely accidential, inessental circumstance. More modestly still, he may say that when he works he is merely amusing himself." (*Principles of Literary Criticism, p. 26*).

The last words of his argument lead us to another controversy, i.e. to whom is the poetry addressed? Whether it is the poet himself who writes for his own self or it is the public in general and whether writing for the general public would not lower down the standard of poetry. According to the celebrated Hindi poet Goswami Tulasidas '*Svantaḥ sukha*' can go hand in hand with "*Sabahi Sulabh*' i.e., accessible to all. But let us not delve ourselves into this controversy and let us turn to the reader who has an important role to play in this whole set-up.

One thing which calls our attention is the remarkable difference in the use of the terms which stand for the recipient of poetry in Western and Indian Poetics. Audience, reader, recipient and spectator, are the four terms that are used by western thinkers, whereas in Indian poetics we find several terms being used and with different connotations. For example, right from the *Kāmasūtra* down to Panditraja Jagannatha we find such terms as *Nāgaraka*, *Sāmājika*, *Bhāvaka*, *Sahṛdaya*, *Pratibhājas*, *Vidagdha*, *Viduṣ*, *Sant*, *Rasajña* and last of all the *Rasika*. One can very easily mark it that the terms used by the Westerners are based on their organic activities. As against this the terms used in Indian Poetics are related to the mental capabilities of the recipient and the terms like *nagarāka*and *sāmājika* try to mark his place in the society. If we go into the detailed history of the use of these terms we will come across the various changes in our society that effected our mode of thinking and looking towards the Art and especially poetry. These terms proved to be self-explanatory and, therefore, it did not seem necessary for us to talk about the 'Ideal reader' quite apart from a reader, and to give him the status of a class-representative or that of an Elite. Kalidāsa considers the dramatic performance *sādhu,* i.e., best and perfect devoid of all the blemishes, only if it was considered so by the learned. (आ परितोषाद विदुषां न साधुमन्ये प्रयोग विज्ञानम.) (1/3) and for *Kāvyas* like *Raghuvaṁśa* and others, he found the Sants reliable (नं सन्त श्रोतुमहन्ति सदव्यक्ति हे म्नं तवः । हे संलक्ष्यते हन्यग्नौ विशुद्धिः कापि वा रघुवशं 1, 10 ।।) but later on, possibly because of the great influence of Ānandavardhana and Abhinavagupta, the term *sahṛdaya* came to stay. The very word *sahṛdaya* gives us, in all its vividness the account of the qualities as well as his relation with the writer. He was considered to be the touch-stone of *kāvyātmā.* Whichever meaning was appreciated or praised by him or whichever *śabdārtha* proved to be pleasant to him it all was accepted as हन्यग्नौ विशुद्धिः कापि वा रघुवशं 1, 10 (1. योऽर्थः सहृदयश्क्ताघ्यः काव्यात्मेति व्यवस्थितः । घ्व 1/2) (2. सहृदयहृदअलादि शब्दार्थमयन्मेव काव्यकथाण्म.). The reader is called a *sahṛdaya* for two reasons: (a) because he has the capacity to understand the poetry through experiencing it emotionally and not as any logician or the Grammarian tries to understand it in piecemeal and is satisfied only if he finds any coherence in it. Contrary to this the *sahṛdaya* enjoys poetry in its wholeness and without wasting his time on searching for the coherence. He knows that poetry does not have the coherence such as the grammatical and logical expression does have.

(b) Because he has the pleasure of experiencing poetry on par with the poet himself and that is because he enjoys to a great extant an equal amount of *pratibha* like that of the poet with a little difference in potential that a poet can express himself whereas a *sahṛdaya* can not. He possesses *bhāvayitṛ pratibhā,* the genius or the faculty of experience while the poet is the possessor of *kārayitṛ pratibhā,* i.e., the Creative faculty, in addition to the *bhāvayitṛ* of course. Because of this *bhāvayitṛ pratibhā* he establishes the rapport in the form of *hṛdaya-samvāda* with the poet. It is noteworthy here that Abhinavagupta states in very clear terms that not always every *sahṛdaya* is able to establish this rapport because one may feel pleasure in reading a *virarasa kāvya* while the same person may not have the same kind of pleasure when he reads a śāntarasa poem.

This very quality of establishing a *hṛdaya śamvāda* is also being appreciated by Richards when he says: "In any case it is certain that no mere careful study of communicative possibilities, together with any desire to communicate, however intense, is ever sufficient without close natural correspondence between the poet's impulses and possible impulses of his reader." (*Principles of Literary Criticism*, p. 28). And Sartre also in his book *What is Literature* talks on page 29 about the "Dialectical Correlative" between the poet and his reader meaning thereby the same thing which we call *hṛdaya samvāda.* We can find some similarity between the 'Ideal' and the 'Elite' reader and the *sahṛdaya,* though not to the extent of considering him as a representative of any special class in the social order, if we follow Abhinavagupta when he enumerates the necessary qualities of a *sahradaya* as "भेषांकाव्यानुशक्तिनवशात ....etc."

But let us not just go through all this account and just have a cursory glance at the Poem itself from the communication point of view. I would like to draw your attention to the discussion of 'Obscurity' by Herbert Read, 'Ambiguity' by William Empson, 'Obliquity' by E.M. Tillyard, 'Difficulty' by Cleanth Brooks and the last of all the theory of 'Silence' as put forward by Susan Santog. It is clear that they are not talking the same thing when they are talking about 'Obscurity' etc., but at the same time they all sincerely feel that Modern Poetry cannot be understood in the same manner as one used to understand traditional poetry. It is because sometimes it is obscure and does not convey the sense very clearly, sometimes it is ambiguous because of the use of so many implications of the words and phrases that one cannot be very sure about the meaning which the poet actually wants to convey, sometimes it is difficult because we are not accustomed to the use of the words and therefore fail to reach the poet's intended meaning. And there are so many other reasons, too, such as the Abstraction, Displacement, Condensation, Distortion, use of Montage-Collage and last but not the least, Mythical Allusions.

However, all of them accept the presence of emotional unity in the poem as such and propose either directly or indirectly to wait and see patiently till all this exercise which makes the modern poetry seem inaccessible to the reader, grows a little old and we become familiar with it. Read indirectly hints at that there are several causes why any particular poem may seem obscure to us. For example, we may not understand and fully appreciate even Dante at first reading or as a native speaker of a language we may not give weitage to others not of the same blood. There are times when we are free from all such limitations, we can even understand and enjoy the foreign poetry even. I wonder if we can interpret him in the fashion of Indian poetics that poetry requires a kind of *saṁskāra Viśesa* and the quality of adaptability to such new things by the reader. While he talks about poetry being obscure by nature, he is just trying to say the same thing which Kuntaka expressed by overlooking the claim of *Svabhāvokti* as against *Vakrokti.* Or whether he was not just hinting at the *Śabda-śaktis* and the *Pratīyamānaartha* when he argued that "The poetry remains in the obscurity is, in some way, the obscurity itself."

Cleanth Brooks, who is so much irritated and annoyed with people asking the poet himself to explain his poem, and complaining against modern poetry for its being difficult, and non-communicable, also repeats almost the same reasons which a *Rasa* theorist in India would like to put forward. He enumerates the reasons as follows:

(a) because is snobbish and definitely wants to restrict his audience (such as our *Alaṅkāra* or Śāstra poets very often did),

(b) because it is bad the total experience remains chaotic and incoherent (it may be covered, I suppose, by *Rasa-Virodha* and the *Kāvyadoṣas*),

(c) because of the special problems of our civilization, (slightly similar to the problem of *mameti-parasyeti vā* and the problem of *deśa-kāla and saṁskār aucitya*), and

(d) because so few people, relatively speaking, are accustomed to reading poetry as poetry.

And Brooks has an answer to all these problems quite similar to that of *Mahākavi* Bhavabhūti and to the theory of Abhinavagupta of *Kāvyānuśīlanābhyāsa etc.* He suggests: "Actually, in a few years, when time has brought its softening changes, and familiarity has subdued the modern poet's frightful mien, and when the tags have been obligingly supplied, we may even come to terms with our moderns" (Essay-'What Does Poetry Communicate?' *in Well wrought Urn*).

I would, however, like to skip over the much talked about theory of Empson and would conclude by saying that Indian Poetics, though has a great potential, is still to develop and though the theorists in the West seem to be coming very near, at times, to the Indian counterparts, there is still a vast gap between the two due to the difference in their cultural backgrounds, and probably the poetry such as that of Spingarn, about which no two critics have the similar opinion, may not be acceptable to the Indian mind. The emotional touch in poetry still plays a very important role and any attempt to include all the varities, old and new, under any one thought, may it be *Dhvani*, will not be fruitful because it will either have to discard the theory of *Rasa Dhvani* as being the best kind of *Kāvya* or it will place most of the new poetry under the category of subordinate *Kāvya*. Inspite of all the obscurity and ambiguity acceptable to the *Ācāryas* of *Dhvani* and *Vakrokti* schools, emotion has been the basic factor which has always worked as the key to communication of poetry in India, however subtle, suggestive, and ambiguous it might have been.

Definition of Poetry Intended by Mammata

G.U. Thite

Mammaṭa defines poetry as follows - *tad adoṣau śabdārthau saguṇāvanalaṅkṛtī punaḥ kvāpi* Thus according to Mammaṭa, poetry consists of word and sense which are faultless, and possessed of qualities, which are further rarely without figures of speech (Kāvyaprakāśa I.4). Viśvanātha critically examines this definition of poetry. He discusses each and every word in this definition. He argues that the word *adoṣau* is not proper in this definition, because if you accept as poetry that alone which is free from fault then the verses like *nyakkāro hyayameva.....* cannot be considered to be poetry which contain a fault. However, this verse has been admitted as a specimen of the best type of poetry as it contains "suggestion". Ānandavardhana accepted this verse as the best type of poetry. Mammaṭa, who also considers Dhvani-kāvya as the best type of poetry (I.4), will have to accept this verse as the best type of poetry. But still according to his own definition (which allows no defect in poetry) this verse will not be poetry at all. This is a discrepancy. Mammaṭa's definition is thus too narrow (*avyāpta*). Viśvanātha further argues that we cannot say that only a part of this verse contains a defect. For, a defect is harmful to the poetry as a whole. Moreover, the very definition of defects depends upon the principle of Rasa which is the most important element in poetry. A defect is a defect only when it affects the Rasa in a poem. It should be further added that it is not always possible to have poetry absolutely free from defects. Viśvanātha has also pointed out that we cannot even say that there should be no defects in poetry "as far as possible". For the defects do not decide whether a verse is poetry or not. It only decides the degree of acceptability of the poetry.

The next adjective *saguṇau,* which makes it essential that there should be qualities in poetry, is also improper. Mammaṭa himself has defined qualities to be the properties of Rasa, which is the soul of poetry according to him (*ye rasasyāṅgino dharmāḥ śauryādaya ivātmanaḥ/utkarṣahetavaste syuracalasthitayo guṇāḥ //* Kāvyaprkāśa VIII. 1). But here, in the definition of poetry, Mammaṭa considers Guṇas to be the properties of words and senses. Guṇas convey the idea of Rasa. Thus it would have been better if Mammaṭa might have said *sarasau śabdārthau kāvyam* Really speaking, that expression might have been more in conformity with the views of Mammaṭa and then the discrepancy might have been avoided. In the case of poetry the possession of Śabda and Artha having Guṇas is not of essence but merely serves to heighten the beauty of poetry. Here we are discussing as to what constitutes the poetry and not what heightens it.

The same argument can be put forth in connection with the words *analaṅkṛtī punaḥ kvāpi.* The poetic embelishments (*alaṅkāras*) also are not the essence of poetry. The poetic embelishments add to the beauty of the poetry. But the beauty itself depends upon the essence of poetry viz. Rasa.

Viśvanātha has thus pointed out that the definition of poetry given by Mammaṭa is not acceptable. It has many discrepancies as far as the nature of poetry understood by Mammaṭa himself is considered.

Some of the modern scholars have tried to defend Mammaṭa's definition of poetry. But these attempts appear to be very feeble. Thus S.K. De tries to defend Mammaṭa by saying that the denition of poetry given by Viśvanātha is also not free from criticism from the other scholars.[1] If is obvious that this is not a logical argument for justifying Mammaṭa. He also says that Viśvanātha has borrowed from Mammaṭa but begins his treatise with a criticism on Mammaṭa.[2] This argument is also illogical and cannot defend Mammaṭa. Similarly the manner of arguing in favour of Mammaṭa adopted by P.V. Kane is also very far-fetched. Thus when he says that because the words like *doṣa, guṇa* and *alaṅkāra* are well-known the definition of poetry based on these concepts becomes easier[3] for understanding on the part of laymen than the definition based upon the concept of Rasa, because the latter is not so well-known. It must be noted that "easy" and "difficult" are relative terms and the criterion of easiness is out of question as far as the definitions are concerned. Secondly, since the concepts of *doṣa, guṇa* and *alaṅkāra* are also defined by Mammaṭa in relation to Rasa, it will not be possible to say that these terms are easier to understand than the term Rasa itself. It seems that S.K. De as well as P.V. Kane are trying to defend a very weak case.

In this connection I want to point out that the nature of poetry intended by Mammaṭa has been defined by Mammaṭa rather indirectly in the first chapter itself where the above mentioned definition is found. For this, we have to read a little carefully the lines in which Mammaṭa shows that poetry is superior to Śāstras and Purāṇas, because it gives moral advice in a very subtle and pleasant way. Thus he says - "*prabhusaṁmitaśabdapradhānaśāstrebhyaḥ suhṛtsaṁmitārthatātparyavatpurāṇāditihāsebhyaś ca śabdārthayor guṇabhāvena rasāṅgabhūtavyāpārapravaṇatayā vilakṣaṇaṁ yat kāvyaṁ lokottaravarṇanānipuṇakavikarma*... Thus poetry is different from the śāstras and Purāṇas. It is a means of manifestation of development of flavour (*rasa*) owing to the subordination of word and sense (in the poetry). The poetry is a creation or work of a poet skilled in (giving) striking or extraordinary description. Thus two things are emphatically mentioned by Mammaṭa. Rasa is the most important aspect of poetry and that it is a product of a poet who should be able to describe something striking or extraordinary. Thus the definition of poetry intended by Mammaṭa will be *śabdārthayor guṇabhāvena rasāṅgabhūtavyāpārapravaṇaṁ lokottaravarṇanānipuṇakavikarma*.

I think that this definition gives a clear idea of the concept of poetry understood by Mammaṭa and not the so-called definition given by him.

REFERENCES

1. S.K. De *History* of *Sanskrit Poetics* (second edition) Calcutta, 1960, p. 224.
2. S.K. De, *The Same*, p. 222.
3. P.V. Kane, *The Sāhityadarpaṇa of Viśvanātha* (reprint) 1957, Notes, p. 16.

Lakṣaṇā as a Linguistic Function and as a Source of Poetic Beauty

M.V. Patwardhan

Lakṣaṇā, i.e., secondary usage, is looked upon by ancient Indian thinkers as a linguistic function (*śabdvṛtti*) of words used in human speech, in addition to *abhidhā* or primary usage corresponding to their literal senses fixed by convention. It is known in Sanskrit by various names such as *guṇavṛtti, bhakti, upacāra, ativacana, adhivacana.* It can also be called *aticāra* (if not *atyācāra*), *vakrokti, paryāyokti* and *atiśayokti.* It conaists in the complete rejection or modification of the primary sense of a word and the adoption of a sense different from the primary sense but connected with it by some relation. The primary sense is superseded. Gerauseit is found to be inconsistent with the context and the other sense is coherent in the context. The reason for resorting to secondary usage is the speaker's desire to impact a striking, arresting, gripping power to what he has to Day. This strikingness is known in Sanskrit under various names such as *vaicitrya, vicchitti, camatkāra, camatkāritva* or *saundarya* - a quality which is at the root of all figures of speech.

Lakṣaṇā corresponds to the etymological sense of the word metaphor which means an extended application of a word to describe something entirely different from what it usually expresses. But by convention the word metaphor means only the extended application of a word based on the particular relation of similarity. In this conventional sense the word metaphor corresponds to *gauṇī lakṣaṇā* which is a particular variety of *Lakṣaṇā* based on similarity. In metonymy and synecdoche the secondary use of a word is based on some relation other than similarity and they correspond to *śuddhā lakṣaṇā* in Sanskrit poetics, Metaphor metonymy and synecdoche are regarded as figures of speech in western poetics, but according to Sanskrit poetics they would be only different forms of the comprehensive linguistic function called *Lakṣaṇā* The word 'indication' usually used by Indian writers to render *Lakṣaṇā*is not a correct equivalent of the word *Lakṣaṇā.*'Secondary usage' would be a better equivalent. The word 'figuration' can also be used for *Lakṣaṇā*in English, because *Lakṣaṇā*is the basis of most of the figures of speech in Sanskrit poetics. What Daṇḍin has said in his *Kāvyādarśa*(I, 100) about the literary excellence called *samādhi*, which corresponds to *gauṇī lakṣaṇā*, i.e., metaphorical secondary usage, holds good of *Lakṣaṇā* in general (तदेतत्काव्यसर्वस्वं समाधिनमि यो गुणः । कविसार्थः समग्रोऽपि तमेनमुपजीवति ।।).

*Lakṣaṇā*is a universal habit or tendency of human speech. It is met with in ordinary colloquial speech as much as in poetic speech, in serious scientific writings as much as in the scriptures. In the words of Daṇḍin (*Kāvyādarśa*, II. 13), *Lakṣaṇā*can be said to reign supreme in scientific writings as much as in poetry (काव्येष्वस्यैव साम्राज्यं शास्त्रेष्वप्येतदीप्सितम) said in the context of the figure of speech called *svabhāvokti* - vivid, graphic description. Almost all the idioms and idiomatic phrases and epigrammatic sayings in any language are based on *lakṣaṇā* Abhinavagupta, a great philosopher and poetician, says that *lakṣaṇā* pervades the three worlds (तदेवम् अनया लक्षणया त्रिभुवनं व्याप्तम्, *Locana*, commentary on *Dhvanyāloka* I). Rājaśekhara's praise of the figure of speech called *upamā* (simile) that it is the crest jewel of all figures of speech, the essence of poetic beauty, and the mother of the race of poets (अलंकार शिरोरत्नं सर्वस्वं काव्यसंप्रदाम् । उपमा कविवंशस्य मातैवेति मतिर्मम ।।) would apply to *lakṣaṇā verbation* The same is the case with Appaya Dīkṣita's observation about *upamā* that it is an accomplished actress assuming ever new faces and playing diverse roles on the stage of poetry and enrapturing the minds of cultured people (उपमैका शैलूणी संप्राप्ता चित्रभूमिकाभदान्। ररञ्जयति काव्यरङ्गे नृत्यन्ती तद्विदां चेतः ।।).

*Lakṣaṇā*is tersely defined as the use of a word to convey something that is different from its literal sense (अतस्मिन् लच्छब्दप्रोगः). This is done in order to extend the properties of one thing to another thing that is entirely different from it (अन्यस्मिन् अन्यशब्दप्रोगः तद्धर्मप्राप्यर्थः). This means that *Lakṣaṇā* is an extended use of a word (in a sense associated with the primary sense) resorted to in order to secure the transfer of the properties of one thing to another, an idea that is conveyed by the word *upacāra* explained by Abhinavagupta (*Locana* I) in the sense of अविशयित व्यवहार and also by the Buddhistic phrases अतिवचन and अधिवचन. *Lakṣaṇā* is to be resorted to only when there is the failure or break-down of the literal sense in a particular context. It is an abnormal procedure, an emergency measure, necessitated by a crisis of the literal sense. This crisis is called *mukhyārtha-vādhā*, and it is obviously the most important precondition for its operation, the other two conditions being (1) some sort of relationship between the raptured primary sense and the inducted secondary sense (मुख्यार्थलक्ष्यार्थसंबन्ध), and (2) the backing of a practice of long standing for the use of the word in that particular secondary sense (*rūḍhi*), or the desire to convey some unique speciality of the secondary sense (*prayojana*, motivating factor behind the secondary usage). *Lakṣaṇā* cannot be resorted to unless these three preconditions are satisfied.

Lakṣaṇā is, as said above, an abnormal, deviant process of words in contrast with *abhidhā* (denotation) which is a normal, natural and straight-line process. *Lakṣaṇā* is open to the drawback called *gauravadoṣa* (round aboutness, indirectness, awkwardness, cumbrousness), while *abhidhā* has the advantage of *lāghavaguṇa* (simplicity, directness, straight forwardness). But in spite of this disadvantage *lakṣaṇā* is resorted to because it imparts an appealing, striking power to human speech and is a very important source of poetic charm, especially when it is not worn out by very frequent use.

By repeated use (प्रोगप्राचुर्य), *lakṣaṇā* loses its charm and degenerates into *abhidhā* and is then called *nirūḍhā* (conventionalised) *lakṣaṇā* Kumārilabhaṭṭa says that such over-used *lakṣaṇās* are as good as *abhidhā* (निरुढा लक्षणाः काश्चित्सामर्थ्यादभिधानवत). A *lakṣaṇa* used for the first time is vibrant with suggestiveness. But by frequent use it becomes desensitised, frozen and petrified as the so-called secondary sense becomes the literal sense for all practical purposes. For example, the words *kuśala* and *lāvaṇya*. *Kuśala* primarily means one who cuts, i.e., plucks with his fingers the blades of the sacred *Kuśa* grass, which have sharp, incisive edges. Such a person has got to be very careful and skilful to save his fingers from being injured. The secondary sense of the word is "skilful in doing any thing undertaken". The primary sense of the word *lāvaṇya* is 'saltiness' which imparts tastiness to food preparations. The secondary sense of the word *lāvaṇya* is "physical charm or loveliness in women" which makes them acceptable and delectable to those who happen to look at them. Thus by constant usage the primary senses of both these words have become defunct and the secondary senses have usurped their places. This phenonenon is so common in every language that it is not necessary to multiply examples.

Though the Dhvani theorists, who have left their indelible mark on Sanskrit poeties, attach the highest importance to the linguistic function called *vyañjanā* (suggestion), they recognise the indisputable role played by *lakṣaṇā* in preparing the ground and setting the stage for the operation of *vyañjanā* in some cases and call such *vyañjanā* as *lakṣaṇā-mūlā vyañjanā.* But they make it absolutely clear that in such cases of *vyañjanā, lakṣaṇa* is responsible for conveying the secondary sease alone and becomes a spent force after doing that. So far as the motivating purpose (प्रयोजन) behind the adoption of *lakṣanā* is concerned, it is *vyañjanā* that is responsible for conveying it. Further, *vyañjanā* has also an independent province for its operation where it is not infrastructured by *lakṣaṇā.* The Dhvani theorists take particular pains to refute the view of the advocates of *lakṣaṇā* that *vyañjanā* is not an independent linguistic function at all, but is rather to be included under *lakṣaṇā* This stance of the advocates of *lakṣaṇā* will be further discussed in the sequel while examining the hypothesis of Mukulabhaṭṭa.

The Mīmāṃsakas propound the view that words have only a single linguistic power, namely, *abhidhā* (denotation, the power of expressing the sense fixed by convention) - a comprehensive power capable of conveying the entire gamut of immediately and mediately understood senses which strike the listener's mind on hearing a word. In this connection they adduce the maxim: यत्परः शब्दः सशब्दार्थः and offer the analogy of the long, far-extending power of an arrow shot by an archer, which by its single activity called velocity achieves a number of successive results, namely, piercing the armour of the enemy, penetrating his chest, puncturing his heart and finally killing him. This analogy is known as *śarasya dīrghadīrghavyāpāra.* According to this view, the literal sense, the secondary sense and the tertiary or suggested sense are all of them conveyed by the single comprehensive linguistic function called *abhidhā*. This view also is refuted at great length by the *Dhvani* theorists who insist on the assumption of three distinct linguistic functions corresponding to the primary, secondary and tertiary senses of words.

Mukulabhaṭṭa (10th century A.D.) was a Mīmāṃsaka by conviction and so he believed that *abhidhā* is the only linguistic function belonging to words. His work called अभिधावृत्तिमातृका glorifies *abhidhā* a the supreme linguistic function. He divides *abidhā* into two functions, namely, principal *abhidhā* (मुख्या अभिधा) and secondary *abhidhā* (लाक्षणिकी अभिधा), subdividing the former into four varieties, corresponding to the linguistic categories जाति (class names), (quality names), क्रिया (action names) and द्रव्य and व्यक्ति (proper names), and the latter into six varieties corresponding to the six divisions of lakṣaṇā mentioned later on by Mammaṭa in the *sūtra* लक्षणा तेन षड्‌ विधा (kāvyaprakāśa, II, 12d, *sūtra* 17). He further says that *abhidhā* mani:fests itself under these ten forms which are only its seeming modifications (*vivartas*). In pursuance of this view he could very well have said that the so-called *vyañjanā* is nothing but वैयण्जिनिकी अभिधा, just as he spoke of *lakṣanā* as लाक्षणिकी अभिधा. But obviously he did not want to show any courtesy for *vyañjanā* even in an indirect and remote manner. He cites well-known examples of factual, imaginative and emotional *vyañjanā* (वस्तुव्यंजना अलंकारण्यन्जना and रसव्यंजना) and tries to show how in all of them the so-called suggested sense is nothing but a secondary sense. He seems to hold the view that for *lakṣaṇā* to come into operation, the literal sense need not be blocked by reason of its incoherence with the context. According to him *lakṣaṇā* is a linguistic function in which a word conveys a sense associated with its primary sense and standing in some relation with it, the failure of the primary sense not being a necessary precondition.

Mahimabhaṭṭa, who lived in the 11th century A.D., was a Naiyāyika. In his work called *vyaktiviveka* he has propounded the view that *abhidhā* is the only linguistic function possessed by words. He refuses to recognise *lakṣaṇā* and *vyañjanā* as linguistic functions at all. He considers them to be intellectual or mental functions and identifies them with logical inference (*anumāna* or *anumiti*) in which the literal sense plays the rôle of the middle term or probeans (लिङ्ग) leading to the inferential cognition of the so-called secondary sense and the so-called suggested sense. In *lakṣaṇā* the so-called secondary sense is understood from the literal sense by presumption (अर्थापत्ति), which is included under *anumiti* (inference) by the Naiyāyikas. In the third chapter of his *vyaktiviveka*, Mahimabhaṭṭa shows how the illustrations of factual suggestion (वस्तुव्यंजना), imaginative suggestion (अलङ्कारव्यंजना) and emotional suggestion (रसव्यंजना) given in the *Dhvanyāloka* can be cast in the form of logical syllogisms, the logic behind them being of course poetic logic (काव्यानुमिति), and not scientific logic (शास्त्रांनुमिति). According to Mahimabhaṭṭa, the assumption of the linguistic functions *lakṣaṇā* and *vyañjanā* is unnecessary, because their results can be very well explained by the already well-known (अन्यथासिद्ध) inferential process (which is an intellectual or mental process). The inference hypothesis was, to our knowledge, first put forward by Śaṅkuka, who tried to explain the aesthetic experience of emotional situations in drama (and also in poetry) as the result of inference. The author of the *Dhvanyāloka* was aware of the inference hypothesis as an anti-*vyañjanā* view and tried to demonstrate its limitations in the matter of explaining the phenomenon of aesthetic experience of emotional situations in poetry and drama. The *Dhvani* theorists were undoubtedly poetically minded thinkers and so they were fascinated with the suggestion hypothasis, because suggestion has a poetical, etherial quality, in contrast with *abhidhā* and *lakṣaṇā* both of which are relatively prosaic, mundane and pedestrian.

There is some grain of truth in the *lakṣaṇā* hypothesis so far as the intimation of the motivating factor in *lakṣaṇā* is concerned. It is very often difficult (even impossible) to identify the motivating factor behind a *lakṣaṇā* and to specify it distinctly from the secondary sense. Even the Dhvani theorists often state the motivating factor as an intensification or augmentation of the secondary sense itself, implying thereby that there is only a difference of degree and not a difference of kind between the two.

Further, *abhidhā*, *lakṣaṇā* and *vyañjanā* are all of them forms of linguistic symbolism, in which a word or an idea stands for and represents another idea. *Abhidhā* is a lower form of symbolism, while *lakṣaṇā* and *vyañjanā* are higher forms. Both *lakṣaṇā* and *vyañjanā* are forms of linguistic deviance (*vakrokti*) and both of them when used in poetry possess the power to give a thrill of delightful surprise to the reader or the listener. Both of them are the outcome of poetic imagination and of skill in the choice of words. Even the proper *abhidhā* requires a lot of skill from a poet. *Abhidhā, lakṣaṇā* and *vyañjanā* form a series of progressively refined and subtle symbolisms. The views of the *Mīmāṃsakas*, Naiyāyikas and the *Dhvani* theorists about *abhidhā, lakṣaṇā* and *vyañjanā* have for us only an academic interest. So far as their contribution to poetic charm goes, they are all equally important.

The Interplay of *Lakṣaṇā* and *Lakṣaṇā* Mūlā Vyañjnā

Sadashiv S. Bhave

It is not necessary for me to explain the phenomenon of '*Lakṣaṇā-mūla Vyañjanā*' It is the 'suggestive force' which is at the root of all instances, except, perhaps, of *rūḍhi-lakṣaṇā*, of the phenomenon of the 'indidative power' of the word. It may be said that it is this 'twin' of *lakṣanā* and *vyañjanā* which is responsible for the miracle of the poetic use of language. The most poignant example of this twin is the '*jahat-ajahat lakṣaṇā*', where there is no '*mukhyārthā-bādhā*'.

It may be argued that the '*mukhyārtha-bādhā*' in even the '*prayojanavati lakṣaṇā*' is not real. It is technical and palpable. The intention, or the '*prayojanā*', of the speaker or of the poet, is to break away from the rigid monotony of general details, and to raise the experience to the conceptual and/or spiritual level. Thus, instead of limiting oneself to only a discriptive phrase like, 'I have read Shakespeare's plays', one moves a few steps higher (or, 'closer', if we confine ourselves to the horizontal context) and says, 'I have read Shakespeare." Here, one hopes to convey, with this '*jahadajahat-lakṣaṇā*') one's experience of having grasped the essence of Shakespeare.

Here, let us ask ourselves a question. Can any linguistic expression, in or outside the spoken or written language, be only descriptive? Or only denotative? We do make a distinction between denotation and connotation. However, the distinction is only for our convenience. In reality, there is this 'twin' of denotation and connotation. However, the distinction is only for our convenience. In reality, there is this 'twin' of denotation and connotation.

Let us examine a few expressions.

(a) 'Thank you'.
(b) 'Bye'.
(c) 'See you'.
(d) 'Enough of it'.
(e) 'Have a nice time'.
(f) 'Sorry. Excuse me'.

These are random samples, noted as they came. Apparently there is no poetry, no narration, no script for performance in these instances. Are these sentences only descriptive? Are the words only denotative? The answer seems to be in the negative. To use an oft-used phrase, 'The expressions convey a lot more than what they actually say.'

The words 'thank', 'enough', 'time', 'we', 'you', are designed to convey much more. The question uppermost in my mind is whether the 'much more' is 'in addition' to, or 'in place' of the original, or denotative, meaning. It would be proper to say that the 'much-more' is conveyed through a subtle negation of the denotative function. By 'negation' I do not mean 'annihilation'. It is flowering into a new form while discarding the earlier form. There is no destruction of the earlier form. There is growth. As if a child grows into a man.

Here, I venture to say that language functions in a series of Lakṣaṇās and thereby achieves different, or higher conceptual levels. In this process, earlier levels are left back, or discarded, or jettisoned, as fresh, new levels are achieved. In climbing a staircase, one has to discard, or leave, the earlier 'step' in order to climb to the next. In launching a spaceship, at every stage, earlier rockets have to be jettisoned while new rockets take over. In the use of language, it is much the same. This may be described as the phenomenon of 'disconnected connections'.

Major stages of the use of language may be indicated below: (At each stage, the 'common' is left out to achieve the 'special'.)

(a) The phonetic expression vanishes indicating a concept. Even this primary use is never descriptive, but 'indicative *and suggestive*' : *Indicative of the concept and suggestive of the ethos.*: The twin play of *Lakṣaṇā and Vyañjanā* which is at its root.

(b) Out of this basic use, representative styles emerge in every social field, such as, government, law, education, art and literature. These styles have the sanction of the cultural tradition, are often impersonal and tend to be pompous. This style rejects the earlier, human, personalised use of language.

(c) While using these 'representative styles' in one or more social fields, a third style emerges. This style bears the personality-stamp of the user. It rejects the impersonal, traditional, pompous use. (When I used 'personality-stamp' instead of 'The stamp of the personality', I have tried a rejection. This stage is the realm of the poet, or writer.

Hence, (i) there is the style of a particular language (*Lakṣaṇā*1);
(ii) there is the literary style of a language (L-2); and,
(iii) there is the style of a particular poet, narrator or a dramatist (L-3). .... and, so on.

At each of the three *Lakṣaṇās*, there is always the attendant *Lakṣaṇā mūlā Vyañjanā*

Consequently, the three major stages in understanding literature are:

(i) The style of understanding, or decoding, a particular language;
(ii) The style of understanding a particular literary tradition;
(iii) The fresh style of understanding required to decode a particular piece of literature, or a particular author.

Generally, there is great resistance for rejecting the earlier framework at every stage. This invariably results in variations of en-coding and de-coding at every stage.

Even if the resistance is eliminated, the resultant multiplicity and complexity in the limitless uses of language shall always lead to a certain confusion in both understanding and discussing literature.

Let us try to minimise the confusion as far as it is possible. Such an attempt on my part brings me to the conclusion of this paper.

Vyañjanā as Reflected in the Formal Structure of Language

Saroja Bhate

The close relationship between poetics and grammar has been often articulated by Indian tradition. Ānandavardhana remarks, for instance, *prathame hi vidvāṁso vaiyākaraṇāḥ* 'the grammarians are the foremost scholars'.[1] The doctrine of *dhvani* owes its existence to the grammarians' doctrine of *sphoṭa* according to Abhinavagupta.[2] Since *śabda* 'word' is the nucleus in both the systems, they share some topics in common. For instance, the diverse types of meanings understood from a word are treated in both, the grammar and the poetics. In addition to the two wellknown functions of word, namely, *abhidhā* 'expressive function' and *lakṣaṇā* 'secondary function', a third one is recognised by the rhetoricians. It is known as *vyañjanā* It is introduced and established by Ānandavardhana in his wellknown treatise, the *Dhvanyāloka* He says that the language of the great poets possesses an extraordinary power of suggestion which pervades the whole poetry like the charm of a beautiful woman which is over and above her limbs and features.[3] The suggested meaning, which is described by Ānandavardhana and his followers as the soul of poetry, is called *dhvani.* It is, on the one hand, 'the manifestation of *pratibhā* 'intuition' of the poet and, on the other, subject to understanding of those listeners or readers who possess *pratibhā* Thus on both the sides it has no concern with ordinary people.

According to the exponents of the *dhvani* theory the hidden beauty of poetry is understood through the function of *vyavjanā* Various kinds of *dhvani* as well as *vyavjanā* are described in different works on poetics.[4] It has been recognised by the *dhvanivādins* that *dhvani* is communicated by both, linguistic and extralinguistic factors. Among the extra-linguistic factors are listed the specific character of the speaker, the listener, the presence of another person, the content, the situation, the place, the time, and the gestures.[5] The linguistic factors that convey *dhvani* are sentence, word, compound, parts of words, suffixes, syntax and the poetry as a whole.[6] Ānandavardhana supplies a number of illustrations to point out how *dhvani* is understood from various linguistic elements. A few illustrations cited by the rhetoricians are given below to make the point clear.

In the *Meghadūtam* of Kālidāsa, the *yakṣa*, while describing his house and the garden around it to the cloud-messenger, draws a beautiful picture of the golden perch in his garden. He says,

तात्कैः शिञ्जद्वलयसुभगैः कान्तया नर्तितो मे
यामध्यास्ते दिवसविगमे नीलकण्ठः सुहृद् वः ।

'(O cloud it is the golden perch in my garden) on which sits the peacock, your friend, who is made to dance every evening by my wife on the rhythms of the clapping of her hands making sweet sound of her tinkling bangles'.

Here according to the rhetoricians the plural ending added after the word *tāla* 'rhythm' suggests the versatile character of the heroine, her artistic talents and thereby the intensity of the pangs of separation experienced by the hero.

Another illustration is from the second act of the wellknown play *Śākuntalam* of Kālidāsa where Duṣyanta, the hero, expresses his dispair over the departure of the heroine, मुखमंसविवर्ति पक्ष्मलाक्ष्याः कथमप्युन्नमितं न चुम्बितं तु ।

'I could somehow lift the face turning towards shoulder (of the beloved) with beautiful eyes, but could not kiss it.'

Here the particle *tu* 'but' conveys dire disappointment of the hero.[7]

Many other examples are cited by various rhetoricians. The two examples mentioned above are enough to show how, according to them, various linguistic elements such as the indeclinable *tu* or the plural case-ending suggest certain feelings. The point to be noted in this connection is that it is implied by all the rhetoricians that the *dhvani* is purely subjective or intuitive. It flashes in the heart of the reader as soon as he reads a particular sentence, word or a word-element. The question, that arises therefore is, do all the readers comprehend the same *dhvani* from a certain linguistic expression? Or does it change from reader to reader? Even if it is admitted that it is only the *sahṛdayas*, the connoisseurs that have the ability to grasp the suggested meaning, do all the asthetes agree in their understanding of the same *dhvani* from an expression?

Generally they do not. The suggested meaning is thus a purely subjective matter. Two readers may not read the same meaning between the lines of a poetry. And more subjective is the appreciation of a literary piece, the less theoretical it turns out to be. This leads to the lack of uniformity, precision and accuracy that is essential to make a system a formal science. It is precisely for this inconsistent and obscure character of the *dhvani* that the *naiyāyikas* 'logicians' like Jayantabhaṭṭa vehemently attacked the *dhvani* theory and rejected *vyañjana* as a separate function.[8] This aspect of the doctrine of *dhvani* and *vyañjanā* seems to lead poetics away from a formal science. It tends to be more intuitive than theoretical.

One therefore wonders if some kind of uniformity can be brought about in the literary evaluation, based on *dhvani*, of a piece of poetry. Apparently diverse emotive and attitudinal meanings cannot be tied down to any linguistic factors, although some of them have been found to be associated with accent and intonation.

More than two thousand years ago, Pāṇini, the foremost grammarian of Sanskrit, analysed the Sanskrit language and successfully handled the suggested meaning at the level of the structure of language. In his *Aṣṭadhyāyī* he showed at least in 200 rules that many emotive and attitudinal meanings were relevant to the form of language. The attitudinal meaning is associated not only with intonation and accent but also with different linguistic elements such as suffixes, prefixes and even augments. A few illustrations will make the point clear.

The preposition *api* in the expression *api stuyād vṛṣalam* 'he may praise even an outcaste' conveys disgust in the mind of the speaker according to P. 1.4.96.[9] When, however, disgust is not intended, the speaker says, *apiṣṭuyād vṛṣalam* 'one may praise an outcaste'.[10] Thus the status of *api* and the consequent phonological change (s—ṣ) are directly connected with the emotive meaning suggested by its use.

Impatience or urgency is conveyed by the *kṛt* suffix *NamUL* according to P. 3.4.52.[11] The illustration given in the commentaries is, *śayyotthāyaṁ dhāvati* '(he) runs straight away from the bed'. The undertone is that he is so impatient that he does not care even to dress up after getting out of bed and runs towards something. If no hurry or impatience is to be conveyed, the expression would be, *śayyāyā utthāyā dhāvati* '(he) runs after having got up from the bed'.

The feeling of appreciation is transmitted through secondary suffixes. The suffix *rūpa* added after the word *vaiyākaraṇa* in the form *vaiyākaraṇarūpaḥ* 'a praiseworthy grammrian' conveys the speaker's appreciation of the grammarian.[12] If there is no appreciation, the speaker uses the form *vaiyākaraṇaḥ* 'grammarian'. These are just a few of the many examples available in Pāṇini's grammar. These illustrations show how minutely Pāṇini has observed the nuances and their correspondence with the formal structure of the Sanskrit language. He has linked many other feelings such as anger, jealousy, love, hatred, insult, etc. with diverse linguistic elements such as primary and secondary suffixes. His treatment of quite a large number of word formations which are linked with the *dhvani* indicates that the emotive and attitudinal meanings can be formalised atleast to a certain extent. Thus *vyañjanā* which often expresses speaker's intention or presuppossion towards an object or a situation, plays a crucial role in the derivational system of Pāṇini. It is incorporated in the formal analysis of the Sanskrit language. In this structural approach the suggested meaning of linguistic expression is fixed and does not vary from listener to listener. The *vyañjanā* theory developed by the poeticians fails to explain this correlation between the linguistic forms and the emotive meanings, which is clearly pointed out by Pāṇini's grammar.

The question that emerges from the foregoing observations is, can the *dhvani* language of the poets, which is deliberately rendered ambiguous to create a charming effect, be put to a uniform objective analysis, at least to a certain extent, as Pāṇini did? Is it possible to bring about uniformity in the comprehension of *dhvani* by all readers by establishing correlation between emotive meanings and the formal structure of the language? Can such formalization render poetics more theoretical than intuitive? Is it really expected to be so?

One has to admit that the structural approach to *vyañjanā* has its limitations. The meaning of a poetry is not a fixed thing and is open to interpretations. The true *sahṛdayas*, people of taste, always consider that poetry the best which, like a veiled beauty, conceals its grace and charm and allows the asthetes to discover it in their own way. The intuitive communication cannot be fastened to the rules of grammar. Nevertheless, a preliminary claim can be made on the basis of the observations made above that the linguistic analysis carried in the Pāṇinian way may provide some insights for the exploration of *dhvani* and bring about uniformity atleast on the initial level in the applied criticism related to Sanskrit poetry.

NOTES

1. The *Dhvanyāloka* of Ānandavardhana, ed. Nagendra, Banares, 1971, p. 53.
2. The *Dhvanyāloka* with Locana, ed. P.N. Virkar and M.V. Patvardhan, Bombay, 1983 pt. 1, pp 233-234.
3. The *Dhvanyāloka*, I. 4:
   प्रतीयमानं पुनरन्यदेव वस्त्वस्ति वाणीषु महाकवीनाम्
   यत्तत्प्रसिद्धावयवातिरिक्तं विभाति लावण्यमिवाङ्गनासु ।
4. The threefold division of *dhvani* into *vastudhvani, alaṁkāradhvani* and *rasadhvani* is based on the nature of content that is suggested, whereas the other threefold division of *dhvani* into *śabdaśaktimūla, arthaśaktimūla* and *ubhāyaśaktimūla* is based on the poetic element- either word or meaning - which is the conveyor. Many other kinds of *dhvani* also have been described. Since it is not the scope of the present paper to present a detailed exposition of the doctrine of *dhvani*, I abstain from giving a full

treatment to this topic.

5. The *kāvyaprakāśa*, ed. Karmarkar, BORI Poona, 1950, p. 72:
वक्तृबोद्धव्यकाकूनां वाक्यवाच्यान्यसंनिधेः
प्रस्तावदेशकालादेवैशिष्ट्यात् प्रतिभाजुषाम्
यद्यर्थस्यान्यधीहेतुर्व्यापारो व्यक्तिरेव सा ।
6. The *Dhvanyāloka*, III. 16:
सुप्तिङ्वचनसम्बन्धैस्तथा कारकशक्तिभिः
कृत्तद्धितसमासैश्च द्योत्योऽलक्ष्यक्रमः क्वचित् ।
7. The *Sāhityadarpaṇa*, ed. Panduranga Javaji, Nirṇayasagar, Bombay, 1931, p. 231.
8. The *Nyāyamañjarī*, ed. K.S. Varadāchārya, Mysore, 1969, p. 129:
एतेन शब्दसामर्थ्यमहिम्ना सोऽपि वारितः
यमन्यः पण्डितंमन्यः प्रपेदे कंचन ध्वनिम् ।
9. P. 1.4.96: अपिः पदार्थसम्भावनान्ववसर्गगर्हासमुच्चयेषु । 'अपि is called when it conveys the meaning of a word, possibility, permission, censure or collection'.
10. Here *s* in the beginning of the form *stuyād* changes into ṣ because it is preceded by *api* which is an *upasarga* and not a *karmapravacanīya*.
11. P. 3.4.52, अपादाने परीप्सायाम् । 'The suffix *NamUL* is added after a root preceded by an *apādāna* (a word in the ablative) when impatience is to be conveyed'.
12. P. 5.3.66, प्रशंसायां रूपप् । 'The suffix *rūpaP* is added after a stem to convey appreciation'.

Aprastuta praśaṁsā and *Vyājastuti*: Is the '*prastuta*', relevant, conveyed by '*Vyañjanā*', word-power of suggestion, or by '*Lakṣaṇā*', word-power of figuration?

V.T. Zambare

The word '*praśaṁsā*' in *Aprastutapraśaṁsā* means a statement or description and not praise. Mammaṭa explains it as '*abhidhānā*',[1] statement and Jagannātha as '*varṇanamātrā*', a description only. He, Jagannātha, warns further that the word '*praśaṁsā*' should not be understood to mean a praise.[2] In *Aprastutapraśaṁsā*, the speaker intends to say something about the '*prastuta*' or '*prākaraṇikā*',[3] the relevant or the matter in hand; but actually describes the '*aprastutā*' or '*aprākaraṇikā*',[4] the irrelevant or the matter not in hand. Hence, in *Aprastutapraśaṁsā*, the '*aprastutā*', the irrelevant, is '*vācyā*', directly expressed and the '*prastuta*', the relevant, is '*vyaṅgyā*', suggested. That is to say, in *Aprastutapraśaṁsā*, the '*aprastuta*', the irrelevant, is conveyed by '*Abhidhā*', word-power denotation of and the '*prastuta*', the relevant, is conveyed by '*Vyañjanā*', word-power of suggestion.

Vyājastuti is explained by Mammaṭa as *Vyājena Vyājarūpā vā Stutiḥ*[5] (The figure is so called because therein is found) either praise in disguise or pretended praise.[6]

Thus, when the speaker intends to praise a certain object or person, he censures it or him or vice versa. Here, superficial praise results in censure or vice versa. Thus when praise/censure is '*vācya*', expressed, censure/praise is '*vyaṅgya*', suggested. As in *Aprastutapraśaṁsā*, in *vyājastuti* also, the not-intended sense is conveyed by '*Abhidhā*', word-power of denotation, while the intended sense is conveyed by '*Vyañjanā*, word-power of suggestion.

It is thus clear that the adherants of the '*Dhvani*' theory consider these two figures, *Aprastutapraśaṁsā* and *Vyājastuti*, as examples of the '*Guṇībhūtaryaṅgya*'[7] poetry, the second division of poetry, the first and the third being '*Dhvani*' and '*Citra*' respectively. In their opinion, in the case of these two figures, the suggested sense is subordinate to the expressed or literal sense. In both these figures, the contextual sense, really intended by the speaker, is suggested by the expressed or literal sense, which is non-contextual. Both these figures come under the '*Vācyasiddhyaṅgā*'[8] variety of '*Guṇībhūtavyaṅgya*' poetry because the suggested sense in both these figures is not '*svamātraviśrāntā*' or '*svamātra-paryavasitā*' i.e. is not autonomous and an end by itself. When the suggested sense is '*svamātraviśrāntā*' or '*svamātraparyavasitā*' i.e. is autonomous and an end by itself, we have the best specimen of poetry-namely, the '*Dhvanikāvyā*'. In '*Guṇībhūtavyaṅgya*' poetry, the literal or expressed sense is not relevant to the context and hence needs to be rationalised by the suggested sense. Thus, in this type of poetry, the suggested contextual sense comes to the help of the literal or expressed sense, which is non-contextual. *Alaṁkāra-ratnākarā*[9] (end of the 12th century A.D.) holds a different view. Though a follower of the 'Dhvani' theory, he expressly states that these two figures, *Aprastutapraśaṁsā* and *Vyājastuti*, are based on *Lakṣaṇā*, word-power of figuration, only and not on *Vyañjanā*, word-power of suggestion.

Śobhākara follows the ancient Aprastutapraśaṁsā,[10] but slightly differs from them in giving its varieties. Traditionally, the figure has five varieties: namely, two based on *Kāryakāraṇabhāva*, effect-cause relation, two on *Sāmānya-viśeṣabhāva*, general-particular relation and one on *Sādṛśyasaṁbandha*, similarity relation. Sobhākara accepts the first four varieties of the figure; but in the fifth variety, he includes all cases of the figure based on *Sādṛśya*, similarity, *Virodha*, opposition and such other relations not conveyed by the earlier varieties.[11]

He then proceeds to show how *Lakṣaṇā* word-power of figuration, - namely, 1) *Mukhyārthabādha*, incompatibility of the literal or primary or expressed sense with the speaker's real intention, 2) *Mukhyārthayoga*, connection of the literal or primary or expressed sense with the non-literal or secondary or indicated sense and 3) *Prayojana*, motive, of the speaker of course, *Ruḍhi*, convention, being out of question, are satisfied here. He argues. If the speaker sets out to describe the '*prastuta*', relevant, also called '*prākaraṇikā*', contextual, but actually describes the '*aprastuta*', irrelevant, also called '*aprākaraṇikā*', non-contextual or anti-contextual, it is nothing short of '*asaṁbandha-pralāpita*', irrelevant speech.[12] As the context goes, it is improper on the part of the speaker to describe the '*aprastuta*', irrelevant. Hence, the '*mukhyārtha*', the primary or literal or expressed sense becomes '*bādhita*', incompatible.[13] The primary sense is connected with the secondary sense by '*Sāmānya-Viśeṣya-saṁbandha*', similarity relation, or by '*Virodha-Saṁbandha*', opposition relation, or by any other similar relation.[14] Hence the second pre-condition, '*Mukhyārtha-yoga*', connection with the primary sense, is also satisfied. As regards the third pre-condition, '*Prayojana*', the speaker's motive, the text runs: '*Cārūḍhapratītyādilakṣaṇe prayojane*'[15] Here, the '*sandhi*', euphonic junction, is evidently to be dissolved as '*catarūḍhapratītyādilakṣaṇe*'. It is not very clear what Śobhākara means by '*rūḍhapratīti*' here. I understand it as '*rūḍhapratītibhinnapratīti*', taking the '*na*', negation, in the sense of '*bhinna*', different. To me, the expression seems to mean 'understanding, different from the normal or traditional understanding'. It is not a straight line approach; it is rather a roundabout manner. This is the '*prayojana*', motive.

And then Śobhākara says emphatically - '*Lakṣaṇāmūlaiva yukta, na tu vyañjanātmikā/Vāsyasyābādhitatvena paryavasite vyañjanasya saṁbharāt/*'[16] Hence, it is proper to consider *Aprastuta-praśaṁsā* as being based on '*Lakṣaṇā*' word-power of figuration, and not on '*Vyañjana*', word-power of suggestion; for, '*Vyañjanā*', word-power of suggestion is possible only when the '*vācyārtha*', expressed sense is '*abādhita*', perfectly reasonable or compatible.

In defining and dividing the figure *Vyājastuti*,[17] Śobhākara follows his predecessors in the field. In the '*Vṛtti*, gloss, that follows, he writes emphatically - '*Eṣāpi Lakṣaṇāmūlaivā*'[18] *Vyājastuti* also, like *Aprastutapraśaṁsā* is based on '*Lakṣaṇā*', word-power of figuration alone and not on '*Vyañjanā*', word-power of suggestion. Therefore, the '*nindā-stuti*', censure/praise, understood from the '*stuti-nindā*', praise/censure, should be considered as '*lakṣyā*', indicated, only and not as '*vyaṅgya*', suggested.[19] As soon as we consider the speaker, the context and so on, we find that there is '*vācyabādhanā*'[20], incompatibility of the expressed sense.

Thus, Śobhākara, who is undoubtedly a follower of the *Dhvani* theory and at the same time an independent thinker, abandoning the beaten track very frequently, emphatically expresses his view that both *Aprastutapraśaṁsā* and *Vyājastuti* are figures based on '*Lakṣaṇā*', word-power of figuration and not on '*Vyañjanā*', word-power of suggestion. In both these figures, '*Lakṣaṇā*', word-power of figuration, comes into operation because of the incompatibility, or breakdown so to say, of the literal sense, which is non-contextual, and hence stands rejected. The literal non-contextual sense is connected with the indicated contextual sense, as pointed out earlier, by '*kārya-kāraṇa-bhāva*', effect-cause relation, or by '*Sāmānya-viśeṣa-bhāvā*', general-particular relation, or by '*Sādṛśya-saṁbandha*', opposition relation in *Aprastutapraśaṁsā* and only by '*Virodha-Saṁbandhā*', opposition relation, in *Vyājastuti*. In *Vyājastuti*, the literal non-contextual sense, either '*stuti*' or '*nindā*', praise or censure, is opposed to the really intended contextual sense, either '*nindā*' or '*stuti*', censure or praise. Thus, for all practical purposes, *Vyājastuti* stands at par with '*Viparīta-Lakṣaṇā*', figuration by opposition, according to Śobhākara.

Jagannātha's definition of *Aprastutapraśaṁsā* contains the word '*praśasyate*'[21], is described, but while giving the divisions of the figure he uses the word "*gamyate*"[22] is suggested, from which it is quite clear that the '*prastuta*', relevant, in *Aprastutapraśaṁsā* is '*gamya*', suggested. Later on, while criticising the opinion[23] that the stanzas '*Yasmin khelati*', '*Digante śrūyante*' and the like are illustrations of *Atiśayokti*, he emphatically declares that the '*prastuta*', relevant, in *Aprastutapraśaṁsā*is '*vyaṅgya*', indisputably suggested.[24]

The phrase '*āmukhapratītābyāṁ*'[25], 'understood at the very outset', occuring in the definition of *Vyājastuti*, is explained by Jagannātha as follows:[26] The adjunct '*āmukhapratītābhyāṁ*', 'understood at the very outset', qualifying '*nindā-stuti*', censure-praise, has '*paryavasānā-bhāva*', 'absence of termination' i.e. they do not continue as '*nindā-stuti*', censure-praise, till the end and therefore, their '*bādhitatva*', incompatibility, is desired. Because in *Dhvani* poetry, through the greatness or strength of *Āgūraṇa* i.e. *Vyañjanā*, powr of suggestion, another sense is suggested by the '*vācyārtha*', expressed sense, which is 'nirbādha', compatible, but it is not so in the present case. Thus this figure cannot come under *Dhvani* poetry. In *Vyājastuti*, the '*vācyārtha*', expressed sense, is '*bādhita*', incompatible.

It will thus be seen that both *Aprastutapraśaṁsā* and *Vyājastuti* are based on *Vyañjanā*, word-power of suggestion and come under the *Vācyasiddhyaṅga* variety of *Guṇībhūtavyaṅgya* in the opinion of Jagannātha and not on *Lakṣaṇā*, word-power of figuration as Śobhākara maintains. It is surprising to note that 'so intrepid a critic and rhetorican'[27] as Jagannātha, who refers to Śobhākara or his work 'in as many as eleven different places, mostly to controvert his views'[28], lets this opportunity slip away and does not criticise Śobhākara for his view of these two figures.

In the case of these two figures only, namely *Aprastutapraśaṁsā* and *Vyājastuti*, Śobhākara's standpoint appears to be rational and hence acceptable; but in all other cases of *Guṇībhūtavyaṅgya* poetry, as the '*vācyārtha*' or expressed sense is everywhere compatible with the context, they, the other cases, cannot be, even according to Śobhākara, said to be based on *Lakṣaṇā*, word-power of figuration.

Aprastutapraśaṁsā and *Vyājastuti* are after all cases of linguistic symbolism. As such, they should be considered as standing at par with cases of '*Lakṣaṇā*', figuration, like '*Gaṅgāyāṁ ghoṣaḥ*', hamlet on the *Gaṅgā*, where the *Gaṅgā* is a symbol for the *Gaṅgātaṭa*, the bank of the *Gaṅgā*. In the same way, in *Aprastutapraṣaṁsā* and *Vyājastuti* also, the non-contextual expressed sense is a symbol for the intended contextual sense. Why does the speaker abandon the direct mode of expression and resort to symbolism in such cases? The purpose underlying the adoption of such symbolism appears to be the speaker's desire to achieve strikingness of expression, variously known as '*vicchitti*', '*vaicitrya*', '*camatkṛti*', '*camatkāra*' and so on. This purpose, namely the speaker's desire to achieve strikingness in his speech, is only inferred according to *Dhvanyāloka* and *Locanā*[29]. But the contextual sense in both these figures is conveyed by *Vyañjanā*, word-power of suggestion, according to the *Dhvani* theorists, while it is conveyed by *Lakṣaṇā*, word-power of figuration, according to Śobhākara.

NOTES

1. *Aprākaraṇikasyābhidhānena prākaraṇikasyākṣepaḥ*/KP, p.618.
2. *Praśaṁsanaṁ ca varṇanamātram, na tu stutiḥ*/RG, p.537.
3. See fn. No. 1 above.
4. See fn. No. 1 above.
5. KP, p.670.
6. KPS, p.670
7. KP, p.21.
8. KP, pp.190 and 205-08.
9. AR, only one printed edition available.
10. AR, *Sūtra* 38, p.61.
11. *Sadṛśaviruddhādeśca*, AR, p.61.
12. AR, p.61.
13. *Prasaṅgenāprastutasyābhidhātumayu-ktatvād bādhitamukhyārthatayā*/AR, p.61.
14. *Sāmānyaviśeṣabhāva-lāryakāraṇatva-sādṛśyavirodhādike sambandhe*/AR, p.61.
15. AR, p.61.
16. AR, p.61.
17. AR, *Sūtra* 39, p.64.
18. AR, p.64.
19. *Tenātra nindāstutyor lakṣyatvenā, na punar vyaṅgyatayā gamyatvāt*/Ar, p.64.
20. *Vaktṛprakaraṇādiparyālocanenāmukha eva vācyabādhanāt*/AR, p.64.
21. RG, p.537.
22. *Aprastutena svasadṛśaṁ prastutaṁ gamyate yasyām ityekā*/RG, p.537.
23. RG, p.546.

24. *Kiṁ cāprastutapraśaṁsāyāṁ prastutaṁ vyaṅgyam iti nirvivādam*/ RG, p.546.
25. RG, p.557.
26. *Āmukhetyādiviśeṣaṇena tayoḥ paryvasānābhāvaṁ vadan bādhitatvamabhipraiti/Ata eva nāsyā dhvanitvam/Dhvanau hi nirbādhena vācyena āgū-raṇamahimnā arthāntaramavagamyate/na caivaṁ prakṛte*/RG, p. 558.
27. AR, Introduction, p.xii.
28. AR, Introduction, p.vi.
29. *Dhvanyāloka* III and *Locana* on it.

BIBLIOGRAPHY

1. C.R. Devadhara: *Alaṁkāra-ratnākara*(AR) of Śobhākara, Oriental Book Agency, Poona, 1942.
2. V. Jhalakikar: *Kāvyaprakāśa* (KP) of Mammaṭa, BORI, Poona, 1965.
3. *Rasagaṅgādhara*(RG) of Jagannātha, Nirnaysagar, 1947.
4. S.S. Sukthankar: *Kāvyaprakāśa* X (KPS), Karnataka Publishing House, Bombay, 1941.
5. *Dhvanyāloka* of Ānandavardhana with *Locana* of Abhinavagupta.

The Merits and Demerits of *Kāvya* According to Bhāmaha and Daṇḍin

G.H. Tarlekar

Earlier than Bhāmaha and Daṇḍin, Bharata has treated the *guṇas* (merits) and *doṣas* (demerits) of Kāvya in the Nātyaśāstra, after giving the four *alaṁkāras* of sense and one of word (i.e. *yamaka*) with their varieties, the ten illustrations. The ten *doṣas* are as follows:-

(1) *Gūḍhārtha* - When the expression contains a synonym that is not well-known, the meaning is considered as concealed (e.g. '*ekādhikanavavimānā*' used for the word Daśaratha).

(2) *Arthāntara* - What need not be described is stated along with what is described.

(3) *Arthahīna* - The meaning is unconnected or is incomplete.

(4) *Bhinnārtha* - The expression is indicative of vulgar and rustic sense or the intended meaning is understood differently.

(5) *Ekārtha* - Many words for the same meaning are used. (e.g. 'white like *kunda* flower, moon, garland of flowers and the laughter of Śiva).

(6) *Abhiplutārtha* - When the meaning stated briefly is complete in each foot of the verse having no mutual connection, this defect arises.

(7) *Nyāyādapeta* - The expression lacks in the logical proof as it is in contradiction to what is found in place, time, sciences and arts.

(8) *Viṣama* - It is metrical deficiency.

(9) *Visandhi* - *Sandhi* is not accomplished where it ought to be there.

(10) *Śabdacyuta* - The syllable is dropped.

Abhinava says that the employment of some of these defects turns out to be non-defects, e.g. the use of Abhiplutārtha in the case of a mad person, Arthahīna in the Comic etc.

The ten *guṇas* are as follows:-

(1) *Śleṣa* - When the well-connected words bring out the intended meaning smoothly, the expression gets the quality of *śleṣa.*

(2) *Prasāda* - It is the quality due to which the meaning is grasped easily without the need of any explanation given by wise persons, as the word and the meaning are happily connected.

(3) *Samatā* - The expression possesses evenness or there is the absence of long compounds; the meaning expressed is significant and the words are not difficult to understand.

(4) *Samādhi* - It is the merit of *Kāvya* when it is endowed with the particularly charming meaning that is grasped by the learned ones.

(5) *Mādhurya* - When the sentence though heard or spoken often being desirable does not cause distress, it possesses *mādhurya.* (Abhinava says that the sentence does not convey doubt or contrary meaning.)

(6) *Ojas* - It is the quality of the expression having many compounds and striking words that are *udāra* (dignified) and have *anurāga* (desirability). *Anurāga* is explained by Abhinava as one syllable having expectancy of another syllable, e.g. in the expression , the syllable expects the presence of the syllable for its having a long vowel. *Udāra* is explained by him as the expression in which many words are used to describe one thing; thus the *Ojas* is of the nature of expansion.

(7) *Saukumārya* - It is that quality when there are words used happily, with properly achieved *sandhis* and having delicate

meaning. The word (used happily) is explained by Abhinava as devoid of *pāruṣya* (harshness) of the word itself or the word joined with *sandhi.*

(8) *Arthavyakti* - When the words employed have well-established usage based on the dealing of the people, this quality arises.

(9) *Udārată* - The expression endowed with divine states (i.e. states in the case of divine characters) that are fit to be found in human characters, manifesting the Erotic sentiment (even having the pathos etc.) and the Marvellous sentiment, with many states (related to the *vibhāva, anubhāva* etc.) is said to have the quality of *udāratā*

(10) *Kānti* - The love-sports of the character described, delight the mind and the ears like the sight of the moon.

(In the case of some of the *guṇas,* there are varient readings also.)

Bharata's main concern was the play proper. Hence, he has stated those defects in the language of the plays that would come in the way of aesthetic delight and those merits of the language that would help the manifestation of the aesthetic delight. Verbal gesticulation was helped by the physical and the temperamental gesticulation. But the later rhetoricians like Bhāmaha and Daṇḍin extended the conception of merits and demerits of the dramatic *Kāvya* to the *Kāvya* in general. The effect of dramatic *Kāvya* was to be achieved by the language of the *Kāvya*. Hence, the treatment of *guṇas, doṣas* and *alaṁkāras* received a wider scope.

Bhāmaha has treated the demerits of *Kāvya* in the first and the fourth chapters of his *Kāvyālaṁkāra* The defects dealt with in the first chapter are - (1) *Neyārtha,* (2) *Kliṣṭa,* (3) *Anyārtha,* (4) *Avācaka,* (5) *Ayuktimat,* (6) *Gūḍhaśabdābhidhāna,* (7) *Śrutiduṣṭa,* (8) *Arthaduṣṭa,* (9) *Kalpanāduṣṭa and* (10) *Śrutikaṣṭa.*

(1) *Neyārtha* - The proper meaning of the poetic expression is apprehended forcibly as per the intention of the learned people as it is not worded justly.

(2) *Kliṣṭa* - There is intervention in apprehending the intended meaning due to another meaning present, e.g. the root '*vi* ś *hṛ*' is used in the sense of removing, the intervention of '*vi*' comes in and the meaning has to be understood with difficulty.

(3) *Anyārtha* - There is the non-apprehension of the intended meaning e.g. '*vi* ś *kṛ*' means to change. If it is used where '*kṛ*' meaning to do is necessary, this defect arises.

(4) *Avācaka* - The use of a word which is not well-known in popular usage; e.g. the word '*himāpahāmitradharaá* used for cloud. Himāpaha means 'destroyer of snow' i.e. fire. Its *amitra,* i.e. enemy is *Jala,* i.e. water. The expression thus means *jaladhara,* i.e. cloud.

(5) *Ayuktimat* - Not logical usage, e.g. the employment of cloud, wind, bee etc. as messengers, as they have no power of speech. As such employment is seen in the works of learned poets, it can be allowed in the case of insane speakers whose mind is overwhelmed by yearning etc.

(6) *Gūdhaśabdābhidhāna* - The word having concealed meaning must not be used. e.g. *asitarti* meaning whose path is black i.e. fire; '*asitartituk*' means Kārttikeya who is the son of fire. (tuk ī child)

(7) *Śrutiduṣṭa* - The words which distress the mind when listened to, bring in this defect, e.g. the use of words meaning excretion, vomitting, organ of generation, etc.

(8) *Arthaduṣṭa* - The words which express vulgar meaning cause this defect.

(9) *Kalpanāduṣṭa* - The joining of two words gives undesired meaning.

(10) *Srutikaṣṭa* - The words are used which are trouhlesome to hear.

But in particular arrangements of words or due to the charm of the thing described, sometimes the defects also become faultless. e.g. *klinna* (wet) and *gaṇḍa* (cheek) are supposed to be avoided; but in the description of elephant the word *viklinnagaṇḍa* (having the temple wet with ichor) gives proper sense.

The fourth chapter treats the following defects of Kāvys which destroy its beauty:-

(1) *Apārtha* - The meaning of words is not apprehended collectively in a sentence.

(2) *Vyartha* - The meaning is contradictory.

(3) *Ekārtha* - Tautology.

The repetition of words in the states of fear, grief, jealousy, joy and wonder is not a defect.

(4) *Sasaṁśaya* - The expression gives doubtful meaning.

(5) Apakrama - The mention as per instruction is *krama*, i.e. order. When such order is not there, this defect arises.

(6) *Śabdahīna* - Ungrammatical usage of words.

(7) *Yatibhraṣṭa* - Wrong break for pause in a verse.

(8) *Bhinnavṛtta* - Metrical defect.

(9) *Visandhi* - Absence of *sandhi* when it is required.

(10) *Deśavirodhi* - Anything in contradiction to what is there in the region (or place).

(11) *Kālavirodhi* - Anything that is in contradiction to time (anachronism).

(12) *Kalāvirodhi* - That which is in contradiction to convention in arts.

(13) *Lokavirodhi* - Contradictory to popular established usage.

(14) *Nyāyavirodhi* - Nyāya means the *śāstric* works relating to *Dharma, Arthā* and *Kāma* which include political science also. Whatever is contradictory to Nyāya.

(15) *Āgamavirodhi* - In contradiction with the practice laid down in Dharmaśāstra.

In chapter five, Bhāmaha has treated the defects arising out of logical fallacies in the case of the *pratijña* (proposition) the *hetu* (logical reason) and the *dṛṣṭānta* (illustration), in detail.

He says that *śāstra* is also useful when it is combined with the sweet *rasa* of *Kāvya*. So *śāstra* also has its own share to offer to *Kāvya*. Hence, the discussion of logic and the means of knowledge become proper in poetics. The *pratyakṣa* would be contradicted when fire is described as cool or the moon as hot. But in *Kāvya*, the rays of the moon prove to be hot for a lover suffering from separation. The sky has no colour, but it is described as having dark colour like that of a sword. The inference as in the statement - there is lake nearby for there is the fragrance of lotuses, finds proper place in Kāvya. The logical reasoning must not create ignorance, doubt and wrong knowledge.

The sixth chapter deals with *Sauśabdya* (the good word) in *Kāvya*. It explains the importance of grammatical purity in *Kāvya*.

Bhāmaha gives only three *guṇas* in brief.

(1) *Mādhurya* - That Kāvya is considered *madhura* in which the meaning is expressed through words which do not have many compounds and which is agreeable to hear.

(2) *Prasāda* - The *prasāda* quality of Kāvya is there when the expression is easily understood by the learned, the women and the *Bālas* (uneducated persons) also.

(3) *Ojas* - Abundance of long compounds is endowned with the quality of *Ojas*.

All the *alaṁkāras* have *vakrokti* at the basis. Bhāmaha says - सैवा सर्वव वक्रर्धक्ति रनयायर्ध विभाव्यत्य यत्लद्यऽस्यां कविना कार्यः कद्यडतुडक्तनरद्यऽनया विना

Vakrokti is a striking mode of speech, differing from the plain, matter of fact, ordinary mode of speech. It is the distinguishing characteristic of *Kāvya* which brings in the special charm. It keeps the distinctions of *Kāvya* from *śāstra* on the one hand and from popular, matter of fact speech on the other hand. "The sun has set, the moon shines, the birds go to their nests" and such other statements are not *Kāvya* but *vārtā* (reporting) according to Bhāmaha as they do not have *vakrokti*.

Daṇḍin has treated the ten qualities of *Kāvya* in the first chapter of his *Kāvyādarśa* and the ten defects of *Kāvya* in the third chapter. He speaks of the two *mārgas* (styles) *Vaidarbha* and *Ganḍa* The ten *guṇas* are the *prāṇas* (life-breaths) of *Vaidarbha mārgas* In the *Ganḍa mārga*, the inversion of these is mostly there - i.e. in some cases there is the complete absence and in some, partial presence of them. The word mostly indicates that in the case of avoiding *grāmyatva* etc. there is oneness of opinion.

(1) *Ślesa* - The expression has no looseness of construction. It has the majority of syllables that are non-conjunct and unaspirates (i.e. pronounced with a slight aspiration) interspered with conjunct consonants and aspirates. The looseness of construction is desired by *Ganḍas* as they have great liking for alliteration.

(2) *Prasāda* - Clarity of expression. *Ganḍas* accept words in the sense of their etymology, though not so well-known in popular usage.

(3) *Samatā* - The composition has evenness. The compositions are three-fold with sonants or surds or with both used evenly. The Ganḍas disregarding evenness resort to unevenness.

(4) *Mādhurya* - It is present in the speech that is agreeable and endowed with *rasa* and in the things described. By this quality the connoisseurs become glad like the bees by honey.

(5) *Sukumaratā* - It is seen in the compositions having soft consonants mostly. If all the consonants are soft the defect 'looseness' of composition occurs. *Ganḍas* do not desire this quality. They employ the quality of *dīpti* (brilliance).

(6) *Arthavyakti* - The meaning being clearly apprehended, no additional help is required. The desired sense is expressed through appropriate words.

(7) *Audārya* - The excellence of some quality is apprehended through the expression. Due to it the Kāvya becomes brilliant. According to some, this quality is there when the expression is

endowed with adjectives that bring out the excellencee of the subject of the poem. In the illustration the excellence of generosity is described.

(8) *Ojas* - The expression has abundance of compounds. This quality is vital for *gadya* (prose). It is accepted by both i.e. *Vaidarbhas* and *Gaṇḍas*. *Gaṇḍas* prefer it in poetry also. It has sometimes the abundance of short syllables or that of long syllables.

(9) *Kānti* - The expression follows the well-established usage in describing things. Hence the meaning that is easily grasped becomes striking. This is the merit of *artha* (sense). It is seen in the expression having the *vārtā* and in the description. According to *Gaṇḍas Kānti* is present in the expression which is endowed with extreme superimposition, beyond the wellknown usage. It is thus fancied by the poet with his inspiration.

(10) *Samādhi* - When the attribute of one is superimposed elsewhere, keeping the bounds of wordly dealings, this merit arises, e.g. in the expression कुमुदानि निमिलन्ति ('the night lotuses fade'), 'निमीलन' (closing the eyelids) which is the attribute of eyes, is superimposed on *kumudas* (night lotuses).

The words expressing such sense as spitting, vomitting, etc. when used in secondary meaning become charming. In fact, *Samādhi* is the quality of sense as the meaning is superimposed. But it is understood as the quality belonging to word, by tradition. When these words are used in the primary sense, the defect *grāmyatā* arises. Even though such words are faulty, when used in their primary meaning, they possess merit when used by indication. The reason for this is the superimposition of identity, which is the result of *Lakṣaṇā* (Indication).

The ten demerits of *Kāvya* -

(1) *Apārtha* - Devoid of the sentence-sense or the sense of the sentences grouped together. Such speech is not a defect if spoken by a mad person or an intoxicated person or children. Due to the absence of propriety, expectancy and continuity

necessary for expressing the sense of a sentence, the sentence loses its meaning.

(2) *Vyartha* - When there is a contradiction between the prior and posterior parts in one sentence or in a group of sentences, this defect arises. Due to the contradictory meaning, the speech becomes meaningless. When the mind is overpowered by unhappiness etc. the contradictory statements also become faultless.

(3) *Ekārtha* - The repetition of meaning or word. But if some particularity like compassion etc. is to be expressed, such repetition is not a defect but it serves as an embellishment.

(4) *Sasaṁśaya* - A doubt is created by the statements used to express definite sense. But if such a doubt is intended to be expressed, it becomes an illustration of *Saṁśayālaṁkāra*

(5) *Apakrama* - What is mentioned in order is not followed by further statements. e.g. the three gods that are the cause of the maintenance, creation and destruction are given as Śambhu, Nārāyaṇa and Brahmadeva respectively. The order ought to have been Nārāyaṇa, Brahmadeva and Śambhu. Sometimes *Apakrama* is not seen as a defect, e.g. "In the triad, 'giving up relations, body and country,' the first and the last create more suffering than the middle one in which case the suffering caused is for a short while." It means that giving up body is better than giving up one's relations or one's own country.

(6) *Śabdahīna* - When the proper precedure of wording is not followed correctly, this defect arises, as such usage is not allowed by the eminent persons. When such an employment of wording is allowed by the learned ones on proper grounds, it is not a defect.

(7) *Yatibhraṣṭa* - The pause after a word in a verse at the fixed place is called *Yati*. When such a pause is not used properly, this defect is seen. Sometimes, due to the observance of *sandhi* rules, there is *yati* in the midst of words combined by *sandhi*. In such cases the *yati* is not disagreeable to hear.

(8) *Bhinnavṛtta* - This defect is a metrical one. When there is deficiency or addition of syllables or improper arrangement of short and long syllables, this defect arises.

(9) *Visandhi* - Non-observance of *sandhi* when it is expected by the rules of grammar. it is not a defect when allowed by grammatical rules.

(10) *Deśa-kāla-kalā-loka -nyāya-āgamavirodhin* The expression that is in contradiction to place, time, conventions of art, popular knowledge, logic, and *śruti* and *smṛti*. All such contradictions sometimes lose their nature of contradiction due to the skill of the poet, e.g. 'Due to the power of that king, the gardens became the place of desire-yielding trees having leaves in the form of wet silken garments (of the beautiful ladies spread over them for being dried.)'. Here the desire-yielding trees that are found only in heaven are described as being there in the gardens situated on the earth. So the defect of contradiction of place arises. But the poet's skill in this description brings out the greatness of the king in a specially charming manner.

The discussion as regards the defects caused in the *pratijñā, hetu* and *dṛṣṭānta* found in Bhāmaha's *Kāvyālaṁkāra* is brushed aside by Daṇḍin saying that such thinking is mostly harsh belonging to the province of *śāstras* only. It has no use in the field of poetics. He accepts the figures *Hetu, Sūkṣma* and *Léśa* as best adornments of speech. The expressions like, 'The sun has set' etc. are striking enough in the poetic speech to create charm as they indicate the specific time, i.e. the evening time.

The exact distinction between *guṇa* and *alaṁkāra* is not made sufficiently clear either by Bhāmaha or Daṇḍin. Bhāmaha's treatment of the three *guṇas* is very brief, and does not give a clear idea. The *mādhurya* defined by him as agreeable to listen to and not having many compounds would be the quality of words in the poetic expression. He states that in *prasāda* also there should not be many compounds as clarity of expression must be there. *Ojas* is characterised by abundance of compounds. The word *guṇa* is found in his definition of *Bhāvikatva*. He says that when the things in the past and the future are perceived as being in the present, it is the *guṇa* Bhāvikatva. It is given as the quality of *prabandha* (continuous composition). It results from the strikingness, sublimity and marvellousness of meaning, effective acting of the story and clarity of words. From this it appears that he has the dramatic composition in mind, while dealing with *Bhāvikatva*. Later writers have treated *Bhāvikatva* as a figure of speech. His treatment of the defects of Kāvya is exhaustive. He does not accept the distinction of dictions as *Vaidarbha* and *Ganḍa* which must have been a topic of discussion in the field of poetics.

Daṇḍin treats the ten *guṇas* as mentioned by Bharata. His *śleṣa* requires the construction to have no looseness. This absence of looseness is, according to him, achieved by the employment of majority of non-conjunct syllables and unaspirates mixed with the conjunct consonants and aspirators. In regard to *mādhurya*, he says that the expression has *rasa*. It is to be understood as the expression is such in which the situation stated effectively evokes *rasa*. The expression has alliteration of consonants uttered from the same place of utterance in the mouth; the vowels may be different. e.g. '*tadāprabhṛti dharmasyā*'. In this expression, there are dentals *ta, da and dha*. This *śrutyanuprāsa* is favoured by Vaidarbhas as it is helpful to *rasa*. We find that Dhvanikāra does not favour the presence of alliteration and *yamaka*, etc. in the Erotic, particularly, *yamaka* etc. in Love-in-separation, for the emphasis on having these is the result of particular effort on the part of the poet. The *dīpti* desired by *Ganḍas* is produced by the abundant use of hard consonants. His explanation of *kānti* and *udāratva* is different from that of Bharata. In *samādhi*, according to him, there is the superimposition of one thing on the other resulting in identity, which is the province of Indication (*Lakṣaṇā*). He has not made clear-cut distinctions between the *guṇas* of words and those of sense. Later, Vāmana treated all the ten *guṇas* as belonging to word and sense both. The two styles (*mārgas*) treated by Daṇḍin were developed into three styles (*rītis*) by Vāmana which he emphasized as 'all-in-all' of Kāvya. Dhvanikāra confirmed Bhāmaha's view of the three *guṇas* and made a distinction between *guṇas* and *alaṁkāras* saying that the former are the inherent qualities like bravery, (generosity, courage) etc. seen in persons, while the latter are the embellishments like the decorative ornaments worn on the body. Daṇḍin's treatment of the defects is similar to that of Bhāmaha. But he is not inclined to allow the *śastric* discussion of logical entities in poetics.

Considering the treatment of the merits and demerits of Kāvya by Bhāmaha and Daṇḍin, it becomes clear that these early rhetoricians tried to fix the criteria for good Kāvya. Bhāmaha tried to establish that Kāvya has its own *śāstra* like other standard *śāstras*. Daṇḍin also tried to find out what makes Kāvya charming and effective. They considered that the beauty of Kāvya is achieved mainly by *alaṁkāras* and hence treated *alaṁkāras* in detail. There is a difference of opinion between them as regards the number of *guṇas* and accepting the *alaṁkāras* like *Hetu*, *Sūkṣma* and *Leśa*. It may be due to their subjective preferences.

The concept of *Vakrokti*- the striking mode of speech-is understood by Bhāmaha as the basis of all *alaṁkāras*. Later, Kuntaka developed it as the all-in-all of poetic compositions.

The medium of literature being language, they made efforts to find out the distinction between the poetic and the *śāstric* expressions, which led them to the conclusion that the *guṇas* and the *alaṁkāras* of words and meaning are essential to *Kāvya*. Among the defects both have pointed out that some defects have exceptions. In some cases, some defects may turn into *guṇas* due to the skill of the poet and the charming nature of the subject of *Kāvya*.

The efforts of Bhāmaha and Daṇḍin served as the basis for the further development of Sanskrit poetics.

The *alaṁkāras* are not understood as mere figures of speech. They have an important function to be fulfilled in *Kāvya*, i.e. making the poetic expression sufficiently effective to produce the desired effect. The concept of *alaṁkāra* as stated by the early rhetoricians has wide scope. Kuntaka says - 'Kāvya is the name of what is adorned. (सालंकारस्य काव्यता)

The *alaṁkāras* should not be called as mere external decorations of *Kāvya* as they are an integral part of the effective poetic expression. It can be said that the *guṇas* have the nature of generality of beautification while the *alaṁkāras*, that of particularity.

NOTES

1. History of Sanskrit Poetics (Third Edition) - by M.M.P.V. Kane Motilal Banarsidass, Delhi-6. 1961.
2. *Kāvyādarśa* - (IInd Edition) - Bhandarkar Oriental Research Institute, Poona, 1970.
3. *Kāvyālaṁkāra*- Bihar -Rashtrabhasha - Parishad, Patna, 1962.
4. *Nāṭyaśāstra*- Vol II -(Chapter XVII) - The Chowkhamba Sanskrit Series Office, Varanasi -1, 1972.

The Concept of *Guṇas* as presented by Paṇḍitarāja Jagannātha in his *Rasagaṅgādhara*

Suneeti Dublay

The people of ancient India have given us a rich heritage in the field of vairous branches of knowledge. There was original thinking in Physics, Chemistry, Medicine, Astronomy, Astrology, etc. as well as Metaphysics, Epistemology, Cosmology, Philosophy and the like. The science of poetry did not lag behind in original thinking. Various technical elements of poetry were given a thorough consideration and a regular science of poetic beauty was put forth. It all started from Bharata and ended with Jagannātha.

Jagannātha is a scholar of great calibre. He is a veritable intellectual giant, has a clarity of vision and a capacity of presenting a thought with logical acumen. In fact, he is a great dialectician. He has originality, erudition and intuitive genius, with which he creates poetry of a high order. He is a great poet-critic, a rare combination of a poet's insight and critical judgement. He is arrogantly aware of his capacities and makes no secret about it. He is the last great author on poetics who finally established the Dhvani theory giving paramount importance to the suggested sense, without neglecting the formal side of the poetic compositions. He has the advantage of being the last one and gives us the gist of throught in the poetic field covering all the salient features of different schools and giving his opinion as a final word after criticising or supporting earlier opinions in a totally unambiguous manner.

I have selected this author for this paper on the concept of Gunas for the reason that the history of the development of this concept could be traced from his work *Rasagaṅgādhara*.

Rasagaṅgādhara, a treatise on Sanskrit Poetics, is 'a most scholarly and authoritative text' and 'admittedly the most difficult one'. Unfortunately, this ambitious work of the worthy author remained incomplete, but whatever is available, is invaluable to any student of Sanskrit poetics. The Indian thought in this field has reached its acme in *Rasagaṅgādhara*. Whatever Jagannātha could do, he has done perfectly logically, giving beautiful suitable examples composed by himself, which are, many times, fine pieces of poetic beauty and command admiration. He has tried to effect a compromise wherever he deemed it necessary, in the views of earlier and later writings by putting forth a theory of his own, making it free from loopholes as far as possible.

He has discussed many concepts which are technical elements of poetic beauty. The concept of Guṇas is one of them. This concept was recognised as a very important element in poetry from very early time in the development of thought in the field of poetics along with the concept of Alaṁkāras (figures of speech). Bharata's *Nāṭyaśāstra* is the oldest extant treatise. It is mainly concerned with dramaturgy. Bharata refers to this concept while discussing the literary aspect of Vācika abhinaya. He speaks about Guṇas along with Doṣas, Lakṣaṇas and Alaṁkāras. He enumerates ten Guṇas which are developed later on by authors like Vāmana, giving us Rīti-school of thought in poetics. Bhāmaha, the first author on poetics proper, cursorily mentions three Guṇas but does not discuss the importance and scope of the concept in the theory of poetic beauty. Then Daṇḍin comes and tells us the importance of this concept. He understands the word Alaṁkāra in the sense, 'that which enhances poetic beauty' and says that every Guṇa is an alaṁkāra, i.e. figure of speech is a Guṇa. He thinks that the presence of Guṇas is absolutely essential for any good poetic composition. He discusses ten Guṇas using the nomenclature of Bharata but having a different content. Then comes Vāmana, the propounder of the Rīti school in Idnian poetics. He is the first author who stresses the importance of this concept of Guṇas. He tells us रीतिरात्मा काव्यस्य । विशिष्टा पदरचना रीतिः । विशेषो गुणात्मा । and काव्याशोभायाः कर्तारः धर्माः । and adds that the Guṇas are the permanent (नित्य) elements in poetry and teaches the inseparable relationship of Guṇas and Ritis. His discussion is chiefly related to the form of poetry; He points out the difference between Guṇas and alaṁkāras as (नित्य) and (अनित्य) elements in poetry, still he clearly regards both Guṇas and Alṁkāras as qualities of word and meaning. Thus we notice that upto this point in the history of this concept it was clearly believed to be an element related to words and meanings.

Then came the epoch-making work *Dhvanyāloka* of Ānandavardhana. It revolutionised the theory of poetry by proposing Dhvani, the suggested sense as the most important element in poetry, the veritable soul of poetry. It was Ānandavardhana, who made a clear-cut distinction between Guṇas and alaṁkāras as तमर्थमवलम्बन्ते येऽङ्गिनं ते गुणाः स्मृताः । अङ्गाश्रिता–स्त्वलंकारा मन्तव्याः कटकादिवत् ।। by which Guṇas are stated as inherent while figures of speech were extraneous elements in poetry. Ānandavardhana, the propounder of the Dhvani school, was followed by Abhinavagupta, Mammaṭa, etc. Mammata did one important thing, viz. he clearly stated that the Guṇas were connected with रसs only (रसमात्रधर्म). That was an important step from formal consideration of literature to the consideration of content. Jagannātha, also, generally follows the Dhvani theorists in the treatment of various poetic elements.

At the beginning of the treatment of the concept of Guṇas, following the earlier authors of the Dhvani-school, Jagannātha tells us the three Guṇas Mādhurya (elegance or grace), Ojas (vigour) and Prasāda (clarity) accepted by them. He says: रसेषु चैतेषु निगदितेषु माधुर्योजःप्रसादाख्यांस्त्रीन् गुणानाहुः । and proceeds to give different opinions as regards their existence in poetic compositions presenting different sentiments, the welknown रसs of Indian poetic theory. Thus he tells us that according to the opinion of certain thinkers the quality of Mādhurya is found in the compositions delineating the sentiments of संयोगशृंगार, करुण विप्रलम्भशृंगार and शान्त in a higher degree respectively, Others opine that there is no difference of degree in करुण विप्रलम्भ and शान्त while a third group of thinkers considers the order to be संयेगशृंगार then करुण and शान्त and then विप्रलम्भ which becomes highest in order. The quality of Ojas must be present in a composition where वीर, रौद्र or बीभत्स sentiments are depicted. Then According to some, Mādhurya and Prasāda both are necessary for the delineation of अद्भुत (marvellous), हास्य (ludicrous) and भयानक (fearful), while others think that only Prasāda will be sufficient. He further states that the quality of Prasāda is common to all the रसs and all expressions of compositions (रचना).

Now, with these three Guṇas माधुर्य, ओजस् and प्रसाद three mental states viz. द्रुति (melting) दीप्ति (excitement) and विकास (expansion) are connected and these mental states are created by the enjoyment (चर्वणा) of रसऽ which are qualified by the respective qualities माधुर्य etc. Thus the Guṇas are the qualities of रसऽ alone and statements such as मधुरा रचना, ओजस्वी बन्धः, etc. are only metaphorical just like a statement आकारोऽस्य शूरः 'His form is heroic' where the form is called heroic in a secondary sense. Jagannātha says that this is the view of Mammaṭabhaṭṭa etc; what is the basis of their assertion that the Guṇas are the essential qualities of रसऽ ? He says if you say that it is self-evident, i.e. proved by direct perception, it is not so, because like the heat (उष्णस्पर्श) of fire which is seen as a quality different from it's effect (कार्य) burning (दाह) we do not experience माधुर्यादि as qualities different from the effects of रसऽ like melting etc. (द्रुत्यादि) of the heart (चित्तवृत्ति). If you say that Guṇas can be inferred as रसधर्मऽ because it is due to the existence of these qualities माधुर्य etc. that the effects like melting etc. (द्रुत्यादि) are experienced, that is, गुणविशिष्टत्व of रस is a necessary condition for being the cuase of द्रुत्यादि, this is not right because by their own nature (प्रातिस्विकरूपेण) are capable of producing the effects melting etc. Such being the cause, imagination of Guṇas for explaining द्रुत्यादि involves the fault of cumbersomeness (गौ रव दोष) Then Jagannātha enters into a hair-splitting disscussion raising possible objections and answering them capably. He says, if you say that it will be more simple if we consider that the Rasas like शृंगार–करुण–शान्त have the quality of माधुर्य and therefore become the cause of द्रुति , than considering each individual रस in its own capacity being the cause, because all the three instances will be covered by taking माधुर्यवत्त्व of these रसऽ as the cause of द्रुतिः . Jagannātha objects to this argument on the ground that according to you there is a difference of degree, viz. मधुर, मधुरतर, मधुरतम and the results are द्रुति, द्रुततर, द्रुततम respectively and, therefore, this fourth variety of general माधुर्य giving rise to general द्रुति will be futile because of these different causes and effects. Therefore, it is proved that our opinion that the रसऽ are directly the cause of द्रुति etc. by their own nature has the quality of brevity (लाघव) and that the Guṇas माधुर्य etc. are identical with the mental states द्रुति etc. These गुणऽ are not a separate element.

Then Jagannātha proceeds by putting forth a very strong argument. He says that you consider रस as the soul of poetry and the soul is devoid of all qualities. Therefore the qualities like माधुर्य etc. can not be qualities of रस which is the soul of poetry. If you say that they will be the qualities of the limiting conditions (उपाधिs) of रसs such as रति etc. we say no, because there is no proof for such an assumption. Secondly, the Ratyādi are themselves the attributes of रसs, hence it will be improper to consider माधुर्यादि as their attributes because an attribute can not be the property of another attribute according to nyāyaśāstra (गुणे गुणानङ्गीकारात् ।).

If you ask, how do you explain the usage like शृंगारो मधुरः । we justify it by telling you tht the capacity of रसs to cause the mental states like द्रुति etc. is called माधुर्य etc. i.e. this माधुर्यादि of शृंगार etc. is द्रुत्यादि itself and is related to रस by the relation of the prompter and the prompted (प्रयोजकतासंबन्ध). This means that the Mādhurya etc. becomes identified with the mental states Druti etc. which again leads to the impossibility of explaining the usages like शृंगारो मधुरः । because the मधुरता becomes the result of शृंगार etc. Jagannātha explains that the usage is to be explained with the help of usages like वाजिगन्धाउष्णा । where the herb Vājigandha which causes heat in the body of the consumer is itself called hot, ie. Vājigandhā which is a prompter or causer of heat is called hot by प्रयद्यजकतासंबन्ध . Similarly रसs are called मधुर etc. as they are the प्रयद्यजकs (prompters) of माधुर्य etc. which are the mental states द्रुति etc. Thus माधुर्य etc. are the attributes of the heart of the appreciative reader and रसs are only the प्रोद्यजकs. Words, meanings, expressions or compositions (रचना) and रसs all can be in a position of having this प्रयद्यजकत्व of mental states. But the mental states can be prompted by fate etc. (अदृष्टादि) also. Therefore जगन्नाथ qualifies this प्रयोजकत्व by the adjective अदृष्टादि विलक्षण. Thus the usage is explained easily without resorting to metaphor or secondary sense. Jagannātha says that according to the thinkers like me, this explanation is valid in connection with words and meanings also.

Thus Jagannatha has put forth a revolutionary theory about the concept of Gunas of the Dhvani school. He has virtually denied their independent existence and identified them with the mental states like Druti etc. But next, beginning with चिरन्तरास्तु meaning thereby the authors like Vamana, Dandin and their followers, he enumerates the ten Gunas by the stanza of Daṇdin श्लेषः प्रसादः समता माधुर्य सुकुमारता । अर्थव्यक्तिरुदारत्वओजः कान्ति समाधयः । and remarks that these are the names of शब्दगुणs and अर्थगुणs both though their difinitions are different and proceeds into a detailed discussion of the ten Guṇas accepted by the ancient theorists and gives his own definitions with appropriate examples composed by himself.

While reading this discussion of the Guṇas by Jagannātha one feels that he is just trying to explain this element with the help of the old and new theorists and wants to effect a compromise as it were. One has a distinct feeling that he considers the Guṇas of the Dhavani theorists and the Guṇas of the older theorists as two different entities. They need not be identified though they bear the same names. He diverges from the Dhvani theorists especially from Mammaṭa onwards and clearly says with reference to प्रसादगुण that it is common to all the रसऽ and all the रचनाऽ, प्रसादस्तु सर्वे रसेषु रचनासु च साधारणः । implying thereby that he does not consider the Guṇas as exclusively belonging to the रसऽ alone (रसमात्रधर्मऽ) but thinks them as connected with शब्द, अर्थ andरचना.

Out of these two sets of Guṇas, the Guṇas of the Dhvanivādins have been totally refused a place of their own, by Jagannātha, in the scheme of elements conducive to poetic beauty. Jagannātha is a scholar, who with his sharp intellect and wit along with his profound knowledge of various sciences is many times capable of taking the view of things in a proper perspective. He clearly shows his awareness of the importance of words and meanings in the theory of poetry. This is evident from his definition of Kāvya as रमणीयार्थप्रतिपादकः शब्दः काव्यम् । whereby the importance of word-structure is stressed. In other words, it means that he is aware of the importance of form in the consideration of poetic beauty. Though he generally follows the Dhvani-theorists, he has a difference of opinion about this concept of Guṇas and he boldly states it. He finds that it will not suffice to restrict the scope of Guṇas to रसऽ alone and says that words, meanings and expressions also are related to Guṇas by प्रयोजकतासंबन्ध.

This all clearly indicates that Jagannātha accepts the ten Guṇas of the Jarattaras on a formal level and equates the three Guṇas of the Dhvani theorists with the effects Drutyādi of the रसऽ refusing them an independent status. This is an improvement on the thought of the Dhvani theorists by Jagannātha. Again, this means that though he is a follower of the Dhvani school, he is not a blind follower. He is bold enough to tell his own opinion when it differs from that of the preceding sires. He tries to incorporate the elements of poetic beauty propounded by the very early writers in his scheme of poetic thought, which proves that he realises the importance of their way of thinking.

However, like the earlier authors, Jagannātha does not refer to the element of Rītis or Mārgas which is invariably associated with the concept of Guṇas in earlier thought. In fact, particular Guṇas are considered as indispensible for a particular Rīti or Mārga, rendered as 'style' in a very general sense of the term. Riti in Indian thought is connected with geographical location more like गौ डी, वैदर्भी, पांचाली than the personal way of expression of a poet. Jagannātha concerns himself with word-structure or expression (रचना) only and not with rīti or style.

With regards to the Guṇas of the Jarattaras, he has not said anything which could be considered as his own valued opinion, but it seems that leaving the Dhvani theorists he has joined hands with the earlier authors like Daṇḍin and Vāmana. This is evident from his elaborate treatment of the ten शब्दगुणs and ten अर्थगुणs while he refuses to accept गुणs as रसमात्रधर्मs. But in this treatment of शब्दगुणs and अर्थगुणs he does not tell anything new. He follows Vāmana and Siddhicandragaṇi, a commentator on the *Kāvyaprakāśa* of Mammaṭa; almost verbatim as shown by Dr. Ramacandrudu in his excellent treatise on Jagannātha.

Now my questions are as follows: can we possibly call a literary piece as excellent unless it has all the necessary technical elements in a perfectly harmonised and balanced manner? Can there be a suggested sense without proper words and meanings? I mean to say that whatever sense is understood by suggestion, must be understood in terms of words and meanings. So to have clarity of suggested sense, perspicuity in words and meanings would be a pre-requisite. How can there be a clear suggested sense if the words and meanings are obscure or ambiguous?

I am not acquainted with modern poetics and so am not aware whether there is any element in modern thought which could be equated with this Indian concept of Guṇas. But if there is such a concept it will be an interesting study to compare the views of Jagannātha on Guṇas with the modern western thought.

In the short duration of time available, it was not possible to go into the details of the discussion by Jagannātha on this concept of Guṇas. This is only a bird's eye-view of the topic. But I sincerely hope that a general idea about Jagannātha's views on this concept will be clear from the above discussion.

Unwritten Sanskrit Poetics

W.K. Lele

Explanation of the Title of the Paper

The title of my papr may seem to be rather perplexing. Let me, therefore, elucidate it at the outset. By unwritten Sanskrit Poetics I mean the concepts of Sanskrit Poetics which have not been stated explicitly in so many words but which are intended to be understood by the studious readers. All Sanskrit poeticians like भामह , दण्डिन , वामन , रुद्रट , राजशेखर , क्षेमेन्द्र , हेमचन्द्र and others did not mention each and every concept or topic expressly and elaborately, but conveyed it through certain devices, to be explained below. They expected their readers to be attentive while reading works on Sanskrit Poetics and to exercise their intellectual and imaginative faculties in understanding them fully and flawlessly. The reasons why the ancient thinkers resorted to 'implication' can be surmized and summarized as under.

Reasons for 'implication'

(*i*) Like all ancient theoreticians in other disciplines, the theorists in the field of poetics also preferred brevity to prolixity.

(*ii*) They addressed their works to diligent readers.

(*iii*) They intended to stimulate the reflective and imaginative faculties of their readers.

(*iv*) They expected their readers to be intellectually independent or self-reliant.

(*v*) They thus sincerely aimed at helping the growth and development of Sanskrit Poetics.

I trust there will not be two opinions over the reasons listed here. I, therefore, pass on to the next point.

Implication through devices of methodology

The implication, the central theme of the present paper, was not an arbitrary phenomenon, but it was achieved by resorting to devices of a comprehensive methodology conceived by ancient Indian savants like कौटिल्य, चरक, सुश्रुत, वाग्भट, नीलमेघ and upheld and meticulously cultivated by their worthy commentators like इन्दु, चक्रपाणिदत्त, डल्हण and अरुणदत्त. This methodology comprised, in all 128 devices, grouped under seven categories, viz., thirty-six तन्त्रयुक्ति, fifteen व्याख्याऽ, seven कल्पनाऽ, twenty आश्रयऽ, seventeen ताच्छिल्य, eighteen शास्त्रगुणऽ and fifteen शास्त्रदोष.[1] Of these 128 devices, the poeticians made use of the following ones to express certain concepts through implication or a slight indication.

अतिदेश - This is one of the thirty-six तन्त्रयुक्तिऽ . The word तन्त्र means a science or a scientific work and the word युक्ति means a device. Thus the compound तन्त्रयुक्ति means a device employed for composing a scientific work. The ancient thinkers, namely, कौटिल्य चरक and others had conceived of thirty-six of such devices. Since these devices went into the making of scientific treatises, their thorough knowledge was a sine qua non for interpreting scientific treatises. अतिदेश, under consideration at present, is one of such indispensable devices. अतिदेश, means proving or establishing a thing with what is already said. In other words, it is the extension of the application of a norm to an analogous topic, कौटिल्य , अरुणदत्त and चक्रपाणिदत्त have defined अतिदेश as under:

कौटिल्य – उक्तेन साधनम् अतिदेश[2]

अरुणदत्त – अतिदेशो नाम, यत् किञ्छिद् एव अर्थजातं उक्त्वा अनुक्तार्थसाधनाय एवं अन्यद्द अपि प्रत्येतव्यम् इति परिभाषायां स्थापति ।[3]

चकपाणिदत्त – अतिदे्गे नाम , यत् किञ्चिद्द एव प्रकाश्य अर्थं अनुक्तार्थसाधनाय एव एवं अन्यद्द अपि प्र प्रत्येतव्यम इति परिभाष्यजते ।[4]

It is evident that the difference in these three definitions is only verbal, their meaning being the same. Let us now turn to the next device, viz., अपवाद

अपवाद - अपवाद also known as अपवर्ग or अपवर्ज is also तन्त्रयुक्ति. Like अतिदेश अपवाद means an exception to a general rule. Both कौटिल्य and सुश्रुत have defined अपवाद in almost identical terms, as is evident from their definitions reproduced below:

कौटिल्य's definition: अभिलुतव्यपकर्षणं अपवर्ग[5] ।
सुश्रुत's definition: अभिव्याप्य आकर्षणं अपवर्ग[6] ।

Now consider the third device.

अर्थापत्ति- Like the previous ones, this too is a तन्त्रयुक्ति . The term अर्थापत्ति is a compound, having two members अर्थ and आपत्ति Of these, अर्थ is meaning and अपत्ति , means obtaining. The compound means 'obtaining the meaning'. As to its nature, कौ टिल्य, सुश्रुत , अरुणदत्त and चकपाणिदत्त hold practically the same view. They have defined कौटिल्य, च्र कपाणिदत्त, सुश्रुत and अरुणदत्त as under:

कौटिल्य – यद्द अनुक्तं अर्थाद्द आपद्यते सार्थापत्तिः[7] ।
सुश्रुत – यद्द अकीपर्तितं अर्थाद्द आपद्यते साऽर्थापत्तिः[8] ।
अरुणदत्त – अर्थापत्तिर्नाम, यद्यऽब्ध्यन अर्थेन उक्तेन ततद्यऽपरद्यऽप्यर्थ्द गदित इव ज्ञायते[9] ।
च्र कपाणिदत्त – अर्थापत्तिर्नाम , यद अकीर्तितं अर्थाद्द आपद्यते साऽर्थापतिः[10] ।

The implied meaning is generally the opposite of the one expressed in words. The next device to be accounted for is ऊह्य.

ऊह्य - This is also a तन्त्रयुक्ति . The word ऊह्य is derived from ऊह (1.u.) meaning 'to guess, to infer by reasoning, to deduce, to imagine, etc.' ऊह्य , therefore, is that which is to be deduced, inferred by reasoning or imagined. There is unanimity of opinion among कौटिल्य , सुश्रुत and चकपाणिदत्त about the nature of ऊह्य. Their definitions respectively are as below:

अनुक्तकरणं ऊह्यम्[11] । यद अनिर्दिष्टं बुद्‌ध्या ऽवगम्यते तद्द ऊह्यम्[12] ।
ऊहां नाम यद्‌ अनिबद्धं ग्रन्थे प्रज्ञया तर्क्यत्वेनेन उपदिश्यते[13] ।

To be taken up after ऊहा is प्रकार .

प्रकार - This is one of the seventeen ताच्छिल्य defined and discussed by अरुणदत्त. The word ताच्छिल्य is etymologized thus: तत शीलं स्वभावः यस्य सः तच्छीलः, वस्य थावः ताच्द्दील्यम‌् । It means the nature of a thing. While defining प्रकारताच्छिल्य, अरुणदत्त says: यो यस्य समानधर्मा स तस्य प्रकारः[14] । which means the mention of one member of a class. The scientific writer leaves it to the intelligent understanding of his readers to know the other members of the same class, not actually mentioned. The next device to be considered is योग.

योग – युज् (7A.) is at the root of the word योग, which etymologically means 'joining, uniting, connecting'. It thus stands for the joining of the words and/or sentences, to yield the intended meaning. कौटिल्य, सुश्रुत &नीलमेघ have offered the following definitions of this तंत्रयुक्तिः:

कौ टिल्य – वाक्ययोजना योगः[15] ।
सुश्रुत – येन वाक्यं युज्यते स योगः[16] ।
नीलमेघ – योगः पदानां एकैकं अथ 'चित्येन योजना' ।।2।।

Thus the purpose of this device is to unite unconnected sentences or to establish a coherent connection between farflung elements.

The last device to be taken into account is विपर्यय.

विपर्यय - This is a तन्त्रयुक्ति, meaning contrariety or inversion. व्यक्तिक्रम & अन्यथाभाव are its synonyms. कौटिल्य, सुश्रुत, इन्दु, नीलमेघ, अरुणदत्त & चक्रपाणिदत्त hold almost the same view about the nature of this device. Their definitions read as follows:

कौटिल्य – प्रतिलोभेन साधनं विपर्ययः[18] ।
सुश्रुत – यद् यत्र अभिहितं तस्य प्रतिलोम्यं विपर्ययः[19] ।
इन्दु – विपर्ययश्च नाम उक्तस्य अन्यथाभावो विपर्ययः [20]।
नीलमेघ – उक्तार्थविपरीत्येन लक्षणं स्याद् विपर्ययः[21] ।
अरुणदत्त – विपर्ययो नाम – यथोपदिष्टविपर्ययेण लक्षणाकिरणम्[22] ।
चक्रपाणिदत्त – विपर्ययो नाम – अपकृष्टात् प्रतीपोदाहरणम्[23] ।

Here one important point is to be borne in mind. In अर्थापत्ति considered under 1.2.3 above, the reader has to infer the opposite meaning from the words actually used. That is to say, the opposite meaning is implied. In the case of विपर्यय, however, the very word विपर्यय or its equivalents like विपरीत & न are expressly used and they signify the opposite meaning which the author intends his readers to understand.

Let us now consider how the ancient poeticians employed the above devices to suggest certain concepts of Sanskrit Poetics. Let us take up the above-mentioned devices, one by one in the same order. Accordingly, the first to be considered is अतिदेश .

अतिदेश & Sanskrit poeticians.

In his काव्यालंकार, भामह has defined संसृष्टि[24] (co-existence of more than one figure of speech) in 3.49, has given two illustrative examples in 3.50, in 3.51 and has then exhorted: अन्येषां अपि कर्तव्या संसृष्टिरनया दिशा । (3.52), meaning, the संसृष्टि of other figures is to be achieved in the same manner. Thus he expects his readers to achieve the उपमा रुपक, उपमा & श्लेष, उत्प्रेक्षा & श्लेष and so on. Such combinations can theoretically be literally numerous and therefore भामह rightly says: कियद् उद् घटितज्ञेभ्यः शक्यं कथयितुं मया । (3.52).

भामह again, in the fourth chapter of his work discusses the demerits of poetry. During the course of that discussion he cites an instance of a demerit concerning the art of music and then observes: अन्यासु अपि कलासु एवं अभिधेया विरोधिता । (4.35). He wants his reader to find out instances of poetic blemishes relating to other fine arts, viz., चित्र, शिल्प, वास्तु etc., which are in number, according to the ancient tradition.

दाण्डिन्, in his काव्यलक्षणम्[25](1.14) lays down a rule thus: आशीर्नमस्क्रिया वस्तुनिर्देशो वापि तन्मुखम् । meaning thereby that a poet should begin a महाकाव्य either with a benediction to his readers or a salutation to his deity or a mention of the subject of his narrative. This rule is to be extended to the other two varieties of creative writing, viz., गद्य & मिश्र. In other words, the गद्यकाव्य as also the मिश्रकाव्य have to be begun with either an आर्शीवचन, or a प्रणाम or a वस्तुकथ. दण्डिन informs us in 1.33 that there are many varieties of प्राकृत, viz., तद्भव, तत्सम, देशी and सर्वशब्दसामान्यः Later in 1.36, he speaks of the अपभ्रंशः What is true of the प्राकृत is also true of the अपभ्रंश. Thus, the अपभ्रंश too has four varieties as above.

In 2.327 he advises his readers अयं एव क्रमोऽन्येषां भेदानां अपि कल्पने । meaning, the process followed in the case of हेतुविशेषोक्ति is to be followed in the case of other varieties of विशेषयक्ति . Thus, the process is to be made applicable to अविरुद्ध – क्रियाविशेषोक्ति, विरुद्धक्रियाविशेषोक्ति, चाटुविशेषोक्ति and so on.

Now let us turn to वामन's काव्यालंकारसूत्राणि[26] . He desires a budding poet to acquire proficiency in many scientific subjects like grammar, prosody, sciences of fine arts, etc. After having actually discussed six of them, he states एवं अन्यासां अपि विद्यानां यथास्वं उपयोगो वर्णनीय इति[27] । What he drives at is that the knowledge of other lores like वेद, स्मृति, निरुक्त, ज्योतिष,

शिक्षा, मोक्षज्ञान, क्रियाविधि, धनुर्वेद, हस्तिशिक्षा, कामतंत्र, लक्षण, पुराण, इतिहास, तर्क, वैद्यक etc. is of immense use to a budding poet.

Another example from वामन's work is worth considering. He mentions two types of अश्लील, viz. असभ्यार्थान्तिरम् & असभ्यस्मृतिहेतुः.[28] Further on, he proposesa three-fold division of अश्लील, namely, व्रीडादायि, जुगुप्सादायि & अमङ्गलातङ्कदायि[29] । The attentive reader has to understand that both असभ्यार्थान्तिर & असभ्यस्मृतिहेतु have three varieties each, stated above.

The following statement made after illustrating अक्षरयमक is a very clear instance of the अतिदेश तन्त्रयुक्तिः

अन्या च वर्णयमकमालया पदयमकमाला व्याख्याता[30] ।

So also the following one made after discussing three types of यमक obtained by splitting:

एतेन इतरौ अपि व्याख्यातौ[31] ।

After having treated of the हनित्व उपमादोष, वामन's comments, तेन अधिकत्वं व्याख्यातम्[32] ।, meaning, just as there are three sub-types, viz., जातिहीनत्व, प्रमाणहीनत्व & धर्महीनत्व, so also there are three sub-types of अधिकत्व , viz., जाति-अधिकत्व, प्रमाण-अधिकत्व& धर्म-अधिकत्व. वामन 's observation तेन वचनभेदो व्याख्यातः[33] ।।15।। is yet one more instance of अतिदेश.

Quotations from works of other poeticians could also be given. But there is no point in multiplying examples for clarifying a point which has hopefully become crystal clear. The अतिदेश, thus, helps the diligent reader comprehend the unsaid.

Let us now turn to the consideration of the employment of अपवाद by the ancient poeticians for the purposes of suggestion.

अपवाद & Sanskrit poeticians.

While defining यमक in his काव्यालंकार[34] (3.1) रुद्रट says: पुनरावृत्तिर्यमकं प्रायः छन्दांसि विषयोऽस्य । रुद्रट contends that though the legitimate sphere of activity of यमक is versified creative writing, it is sometimes found to have been used even in prose writing. This exception has been suggested by the word प्रायः , meaning generally.

Let us peruse वाग्भटालंकार[35] in this respect. वाग्भट permits a poet to accept the meaning of another's poem during समस्यापूर्ति (completing part of a stanza proposed by another). He says: परकाव्यग्रहद्यऽपि स्यात्, समस्यायां गुणः कवेः[36] । But the reader is supposed to interpret this line very cautiously. वाग्भट, it is to be borne in mind, does not recommend here the accepting or borrowing of the whole stanza composed by another poet. Such a borrowing is not at all a गुण , but verily a दोष. The borrower should borrow one, two or at most three lines of another's stanza. Thus this exception has to be carefully understood.

Again, वाग्भट further exhorts: पदाद न च वक्तव्याशृवादयः प्रायशो बुधैः[37] । meaning, the wise should not generally employ the words like आदि etc. at the beginning of a line of a verse. The word प्रायशः implies an exception, viz., the words like रे, धिक, हा, किं, न, आः, and others may be used. Such usage is not faulty.

Let us now pay attention to a very important instance of अपवाद which has occurred in दण्डिन's काव्यलक्षणम्. The कारिका listing the ten qualities (श्लेष etc.) of the वैदर्भमार्ग is followed by the कारिका reproduced below:

इति वैदर्भमार्गस्य प्राणा दशगुणाः स्मृताः ।
एषां विपर्ययः प्रायो दृश्यते गौडवर्त्मनि[38] ॥42॥

Here दण्डिन has resorted to अपवाद by using the word प्रायः. What दण्डिन desires to convey thereby is that the contrary qualities of some of the ten गुणs are to be met within the गौडमार्ग and some of the qualities of the वैदर्भमार्ग are retained in their original form in the गौडमार्ग. Thus, the qualities of अर्थव्यक्ति, उदारत्व & समाधि of the वैदर्भमार्ग are dear to the गौडमार्ग also. The opposites of the remaining seven qualities only find favour with the गौडमार्ग.

The works of भामह, वामन, केशवमिश्र, राजशेखर and others abound in instances of अपवाद , no doubt. But these authors have themselves explained the अपवाद to the general rule.[39] But here we considered only such instances of अपवाद which are implicit and therefore to be interpreted by an attentive reader. While closing the discussion on this point we may assert that the ancient Sanskrit poeticians hinted at some concepts through the medium of अपवाद तन्त्रयुक्ति as well Now comes the turn of अर्थापत्ति.

अर्थापत्ति & Sanskrit poeticians.

Let us begin our survey by the consideration of भामह's work. To avoid prolixity, below are reproduced some of भामह's statements against which their implied meanings only have been given:

(i) अज्ञस्य इव प्रगल्भत्वं अकवेः शास्त्रवेदनम्[40] ।: Only a poet's acquaintance with various scientific subjects is fruitful.

(ii) यत्नो विदितवेद्येन विधेयः काव्यलक्षणः[41] ।: One should not attempt at composing poetry without first acquiring knowledge of various subjects.

(iii) सर्वथा पदं अपि एकं न निगाद्यं अवद्यवत्[42] ।: The entire poem should be flawless.

(iv) सर्गबन्धो महाकाव्यं महतां च महत् च यत्[43] ।: An epic poem must never describe a non-celebrity or a most ordinary person and it must also not be inconsiderably small.

Let us now focus our attention on दण्डिन 's work in this respect. The method of treatment will be the same as above.

(i) गुणदोषान् अशास्त्रज्ञः कथं विभजते जनः[44] ।: Only a knower of poetics can efficiently distinguish between merits and demerits of poetry.

(ii) सा विद्या न विविक्षूणां गम्भीरं काव्यसागरम्[45] ।: Those desirous of composing poems must intently and respectfully study prosody.

(iii) सर्गैः अनतिविस्तीर्णैः...[46]। The cantos of an epic poem should be medium in length, so that they will sustain the reader's interest in the poem, and will not tire him out.

(iv) काव्यं कल्पान्तरस्थायि जायते सदलंकृति[47] ।: The embellishing features should be fittingly or appropriately used, for then alone they adorn a piece of creative writing.

(v) यदि उपात्तेषु संपत्तिः आराधयति तद्विदः[48] । If the wealth in the form of various features of an epic poem does not entertain the learned, then they regard such a poem as faulty and discard it.

(vi) तद ् एतत्त काव्यसर्वस्वं समाधिनमि यो गुणः[49] । The quality समाधिः is the quintessence of all types of poetic (literary) compositions, like prose, verse, and mixed.

Now let us consider रुद्रट's work, following the same procedure as above.

(i) सुविहितपदभङ्गं सुप्रसिद्धाभिधानं । तदनु विरचनीयं सर्गबन्धेषु भूम्ना[50] ।।59।। The यमकऽ which do not contain pleasing पदभङ्गऽ and which contain unpopular descriptive words should be avoided. Again, such यमकऽ should be very sparingly used in the नाटक, कथा & आख्यायिका.

(ii) प्रकृतिप्रत्यमूल्यं व्युत्पत्तिर्नास्ति यस्य देश्यस्य । तन्मड्हादि कथंचन रुढिरिति न संस्कृते रचयेत ्[51] ।।27।। : A देशी word, the etymology of which can be satisfactorily advanced may be used, in a Sanskrit composition.

Let us now turn to वाग्भट'ऽ work. He prescribes:

(i) साधुशब्दार्थसन्दर्भगुणालंकारभूषितं । स्फुटरीतिरसोपेतं काव्यं कुर्वीर्ति कीतये[52] ।।2।। : A composition which contains ungrammatical words, which is devoid of गुणऽ, अलंकारऽ, रीति, & रसऽ, will put the poet to shame.

(ii) वाग्भट exhorts:

अनारतं गुरुपान्ते यः काव्ये रचनादरः। तं अभ्यासं विदुः तस्य क्रमः कोऽप्युपदिश्यते[53] ।: He who sits at the feet of the teacher only once, intermittantly or occasionally to learn the art of composing poetry cannot be said to be doing any practice at all.

In the end, let us go through क्षेमेन्द्र'ऽ औ चित्यविचारचर्चा[54]

(i) यस्य जीवितं औ चित्यं विचिन्त्य अपि न दृश्यते[55] ।: Propriety, the very life of poetry, should be easily perceptible. In other words, the reader should be able to discern at a single glance whether a particular poetic composition is appropriate or otherwise.

(ii) अलङ्कारास्त्वलङ्कारा: गुणाः सदा ।: Neither गुणऽ nor अलङ्कारऽ can ever become the life of a poetic composition. A composition full of गुणऽ and अलंकारऽ but devoid of औ चित्य is verily lifeless.

The above discussion will convince us that the present device goes a long way in formulating some principles of creative writing and criticism. The device to be considered hereafter is ऊह्य .

ऊह्य & Sanskrit poeticians.

Let us first of all examine भामह's work. While concluding the second chapter of his work, भामह somewhat apologetically says:

समासेन उदितं इदं धीखेदाय विस्तरः ।
असङ्गृहीतं अपि अन्यद्, अभ्यूह्यं अनया दिशा[57] ।।95।।

Here the reader is experted to imagine the figures of speech other than the ones discussed by भामह either by bringing into play his own intellectual faculties or by taking one from the works of रामशर्मा, मेधावी, शाखावर्धन & many others who preceded भामह and who have been referred to by him.

There are several instances of this device in दण्डिन्'s work. Let us consider some of them.

(i) At the end of the रुपकचक्र, दण्डिन् says:
न पर्यन्तो विकल्पानां रुपकोपमयो अतः ।
दिङ्मात्रं दर्शितं धीरैः अनुक्तं अनुमीयताम्[58] ।।96।।

According to him there is no end to the types and subtypes of रुपक & उपमा. He has, therefore, hinted at a few ones only. He expects his intelligent reader to infer the unsaid. The reader has to press into service his own imaginative faculty or seek some guidelines from the works of दण्डिन्'s predecessors.

(ii) Similarly, he suggests to his reader to conceive of several other varieties of दीपक (2/102), आक्षेप (2/166), अर्थान्तरन्यास (2/169) ज्ञापकहेतु (2/44) &, अपन्हुति (2/307).

Let us turn to वामन 's work. While discussing अवेक्षण, i.e. removal on insertion of words, he puts forth the concept of शब्दपाक.[69] The imaginative reader is supposed to conceive of the similar idea of अर्थपाक and has to deduce that as long as a poet cannot decide whether a particular thought or idea could or could not be expressed, its insertion and cancellation continues. It comes to an end the moment the poet decides upon it.

We come across a very interesting example of ऊह्य in क्षेमेन्द्र's कविकण्ठाभरण.[60] After having enumerated and illustrated ten varieties of चमत्कार, he observes: इत्युक्त एष सविशेषचमत्कृतीनां । सारः प्रकारपरभागविभाव्यमानः[61] ।। Here क्षेमेन्द्र advises his alert readers to find out the चमत्कार lying dormant in other features of poetry, like वाक्य, प्रबन्धार्थ गुण, क्रियापद, लिंग, वचन, विशेषण, काल, देश, अभिप्राय, स्वभाव etc.

क्षेमेन्द्र ends his औचित्यविचारचर्चा saying: अन्येषु काव्यगिषु अनयैव दिशा स्वयं अ ौचित्यं उत्प्रेक्षणीयम[62] । He has said this after considering no fewer than 27 cases of अ चित्य . He expects his reader to find out for himself other काव्यांगऽ where औचित्य or अनौचित्य could be met with. The following could be suggested as the probable काव्यांगऽ:

(a) Descriptions of चर्तुवर्गफलप्राप्ति, नगर, आश्रम, शैल, सैन्यावास, अर्णव ऋतु, रात्रि, दिवस, चंद्रोदय, कुमारप्राप्ति, बनविहार, जलक्रीडा, मधुपान, सूर्यास्तसमय, स्त्रीलाभ etc.;

(b) Diction suitable to the sentiment to be expressed;

(c) The metre suitable to the sense to be expressed (e.g. the द्रुतविलंबित suits शृंगार, वसन्ततिलका suits वीर, वैतालीय suits करुण, स्रग्धरा suits रौद्र , and so on).

रुद्रट offers a very typical example of the present device. He has to offer the following advice to the poets in regard to theग्राम्यदोषः

एतद्विज्ञाय बुधैः परिहर्तव्यं महीपयसो यत्नात[63] ।
नहि सम्यग्विज्ञातुं शक्यं उदाहरणमात्रेण ।।11।।

रुद्रट wants his enlightened readers to put in great efforts to ward off the ग्राम्य दोषः. He expects them to read the poetic compositions of the past generations, to pay minute attention both to the लोकव्यवहार & कविसमय and to make use of their imagination. This three-fold महीयस् यत्न will enable the readers to know well the real nature of the ग्राम्य दोषः. Therefore, he refrains from giving illustrations only.

Before we wind up the discussion on ऊह्य , let us consider one more example from वाग्भट's काव्यालंकार . The concluding verse of the fourth chapter of his work reads as under:

अर्थेन येन अतिचमत्करोति प्रायः कवित्वं कृतिनां मनःसु[64] ।
अलङ्क्रियात्वेन स एव तस्मिन् अभ्यूह्यतां हन्त दिशानयैव ।। 52 ।।

वाग्भट here wants his reader to note that the number of figures of speech is not restricted to 35 only. An imaginative reader can, in fact should, conceive of many other pleasing turns of expression. For whatever, he maintains, pleases a learned lover of poetry and whatever is aesthetically attractive should be regarded as an embellishment of creative writing and should find a place of honour in works on poetics. Although वाग्भट's above view is not altogether new, for we are familiar with दण्डिन्'s assertion that none can interminably enumerate the beautifying features of poetry ते च अद्यापि विकल्प्यन्ते कस्तान् कात्स्न्येंन वक्ष्यति ।।, it is clear that the poeticians helped promote the conceptual development of Sanskrit poetics by judiciously making use of the उह्य तंत्रयुक्ति.

We now pass on to the next device, viz; प्रकार.

प्रकार & Sanskrit poeticians.

It is relatively a minor dvice, yet helps reveal some concealed meanings. Generally the word आदि represents the present device. The word आदि at the end of a compound means 'etcetera', ' and the rest', and so on (of the same nature or kind), 'such like'. It thus denotes members belonging to the same class or group as spoken of earlier. Let us persue a few examples.

(*i*) When दण्डिन says:
सौरसेनी च गौडी च लाटी चान्या च ताहशी[66] ।
याति प्राकृतं इति एव व्यवहारेषु सन्निधिम् ।।35 ।।

He wants his reader to understand that पांचाली & मागधी, the अन्या भाषा , which too are known as the प्राकृत languages, for they are belong to the category of the सौ रसेनी & others.

(*ii*) The word आदि appearing at the end of the compound लास्यच्छलिनशम्यादि[67] in 1.39, denotes स्कन्धक . Thus the reader has to understand that the स्कन्धक is meant for viewing (प्रेक्षार्थम्).

(*iii*) Similarly, आदि in कल्पदेशीयदेश्यादिः (2/60) and शशाङ्कवदनादिषु[68] (2/61) stands for 'बहुजादि' and उत्पलाक्ष्यादि respectively, as pointed out by रत्नश्रीज्ञान , the learned commentator of दण्डिन्. Again, in नूनं इति एव आदिभिः[69] (2/232), the word आदि denotes तर्कयामि, कल्पयामि, उत्पश्यामि which are similar to मन्ये, शङ्के and others. So also in गुणजातिक्रियादीनां (2/321), the word आदि represents द्रव्य which belongs to the same class as गुण, जाति & क्रिया.

(*iv*) रुद्रट, like all other poeticians, holds that पुनरुक्त is a poetic blemish. But he mentions an exception to this general rule, saying that in certain contexts, the पुनरुक्त is not a दोष. He enumerates those contexts thus: वक्ता हर्षभयादिभिः आक्षितमनाः तथा स्तुवन्निन्द .[71] । The आदि used herein denotes विस्मय, शधक, त्वरा, अर्थातिशय, दैन्य, कधप, & अर्वचारण . The reader has, therefore, to take into consideration the sentiment expressed by the poet and then to decide whether the पुनरुक्ति made by the poet is सदोष or निर्दोष

(*v*) रुद्रट has composed the following कारिका to describe the varieties of द्रव्यः

नित्यानित्यचराचरसचेतनाचेतनैर्बहुभिः[72] ।
भेदैद, विभिन्न एतद, द्विधा भूरिशो भवति ।।3।।

The बहुभिः भेदैः referred to herein are सवचन + अवचन, व्यक्त + अव्यक्त, सूक्ष्म + स्थूल, नक्तंचर + दिवाचर & ' स्थलज + जलज. These additional ones complete the list of the भेदs of द्रव्य.

(*vi*) The word आदि used by रुद्रट in प्रशस्तिकुलकादि[73] points to मुक्तक, संदानितम , विशेषक, कलापक कोष & परिकथा, which all belong to the कुलक class.

(*vii*) वाग्भट too has employed this device. While defining व्युत्पत्ति, he uses the word आदि in शब्दधर्मार्थकामादि[74] (1.5) and suggests that a would-be poet must read other शास्त्र s, like छन्दस, अलंकार, अभिधान, गजशिक्षा, अश्वशिक्षा, रत्नपरिक्षा, & दर्शनाभिधायक शास्त्रs.

(*viii*) We cite one more instance from वाग्भट's work and end the discussion of the present device. The word आदि appearing in the definition of the figure स्वभावोक्ति हीनत्रस्तार्भकादिषु [75](4.47) alludes to मत्त & कुपित also, for their natural description lends charm to poetry.

Thus the प्रकार device acquaints the reader with some additional concepts of Sanskrit poetics and thereby lends completeness to his knowledge of the subject.

We now turn to the penultimate device, viz., योग.

योग & Sanskrit poeticians

Let us start our study with the examination of भामह's work. Read the following two कारिका's

> शब्दार्थ 'सहित काव्यं, गद्यं पद्यं च द्विधा ।
> संस्कृतं प्राकृतं चान्यद् अपभ्रंश इति त्रिधा ।।16।।
> वृत्तदेवादिचरितशंसि च उत्पाद्यवस्तु च।
> कलाशास्त्राश्रयं च इति चतुर्धा भिद्यते पुनः[76] ।।17।।

These two stanzas are to be joined together. This done, they yield the following varieties of compositions:

1 गद्य – संस्कृत – वृत्तदेवादिचरितशंसि, 2 गद्य – संस्कृत – उत्पाद्यवस्तु, 3 गद्य – संस्कृत – कलाश्रय, 4 गद्य – संस्कृत – शास्त्राश्रय, 5 गद्य – प्राकृत – वृत्तदेवादिचरितशंसि, 6 गद्य – प्राकृत – उत्पाद्यवस्तु, 7 गद्य – प्राकृत – कलोश्रय, 8 गद्य – प्राकृत – शास्त्राश्रय, 9 गद्य – अपभ्रंश – वृत्तदेवादिचरितशंसि, 10 गद्य – अपभ्रंश – उत्पाद्यवस्तु, 11 गद्य – अपभ्रंश – कलाश्रय, 12 गद्य – अपभ्रंश – शास्त्राश्रय,& 12 varieties of पद्य on the same lines, throwing up, in all, 24 varieties of composition.Such a comprehensive list can be raised only if we understand that भामह has used the योग तंत्रयुक्ति.

दण्डिन 's following two कारिका s are also to be connected with each other:

> पद्यं गद्यं च मिश्रं च तत् त्रिधा एव व्यवस्थितम्[77] ।
> & तदिदं वाङ्मयं भूयः संस्कृतं प्राकृतं तथा ।
> अपभ्रंशश्च मिश्रं च इति आहुः आप्ताः चतुर्विधम्[78] ।।

Thus connected, they give rise to four language-based varieties each of गद्य, पद्य & मिश्र compositions. Elaborately enumerated, they will be as under:

1 संस्कृत – गद्य, 2 प्राकृत – गद्य, 3 अपभ्रंश – गद्य, 4 मिश्र – गद्य, 5 संस्कृत – पद्य, 6 प्राकृत – पद्य, 7 अपभ्रंश – पद्य, 8 मिश्र – पद्य, 9 संस्कृत – मिश्र, 10 प्राकृत – मिश्र, 11 अपभ्रंश – मिश्र, & 12 मिश्र – मिश्र. The last variety contains a mixture of languages and a mixture of गद्य – पद्य

We thus come by all the probable varieties of verbal compositions only after we understand the use of the योग तंत्रयुक्ति as shown above. Having thus finished योग, we now take up the consideration of the last device, viz., विपर्यय.

विपर्यय & Sanskrit poeticians.

भामह mentions in the following two verses the characteristics of a bad poetic composition.

अपुष्टार्थं अवक्रोक्ति प्रसन्नऋजुं कोमलम् ।
भिन्नं गेयं इव इदं तु केवलं श्रुतिपेशलम् ।।
अलङ्कारवद् अग्राम्यं अर्थ्यं न्याय्यं अनाकुलम् ।
गौडीयं अपि साधीयोवैदर्भं इति न अन्यथा[79] ।।35 ।।

By inverting these statements we obtain the characteristics of a good poetic composition, they are: पुष्टार्थ, वक्रोक्ति, प्रसन्न, ऋजु, कोमल, श्रुतिपेशल, अलङ्कारवत्, अग्राम्य, अर्थ्य, न्याय्य & अनाकुल.

Through the कारिका 'प्रतीतशब्दं ओजस्वि'...' etc. (2/18), भामह has suggested that a यमक which contains unfamiliar words, clumsy euphonic coalitions, unintelligible, & bad predications is to be regarded as a discardable यमक.

वामन gives two definitions of the poetic quality समता. They are (i) अवैषम्यं प्रक्रमाभेदः समता । & (ii) सुगमत्वं वा अवैषम्यम्[80] ।. While closing this topic he says: प्रत्युदाहरणं सुलभम्, meaning thereby that a composition hard to understand is faulty. This is the विपर्यय of समता.

The following quotations from वामन 's work contain the use of the very word विपर्यय :

(i) पूर्वं शिष्याः विवेकित्वात् ।।2।। ... नेतरे, तद्विपर्ययात्[81] ।।3।।

(ii) अनाविद्धललितपदं चूर्णम् ।।24।।... विपरीतं उत्कलिकाप्रायम्[82] ।।25।।

(iii) पृथकपदत्वं माधुर्यम् ।।20।। ... विपर्ययस्तु यथा –[83] ।

(iv) अजरठत्वं स ौकुमार्यम् ।।21।।... विपर्ययस्तु यथा –[84]

(v) अनुल्बणो वर्णानुप्रासः श्रेयान् न श्रेयान् । उल्बणस्तु नश्रेयान्[85]न।।

(vi) न कर्मधारयो बहुव्रीहि प्रतिपत्तिकरः ।।7।। ... तेन विपर्ययो व्याख्यातः[86] ।।8।।

In the above statements वामन has either stated the contrary concept or has coined the definition of a concept through inversion.

रुद्रट has listed the वाक्यगुण्s in the following कारिकाः:

अन्यूनं–अधिक–वाचक–सुक्रम–पुष्टार्थ–शब्द–चारुपदम् ।
क्षोदक्षमं अक्षूणं सुमतिर् वाक्यं प्रयुञ्जति[87] ।।

नमिसाधु has shown in his gloss on this कारिका that रुद्रट has used the words अन्यून and others to leave off their opposites. The relevant portions of नमिसाधु 's gloss read as under:

(i) तत्र अन्यूनग्रहणाद्, यत्र कंचित्, शब्दं बिना दुष्टार्थप्रतीतिर विवक्षितार्थाप्रतिपत्तिर, एव वा भवति तश्च न्यूनपदं वाक्यं निरस्तम्.[88] ।

(ii) अधिकग्रहणाद्, यत्र शब्दान्तरेण उक्तेऽप्यर्थे पुनस्, तदर्थतदं प्रयुज्जयते तन्, निरस्तम्.[89] ।

(iii) वाचकग्रहणम् अवाचकनिवत्यर्थम्.[90] ।

(iv) सुक्रमग्रहणं दुष्टक्रमनिकृत्यर्थम्.[91]।

(v) पुष्टार्थग्रहणं अपुष्टार्थनिवृत्त्यर्थं एकशब्दप्रतिपाद्यार्थे निरभिप्राय बहुशब्द – प्रयोगाद्, अपुष्टार्थता जायते[92]। (vi) शब्दग्रहणं अपशब्दनिरासार्थम्.[93] ।

(vii) चारुग्रहणं बर्बष्टीत्यादि दुःश्रवशब्दनिवृत्त्यर्थमिति[94] ।

नमिसाधु has evidently resorted to विपर्यय while writing the above gloss.

Thus the विपर्यय enables us to know the opposites of the expressed meanings, which former are very much necessary for the fuller understanding of a scientific text.

Conclusions

(*i*) Sanskrit poeticians did express certain topics through Implication

(*ii*) They accomplished this task by resorting to seven devices which were the constituents of a comprehensive Methodology of Composing and Interpreting ancient theoretics-scientific Treatises".

(*iii*) The seven devices were अतिदेश, अपवाद, अर्थापत्ति, ऊह, प्रकार, योग & विपर्यय. Of these प्रकार is a ताच्छिल्य, the rest areतंत्रयुक्ति.

(*iv*) These devices throw light upon (a) the subtle as well as broad-based ideas of ancient Indian thinkers and (b) the mechanism of their faculties of thinking and imagining.

(*v*) The *implication* achieved by means of these devices helps complete Sanskrit Poetics deliberately left incomplete by the ancient poeticians. Also it extends a hearty welcome to new ideas which help promote advancement of Poetics.

(*vi*) The above devices furnish the literary student, the creative writer and the discerning critic with the knowledge of (a) prerequisites and practices of imaginative writing, (b) essential characteristics of some species of writing, and (c) some norms and notions of 'ideal literature'.

(*vii*) The above devices enable a literary practitioner to know what is to be done and what is to be shunned in respect of certain aspects of creative literature.

(*viii*) The *implication* calls upon the reader (a) to make judicious use of the knowledge of Poetics he has acquired in the past and (b) to press into service his own imaginative faculty for a flawless and fuller understanding of sanskrit Poetics.

(*ix*) It provides the literary critic with some hints on what is to be allowed to pass and what is to be criticized.

(*x*) In fine, the above devices play an important and indispensable role in discovering 'Unwritten Sanskrit Poetics.'

NOTES

1. For a detailed knowledge and treatment of these devices, the interested readers are advised to consult the following:
   (a) तन्त्रयुक्तिविचारः - by नीलमेघ, ed. by N.E.Muthuswami (Govt. of Kerala, Trivandrum, 1976);
   (b) *The Doctrine of the Tantrayuktis* by W.K. Lele (Chaukhamba Surabharati POrakashan, Varanasi, 1981);
   (c) प्राचीन शास्त्रीय ग्रन्थोंका निर्माणतन्त्र-वामन केशव लेले (Ganganath Gha Kendriya Sanskrit Vidyapeetha, Allahabad, Vols. XXXVIII and XXXIX, pp. 73.79).
2. तन्त्रयुक्तिविचारः, cited above, Appendix, p. VI
3. Ibid., p. X
4. Ibid., p. XXVI
5. Ibid., p. VI
6. Ibid., p. XXXV
7. Ibid., p. VI

8. Ibid., p. XXXVI
9. Ibid., p. X
10. Ibid., p. XXVII
11. Ibid., p. VII
12. Ibid., p. XLI
13. Ibid., p. XXVIII
14. Ibid., p. XXII
15. Ibid., p. V
16. Ibid., p. XXXII
17. Ibid., p. 3.
18. Ibid., p. VI
19. Ibid., p. XXXVI
20. Ibid., p. III
21. Ibid., p. 15
22. Ibid., p. XI
23. Ibid., p. XXVII
24. आचार्य – भामह – विरचित काव्यालङ्कार, भाष्यकार देवेन्द्रनाथ शर्मा (बिहार राष्ट्रभाषा – परिषद पटना, 1962)
25. दण्डिकृतं काव्यादर्शापिराभिधम् काव्यलक्षणम्, संपादक – अनन्तलाल ठक्कुर ' उपेन्द्र झा (मिथिलाविद्यापीठ प्रकाशन, दरभंगा, 1957)
26. पण्डितवरवामनविराचितानि काव्यालंकारसूत्राणि, संपा. ना. रा. आचार्य (निर्णयसागर प्रेस, मुंबई, 1953)
27. Ibid., p. 10
28. Ibid., p. 18
29. Ibid., p. 19
30. Ibid., p. 45
31. Ibid., p. 46
32. Ibid., p. 52
33. Ibid., p. 54
34. श्रीरुद्रटप्रणीतः काव्यालंकारः नमिसाधुकृतया टिप्पण्या समेतः, संपा. दुर्गाप्रसाद ' पणशीकर (निर्णयसागर प्रस, मुंबई, 1928)
35. श्रीवाग्भटप्रणति वाग्भटालङ्कारः हिन्दीटीकाकार सत्यव्रतसिंह, (चौखम्बा विद्याभवन, वाराणसी, 1957)
36. Ibid., p. 8
37. Ibid., p. 11
38. काव्यलक्षणम्, cited above, p. 29

39. It is precisely for this reason that a useful paper could be done on "Optional Rules of Sanskrit Poetics".
40. टभामहविरचित काव्यालंकार, cited above, p. 2
41. Ibid., p. 4
42. Ibid., p. 6.
43. Ibid., p. 11
44. काव्यलक्षणम्‌ cited above, p. 5.
45. Ibid., p. 8
46. Ibid., p. 13
47. Ibid., p. 13
48. Ibid., p. 14
49. Ibid., p. 56.
50. श्रीरुद्रटप्रणीतः काव्यालंकारः, cited above, p. 35
51. Ibid., p. 68
52. वाग्भटालङ्कारः, cited above, p. 3.
53. Ibid., p. 5
54. क्षेमेन्द्रप्रणीतऔचित्यसिद्धदान्त आणि औचित्यविचारचर्चाः समीक्षक व संपादकः वा. के. लेले (अभिजात – ग्रन्थावली – प्रकाशन, वाराणसी, 1966)
55. Ibid., p. 4
56. Ibid., p. 6
57. भामहविरचित काव्यालंकार, cited above, p. 66.
58. काव्यलक्षणम्‌, cited above, p. 94
59. काव्यालंकार सूत्राणि, cited above, p. 11.
60. महाकवि क्षेमेन्द्रकृत कविकण्ठाभरणं, संपादक वा. के. लेले (मोतीलाल बनारसीदास, दिल्ली – पटना–वाराणसी, 1967)
61. Ibid., p. 85.
62. क्षेमेन्द्रप्रणीत औचित्यविचारचर्चा, cited above, p. 156.
63. श्रीरुद्रटप्रणीतः काव्यालंकारः, cited above, p. 143
64. वाग्भटालंकार, cited above, p. 97
65. काव्यलक्षणम्‌, cited above, p. 67
66. Ibid., p. 24
67. Ibid., p. 26
68. Ibid., p. 85
69. Ibid., p. 145
70. Ibid., p. 178
71. श्रीरुद्रटप्रणीतः काव्यालंकारः, cited above, p. 68
72. Ibid., p. 74

73. Ibid., p. 172
74. वाग्भटालंकार, cited above, p. 5
75. Ibid., p. 59
76. भामहविरचित काव्यालंकार, cited above, pp. 9-10
77. काव्यलक्षणम्, cited above, p. 8
78. Ibid., p. 23.
79. भामहविरचित काव्यालंकार, cited above, p. 18.
80. पण्डितवरवामनविरचितानि काव्यालंकारसूत्राणि, cited above, p. 39
81. Ibid., p. 3
82. Ibid., p. 12
83. Ibid., pp. 33-34
84. Ibid., p. 34
85. Ibid., p. 47
86. Ibid., p. 70
87. श्रीरुद्रटप्रणीतः काव्यालंकारः, cited above, p. 11.
88. Ibid., p. 11
89. Ibid.
90. Ibid.
91. Ibid., p. 12
92. Ibid.
93. Ibid.
94. Ibid.

Concept of 'Polishing' in Sanskrit Poetics vis-a-vis Western Stylistics

W.K. Lele

Polishing / Refinement / Revision

The word polishing is derived from the verb 'to polish', which ordinarily means 'to make smooth and glossy usually by friction'.[1] But in stylistics, the word 'polishing' has assumed a special or a somewhat technical meaning. In stylistics, the word polishing means 'softening or refining in condition or bringing to a highly developed, finished or refined state.' Polishing is sometimes substituted by the word refinement, a derivative of the verb 'to refine', which means 'to improve or perfect by pruning or polishing. And a poetic style has to be free from what is coarse, vulgar, or uncouth. The word polishing has yet one more synonym in the word 'revision', which is a formation of the verb 'to revise', which means 'to look over again in order to correct or improve a manuscript. Thus the notion underlying polishing is freeing the manuscript of a piece of creative writing from grammatical and metrical inaccuracies, removing whatever is coarse and aesthetically harmful and perfecting it in all other respects so that it gladdens (and possibly maddens) the lovers of imaginative literature. The present paper proposes to examine the concept of polishing in Sanskrit poetics as compared with western stylistics.

Complete Flawlessness: the Aim of Writers

Interestingly, both ancient Indian poeticians and western stylisticians rather dogmatically believe that any literary piece must be completely free from blemishes. This conviction of theirs can be found in many of their utterances. To quote a few: भामह asserts: पदं एकं परं साधु न

अर्वाचीन–निबन्धनम्[4] (5.61), meaning 'I shall prefer even a single flawless inflected word to a long poem full of blemishes.' दण्डिन्'s following oft-quoted verse is very clear on this point:

तद् अल्पं अपि नोपेक्ष्यं काव्यं दुष्टं कथश्चन ।
स्याद् वपुः सुन्दरं अपि श्रिवत्रेण एकेन दुर्भगम् ।।9.7।।

दण्डिन् is not willing to connive at even an insignificant blemish in a poem, for he considers such a blemish as similar to a leprous spot on the body of a lovely person. केशवमिश्र very emphatically exhorts:

दोषः सर्वात्मना त्याज्यो रसहानिकरो हि सः ।
अन्यो गुणोऽस्तु वा मारस्तु महा नु निर्दोषता गुणः ।।

A poetic blemish is to be totally avoided, for it injures the sentiment expressed in the poem. Any other quality may or may not be there in a poem, but the greatest quality, viz., absolute flawlessness, must invariably be there.

Ancient Indian poeticians held that a faulty poem was nothing less than death. Here are a few utterances which equate कुकवित्वं with मरणत्.

भामह says: कुकवित्वं पुनः साक्षान् मृतिं आहुर मनीषिणः [7] (1.12) राजशेखर reiterates भामह, above view thus: वरमकविर्न पुनः कुकविः स्यात् । कुकविता हि सोच्छ्वासं मरणम् ।

What the ancient poeticians maintain is that a literary artist must aim at removing all defects from a piece of writing and aim at making it a perfectly beautiful piece of writing. The same view is upheld by western stylisticians. For instance, Hough says: "...Secondly, and above all, he uses language with an aesthetic intention; he strives to create beauty with words, as a painter does with colours or a musician with sounds"[9]. Vallins also speaks of a writer's instinct for the aesthetic quality thus: "with this instinct (the instinct for language), however, goes another - the instinct for the aesthetic quality of the sentence and the paragraph."[10] The western thinkers, while welcoming aesthetically good writing, disapprove of its opposite, viz., bad writing. For example, while defining bad writing, Chadburn says: "... and by bad prose I mean what is affected, or redundant, or straggly, or confused, or illogical. Then if the student keeps clear of these things, and of pedantry, he will be on the way to writing well."[11] M. Boulton considers the bad novel as a representative of cheap and nasty style and decries it in these words: "The bad novel is another ever flowing spring of cheap-and-nasty-style, for the writer who turns out tripe by the yard has no time to make the necessary effort to write the common style. In the bad thriller there are usually far too many exclamation marks; all the characters speak alike; words are used inaccurately by a writer who obviously never looks in the dictionary when he is in doubt about a word, because he has not enough feeling for words to be in doubt about any of them."[12] C. Isaac, W.S. Maugham, G. Brandreth, M. Beulton, K. Morrison, J.R. Kreuzer, L. Cogan, A. Quiller-Couch, B.B. Cohen and a host of other thinkers regard ungrammaticalness, unintelligibility, repetition, padding, euphemism, cliches, verbiage, jargon as traits of bad writing, no doubt, but it needs to be especially noted in this context, that none of the western thinkers has condemned bad writing (कुकवित्व) as vehemently and as bitterly as the ancient Indian thinkers have done. This reality leads one to infer that the 'God of Creative Writing', which the ancient Indian poeticians have kept before them is loftier than the one the western stylisticians have kept.

The First Draft

Polishing or revision presupposes written matter. Polishing is carried out only after something is put into black and white. This something is called the first draft. Both the groups of thinkers under consideration have expressed their views about this first draft. राजशेखर advises the poets to write the first draft in the second one-eighth part of the day द्वितीये काव्यक्रियाम्।[13]. He expects the poet to get up at day-break, say, at 5 o'clock in the morning. Then during the first three-hour period, the poet is supposed to offer सन्ध्यावन्दना, recite सारस्वतसूक्त & study principal and subsidiary lores.[14] Thereafter and before taking bath and meals, the poet is supposed to write the first draft of his poem i.e. between 8 a.m. and 11 a.m. Among the western stylisticians, P. Hogrefe advises, 'Write the first draft of your story at a single sitting if possible',[15] without specifying the time suitable for writing. राजशेखर describes the mental state in which the first draft is made: रसोवेशतः काव्यं विरचयतो न च विवेक्त्री दृष्टिस्, तस्माद्, अनुपरीक्षेत ।[16] That is, the mental eye of the poet composing under excitement of sentiment cannot exercise discriminating judgement. As a result, the poet is likely to fall into many lapses, like using ungrammatical forms of words, employing words whose meanings are doubtful, violating consistency of meanings, flouting poetic conventions, using यमक s harmful to sentiments, peverting the norms relating to the science of music, dance, drama, painting and other fine arts, committing उपमादघष and so on. Eventually these lapses defile the beauty of poetry. The sentimental excitement and the consequential inattention, of which latter वामन has expressly spoken (अवहितं हि चिन्तम् अथा 'नु पश्यति । [17] i.e. only an attentive mind- 'inward eye' - sees thoughts and ideas in their proper perspective) are responsible for this impairment.

The western stylisticians have also accounted for the imperfection of the writer's first draft in more or less the same words as used by Sanskrit poeticians. S. Ives describes the writer's first draft saying, 'His first draft is rather like a road under construction. A reader, like a motorist, would have to go slow and watch for obstrictions.'[18] Ives, thus, likens the first draft with an uneven road: M. Boulton, like राजशेखर, attributes the lapses in the first draft to the sentimental excitements of the creative writer. She says: 'The poet may find that in the excitement of composition he has wrenched an accent unnaturally or committed some inaccuracy of fact; he may become doubtful of the strict meaning of a word, or its accentuation..."[19] C. Brooks and R.P. Warren have pointed out in the words quoted below that even eminent writers are prone to such pitfalls:

> "It is, however, our great variety of movable modifiers that most often leads us into this kind of blundering.
>
> We write, for example:
>
> Being lazy by nature and because I am clumsy,
>
> I have never liked tennis.
>
> Such violations of parallelism easily creep into *first drafts* - even into the first drafts of a good writer.''[20]

Thus there is unanimity of opinion among eastern and western thinkers over two points, viz. (i) the first draft is made generally under a surcharged mental state and (ii) it is, as a result, liable to be imperfect.

The western stylisticians, have, however, stated one basic and therefore important point which does not find mention in any work on poetics. According to the former, we human beings, are by nature incapable of speaking or writing anything worth its while, without revision. Summer Ives says, "...Hardly anyone consistently writes good sentences without revision."[21] A.H. Gardiner also holds the same view. He says: "It is.. a true and lamentable fact that, in ultimate analysis, one cannot speak about anything without altering it to some extent."[22] This point is a definitive contribution of the western thinkers.

When to carry out revision ?

Since, as stated above, the first draft is imperfect, it cannot be passed on to the reader as it is. It needs revision. On this point, there is complete agreement between eastern and western thinkers, as will be evident from the following quotations. राजशेखर says, तस्माद् अनुपरीक्षेत ।[23] meaning, therefore closely examine it later to find out the lapses that have crept in it. Brooks and Warren firmly opine saying, 'Careful rewriting is the answer"[24] (to remove the blundering). Similar is the advice given by Pearl Hogrefe. She says: "If you and your readers are not completely satisfied, rewrite the whole story or at least the weaker sections. Unless you are semiprofessional you will be doing very well to get a good story in two or even three or four writings."[25] Marjorie Boulton also speaks of the process of revision. She observes: "However, if we look at a manuscript left by any well-known poet we shall nearly always find that the poet has made many erasures and alterations before arriving at the final version. This process of polishing is very important."[26] The point very closely connected with the necessity of revision is the hour or mood fit for effecting it. राजशेखर recommends that the fourth याम of the day is ideal for this purpose. He states: 'चतुर्थ एकाकिनः परिमित् परिषदो वा पूर्वाह्णभागविहितस्य काव्यस्य परीक्षा ।[27] meaning, the poet should either sit alone or in the midst of a few friends and knowers of the art and craft of poetry to examine the poetic piece composed in the third याम of the day. If the poet does the work of scrutinizing the poetic piece all alone, he is likely to miss or overlook some lapses. Besides, he stands to be deprived of the expert suggestions which his literary friend/s is/are likely to offer. Though his sitting all alone for revision is thus disadvantageous in some respects, it is advantageous in one respect, viz. that he can concentrate on the first draft, as there will be none to disturb him. राजशेखर has, however, offered an optional advice to the poet in this connection, by saying that the poet may sit with a few friends of his for the purposes of revision. But राजशेखर has very cautiously used the word 'परिमितपरिषिदः', implying thereby that the friends, admirers or advisors should be very few in number. That is to say, there should not be a large gathering around the poet, for such a gathering is likely to defeat the very purpose of revision. The reason why राजशेखर prefers the चतुर्थ याम for the work of revision can be conjectured easily. According to राजशेखर' s daily routine of the poet, the composer is supposed to make the first draft in the third याम of the day, then to take meals and rest and thereafter to sit at the table for revision in a very composed state of mind. Pearl Hogrefe has also to offer more or less the same advice. She exhorts, 'After your work has cooled, read it critically. Read it aloud. Prune unessential words...[28].

Modes of Revision

Before a poet sets out to revise, he has to decide upon the models of revision. On this point, the ancient Indian thinkers are surprizingly silent. Surprizingly because when the ancient poeticians could conceive of a state/stage as हृदयकविः (यो हृदय एव कवते निह नुते च स हृदयकविः ।) [29], a very subtle and fleeting notion, they could have well conceived of another subtle notion, viz., the revision carried out inwardly. But they have not. The western thinkers, have, however, conceived of two modes of polishing, polishing in mind and polishing on paper. In this context, Herbert Read has quoted Gibbon who writes: "It has always been my practice to cast a long paragraph in a single mould, to try it by my ear, to deposit it in my memory, but to suspend the action of the pen till I had given the same view. He says: "Most writing involves a process of revision, conducted either on paper or in the mind before anything is written down"[31] After finalizing the mode of revision, the actual operation of revision begins. What process do the creative writers follow to perform this operation? The answers provided by both the groups of thinkers will now be considered.

Process of Revision

राजशेखर has proposed a four-fold process as under: 'अधिकस्य त्यागो, न्यूनस्य पूरणम्, अन्यथास्यितस्य परिवर्तनं, प्रस्मृतस्य अनुसन्धानं चाइतिअहीनम्।'[32] that is, dropping the additional, supplying the wasited, changing the one used in a wrong place and inspecting the one totally forgotten. Thus it is completed. With a little imaginative thinking, the details of the above four members of revision could be suggested as below:

अधिकस्य त्यागः

The पदोषs, [33] अनर्थक (पादपूरणमात्रार्थ), अपुष्टार्थ (तुच्छाभिधेय) क्लिष्ट (दूरे यस्यार्थसंवित्तिः), नेयार्थ (स्वसंकेतप्रकृप्तार्थ), अप्रयोजक (अविशेषविधायक), वाक्यदोषs, पुनरुक्तिमत (पदार्थश्रचाभिन्नो) वाक्यगर्भित (वाक्यान्तर सगर्भ), अधिकोपमम् (अधिकोपमानविशेषणम्) the वाक्यार्थदोष, व्यर्थ (गतार्थ, निष्प्रयोजक), एकार्थ (उक्त्यभिन्नार्थ), परूष (अत्यर्थ- क्रूरार्थ), अधिकोपमम्),all these contain some element which is surplus and therefore required to be eliminated. Besides the above ones, the व्यायता (unduly and unreasonably long poetic composition) which has been condemned by भामह in 'कुर्वन्ति काव्यम् अपरे व्यायताभीप्सया यथा।' [34] can also be considered under the present head.

न्यूनस्य पूरणम्

पददोष, देश्य (अव्युत्पत्तिमत) the वाक्यदोषs , न्यूनोपमम् (न्यूनमुपमानविवेषणम्), अशरीर (क्रियापदविहीन), and the अर्थदोष अषार्थ (समुदायार्थशून्य) (हीनोपमानम) निरलङ्कार 35 (अलङ्कारहीन) all these are cases of deficiency which is required to be made good. क्षमेन्द्र in his कविकण्ठाभरण [36] has spoken of two more cases, viz., व्यंजनाराहित्य and प्रसादशून्यता which too can be considered under the present head.

अन्यथास्थितस्य परिवर्तनम्

It can be a very large section, the list of cases being quite long.

The पददोषs: असाधु (शब्दशास्त्रविरूध्द) अप्रयुक्त (कविभिर् न प्रयुज्यते), कष्ट (श्रुतेः असुखद), अन्यार्थ रूढिच्युत) , असमर्थ (असंगतपद), अप्रतीत (शास्त्रे एव प्रसिद्ध) गूढार्थ (अप्रसिद्धार्थ प्रयोग), सन्दिग्ध (अनिश्चकृत) विरूद्ध (विपरीतार्थप्रकष्यन), ग्राम्य (अश्लील – अमंगल – घृणावत), the वाक्यदोषs : शब्दहीन (अपशब्दवत), क्रमभ्रष्ट (अक्रम), व्याकीर्ण (विभक्तिनामसंगतिः), संकीर्ण (वाक्यान्तर पदैर् मिश्र), अपद (विभिन्नप्रकृतिस्थादि पदयुक्ति), भिन्नलिंग (भिन्नलिंगोपमा), भिन्नवचन (भिन्नवचनोपमा), भग्नच्छन्द छन्दोभंगवत) भग्नयति (अस्थाने विरतिः), अरीतिमत् (गुणाना विपर्ययः), श्लेषविपर्यय, समताविपर्यय, सौ कुमार्यविपर्यय, प्रसादविपर्यय, अर्थव्यक्तिविपर्यय , कान्तिविपर्यय,

ओजोविपर्यय, माधुर्यविपर्यय, औ दार्यविपर्यय and the वाक्यार्थदोषs, सन्दिग्धार्थ (ससंशय), अपक्रम (क्रमभ्रष्ट), (खिन्न) (अनिर्व्यूढ अतिमात्र) (सर्वलोकातीतार्थ), विरस (अप्रस्तुतरस), असहशोपमम (अतुल्योपमानम), अश्लील (अश्लीलार्थप्रतीतिकृत), प्रत्यक्ष – अनुमान–आगमविरूद्ध[37] all these are अन्यथास्थित i.e. wrongly placed and therefore deserve to be changed suitably. Besides these, the अनवस्थितपाक[38] as mentioned by राजशेखर, असंवादार्थसंगति and विरोधरसव्यक्ति[39] as implied by क्षेमेंद्र, the poetic conventions enumerated by हेमचन्द्र,[40] and the यमक used in the sentiments of श्रृगार and करुण as rejected by रूद्रट[41] are all instances in point.

प्रस्मृतस्य अनुसन्धानम्

The वाक्यदोष विसन्धि (विरूपसन्धि as well as विसहिता) and the वाक्यार्थदोष अप्रसिद्धोपम (अप्रसिद्धोपमान) [42] are the two cases which belong to this group.

This is Indian thinking in the matter. Turning to the western thinking on the point, we find Brooks and Warren telling us: "...And in our writing, and especially in our rewriting, we need to see that we have avoided irritating monotony of sentence length or a sentence structure."[43] P. Hogrefe exhorts: "Prune unessential words."[44] S. Ives has discussed this point in somewhat detail, as follows: "Skilful writers allow the first suggestion of a pattern to come from the continuity of the passage and then try to fit the material for the new sentence into this pattern. If it does not fit, the writer runs through his inventory of available patterns, seeking the one best suited for the immediate material and the total context. In this process, he may revise his original structures to fit the final pattern. For example, he may reduce an adverbial clause to a prepositional phrase, or expand a phrase to a clause. He may reduce an adjectival phrase to a modifying participle, or add a subject that will make a modifying verb into a finite verb. The possibilities are limited only by the resources of the language and the exigencies of the design..."[45] The same authoress elsewhere observes as under:

"A writer, like a builder, must smooth out the bumps and fill in the holes. The final version seems to be effortless because the verbal impediments have been removed and the mental gaps have been bridged."[46] About the revision conducted by a poet, Marojorie Boulton writers "During the polishing, the poet is usually dealing with individual words; he may exclude a word because its sound echoes or clashes with the sound of another where such an effort is not wanted.[47] M. Boulton, again, observes: 'The words that can most easily be altered in polishing a poem are adjectives and adverbs...' It is interesting to notice that the above quotations reverberate the same notions of अधिकस्य त्यागः, न्यूनस्य पूरणम्, अन्यथास्थितस्य परिवर्तनम् and प्रस्मृतस्य अनुसन्धानम् as conceived of by the Indian thinkers. But one remarkable feature of the Indian thinking is that it is quite systematic and disciplined, it is, as though, aphoristic in nature.

Law of Revision

The ancient Indian thinkers have literally provided us with a सूत्र (Law) of revision. The revision, according to them, is not to be conducted interminably, but to a limit, beyond which it must be stopped. This Law of Revision has been first propounded by वामन in his काव्यालंकारसूत्राणि and later reiterated by राजशेखर and क्षेमेन्द्र. वामन has, while treating of the प्रकीर्ण काव्याङ्ग, exposed the concept of अवेक्षण in the following words:

वामन's concept of शब्दपाक

"पदाधानोद्धरणमवेक्षणम् ।। 15 ।।

पदस्य आधांन न्यासः उद्धरणं अपसाणम् ! तयोःखलु अवेक्षणम् ।

अत्र श्लोक –

'आधानोद्धरणे तावद् यावद् दोलायते मनः ।
पदस्य स्थापिते स्थैर्ये हन्त सिद्धा सरस्वती ।।
यत्पदानि त्यजन्ति एव परिवृत्तिसहिष्णुताम् ।
तं शब्दन्यासनिष्णाताः शब्दपांक प्रचक्षते ।।'[49]

It means: The placement and removal of an inflected word is called Consideration'.

Placing of an inflected word is its employment. Taking it out is its removal. Consideration, indeed, of these two is what is intended here. Here are two traditional verses in this context-

The placement and the removal (of the inflected word continues) as long as the mind oscillates (i.e. the mind is unstable). The movement the word is established, ahū the favour of the Goddess of Learning is won Those proficient in the placement of words define the Perfection of

Diction as that state of the inflected words which gives up for ever the tolerance for change.

The 'mental eye' oscillates in and out as long as it cannot determine whether a particular word is अधिक, न्यून, अन्यथास्थित or प्रस्तुत. The moment it makes sure of either of these, its irresolution comes to an end. Once a word gains its proper position, it becomes firmly rooted there. As though it then loses its elasticity or tendency to change. When all the words in a composition occupy their proper places, the composition is said to be verbally perfect.

This is precisely the same as the concept of mot juste as advocated by the western stylisticians. For example, M. Boulton informs us: 'but most polishing is probably done in search for the mot juste, the most exact and effective word possible in the context.'[50]

राजशेखर's concept of दशविध पाक

राजशेखर has not only pursued the concept of पाक but has elaborated it and lent one more dimension to it, as will be evident from the following long quotation from his work:

"सततं अभ्यासवशतः सुकवेः वाक्यं पाकं आयाति । "कः पुनर् अयं पाकः ? इति आचार्याः। परिणाम" इति मङ्गलः । "कः पुनर् अयं परिणामः ?" इति आचार्याः । "सुपां तिङां श्रवः या एषा व्युत्पतिः " इति मङ्गलः । सौशब्द्यं एतत् । पदनिवेशनिष्कम्पता पाकः" इति आचार्याः। तद् : आहुः–

"आवापोध्दरणे तावद् यावद् दोलायते मनः
पदानां स्थापिते स्थैर्ये हन्त सिद्धा सरस्वती।।"

"आग्रहपरिग्रहाद् अपि पदस्थैर्यपर्यवसाय : तस्मात् पदानां परिवृत्ति–वैमुख्यं पाकः इति वामनीयाः । तद् आहुः –

"यत्पदानि त्यजन्ति एव परिवृत्ति सहिष्णुताम् ।
तं शब्न्एयाय (स) निष्णाताः शब्दपाकं प्रचक्षते ।।"

"इयं अशक्तिर् न पुनः पाकः" इति अवन्तिसुन्दरी । यद् एकस्मिन् वस्तुनि महाकवीनां अनेकोऽपि पाठः परिपाकवान् भवति । तस्माद् रसोचित शब्दार्थसूक्तिनिबन्धनः (नः) पाकः । यद आह–

"गुणानलङ्कार रीत्युक्ति शब्दार्थग्रथनक्रमः ।
स्वदते सुधियां येन वाक्यपाकः स मां प्रति ।।"

तद् उक्तम् –

"सति वक्तरि सति अर्थे शब्दे सति रसे सति ।
अस्ति तन्न विना येन परिस्रवति वाङ्मधु ।।"

"कार्यानुमेयतया यत् –तत् –शब्दनिवेद्यः परं पाकोऽभिधाविषयः । तत् सहृदय प्रसिद्धिसिद्ध एंव व्यवहाराङ्गम् अस ौ इति यायावरीयः ।

स च कविग्रामस्य काव्यं अभ्यस्यतो नवश्चा भवति । तत्र आद्यन्तयोर् अस्वादु पिचुमन्दपाकम्, आदौ अस्वादु परिणामे मध्यमं बदरपाकम्, आदौ अस्वादु परिणामे स्वादु मृद्वीकापाकम्, आदौ मध्यमं अन्ते च अस्वादु वार्ताकपाकम्, आद्यन्तयोर् मध्यमं तिन्तिडीकपाकम्, आदौ मध्यमं अन्ते स्वादु सहकारपाकम्, आदौ उत्तमं अन्ते अस्वादुं क्रमुकपाकम्, आद्यन्तयोः स्वादु नालिकेरपाक इति । तेषां त्रिषु अपि त्रिकेषु पाकाः प्रथमे त्याज्याः । वरम् अकविर् न पुन कुकवि : स्यात् । कुकविता हि सोच्छ्वासं मरणम् । मध्यमाः संस्कार्याः । संस्कारो हि सर्वस्य गुणं उत्कर्षति । द्वादशवर्णं अपि सुवर्णं पावकपाकेन हेमीभवति । शेषा ग्राह्या । स्वभावशुद्धं हि न संस्कारं अपेक्षते । न मुक्तामणेः शाणः तारतायै प्रभवति । अनवस्थितपाकं पुनः कपित्थपाकं आमनन्ति । तत्र फलालधूतन अन्नकणलाभवत् सुभाषितलाभः ।

सम्यग् अभ्यस्यतः काव्यं नवधा परिपच्यते ।
हानोपादानसूत्रेण विभजेत् तद् हि बुद्धिमान् ।।
अयं अत्र एव शिष्याणां दर्शितस् त्रिविधो विधिः ।
किन्तु वि (त्रि) विधम्प्येतत् : त्रिजगति अस्य वर्तते ।।"

The views contained in the above excerpt can be summarized as under:

(i) Continuous practice at writing is necessary for good poetic compositions;

(ii) Different poeticians held varying views about perfection of diction;

(iii) वाक्यपाक perfection of the sentence lends the pleasure giving faculty to a literary composition;

(iv) पाक the perfection can be deduced from the function of the composition;

(v) The compositions which bear the tastes of grapes, mangoes and cocoanuts are ecstatic, because they are by nature chaste;

(vi) A composition devoid of perfection extremely rarely contains fineness.

It is to be noted that राजशेखर is conversant with वामन'sviews and verses.

क्षेमेन्द्र and the concept of revision

During the couse of his a hundred item advice (शिक्षाणां शतं इति उक्तं युक्तं प्राप्तगिरः कवेः ।। 22 ।।)[52] क्षेमेन्द्र refers to the concept of अवेक्षण in the following words:

आधानोद्धरणप्रज्ञा कृतसंशोधनं मुहुः ।[53]

Here क्षेमेन्द्र has advised the poet to conduct revision of a literary composition over and over again.

The concept of अर्थपाक

As shown above, वामन has discussed शब्दपाक and राजशेखर वाक्यपाक. Since every शब्द expresses some meaning or the other and since every अर्थ (meaning) is expressed through some word or the other, it is quite fit and proper to conceive of the notion of शब्दार्थ . Similarly, it is in the fitness of concepts to formulate the notion of वाक्यार्थ. In fine, the conception of the notion of अर्थपाक has full justification. In fact, it has actually been upheld by गद्यपेन्द्रत्रिपुरहरभूपाल, the commentator of वामन काव्यालंकारसूत्रवत्ति, who distinctly says: 'इत्थं अर्थपाकोऽपि समर्थनीयः ।।' [54]. Keeping this in view, the वांक्यार्थदोषs have also been listed under 1.5.1. to 1.5.4 above.

What does Revision achieve?

The revision is conducted to achieve perfection - perfection of diction (शब्दपाक) and perfection of meaning (अर्थपाक) as explained above. The perfection makes the composition flawless. राजशेखर has categorically said so in the words इति अहीनम् ।, quoted under 1.5 above. This complete flawlessness is held by केशवमिश्र (see 1.1 above) and other poeticians as the great quality of any piece of creative writing. In other words, the four-pronged revision as proposed by राजशेखर if attentively conducted, makes a qualitative improvement in a literary composition. This, in a nutshell, is the view of the eastern scholars.

Among the western stylisticians, Brooks and Warren[55] are of the view that revision avoids irritating monotony of sentence length or of sentence structure. In this connection W.S. Morgan observes: "Revising is a conscious and careful attempt to make your writing good."[56] According to Summer Ives,[57] revision removes verbal impediments and bridges mental gaps. B.B. Cohen is of the opinion that "In some cases the changes an author made in the text of his work can provide insight into meaning and technique.[58] Graham Hough has to offer some thought provoking comments on the present point. He writes:

"The organic unity of a work of literature is not something readymade; it is not an entire and perfect chrysolite found lying about in nature; it is something achieved. This organic whole may be arrived at in a variety of ways.... Most writing involves a process of revision, conducted either on paper or in the mind before anything is written down. There is some evidence that different writers look on this revising process in very different lights; some see it as the progressively more accurate embodiment of a preconceived meaning; some see it as a continual change and modification of meaning itself. In either case it is best for the critic to look at the matter prospectively."[59]

Although there is unanimity between eastern and western groups of thinkers about the view that the revision brings about a qualitative improvement in a literary work, the latter group of thinkers has to offer a few penetrating notional details in the course of the discussion on this point. These details are not to be found in the eastern thinking. Before concluding, it is necessary to consider the last point concerning the concept of polishing.

Polishing: Ideal And Avoidable

Only the western thinkers have paid attention to this point. Polishing frees creative writing from all blemishes and enhances its aesthetic value, no doubt. Still some form of polishing is, according to the western stylisticians, undesirable, Hence the need to consider this point.

Pearl Hogrefe disapproves of tinkering and proposes revisualization. She says: "If your work needs much revising, do not be satisfied with mechanical tinkering. Revisualize until it becomes an imagined experience. Then rewrite."[60] Hogrefe has repeated this advice in the context of story-writing in these words; "But if you are doing much revision, revisualize and let the story grow from within you as you rewrite it. Avoid a mere detached tinkering."[61] What Steichen says about one of Matisse's greatest paintings in the words reproduced below applies wholly and aptly to any creative writing as well:

"I remember one of Matisse's greatest paintings, called *The Dance*... I saw the effort and turmoil and the changes and changes that he made. It was gradual, almost as gradual as the development of the baby that's under a woman's apron. And then came the final burst of passion. Within a few days he changed the whole painting; the figures become brilliant vermilion, the background a deep Prussian blue. It was a moment of exaltation - a child being born, a work of art being born"[62]

The polishing brings about this miracle. Revision earnestly and masterly conducted, transforms the first draft into a perfect, fresh and pulsating piece of art.

Conclusions

(i) In stylistics, polishing, the same as revision, or refinement, means freeing the first draft of creative writing from lapses, perfecting it aesthetically and making it pleasant for acceptance.

(ii) Both eastern and western thinkers have advocated good writing and condemned bad writing.

(iii) The eastern thinkers' notion of the 'Goal of Creative Writing' is relatively loftier than that of the western thinkers.

(iv) The Indian poeticians have laid down specific time as the ideal time for wirting the first draft.

(v) The sentimental excitement and the consequential inattention at the time of composition are held as factors responsible for imperfection of the first draft.

(vi) The western stylisticians have attributed man's inability to speak or write anything without revising it to some extent as an additional cause for imperfection of the first draft.

(vii) Both eastern and western thinkers have recommended revision of the first draft.

(viii) The easterners have specified time and mental state fit for revision, the westerners have specified the mental state only.

(ix) The western thinkers have advocated two modes of revision - inward and outword. This concept is absent in the eastern thinking.

(x) राजशेखर has proposed four सूत्रs of revision. The western thinking is wanting in the subtlety and systematicness.

(xi) वामन , who flourished about 800 A.D., has been the first Indian poetician to state the Law of Revsion, अवेक्षण.

(xii) Both eastern and western thinkers have insisted upon the search for the mot juste in polishing.

(xiii) The concept of शब्दपाक can well be extended to the concept of अर्थपाक i.e. maturity of meaning.

(xiv) The western thinkers have provided us with some significant details about qualitative improvement. The eastern thinkers have not paid attention to this point.

(xv) The western thinkers have advanced two more concepts, viz., (a) the avoidable and ideal polishing, (b) revision & transformation of the first draft into a live piece of beauty. These concepts constitute the admirable notional contribution of the western thinkers to the subject of polishing.

NOTES

1. *Webster's New Collegiate Dictionary,* A. Merriam-Webster (G. m C. Merriam Company, Springfield, U.S.A. © 1975), p. 890.

2. Ibid, p. 971.
3. Ibid, p. 992.
4. आचार्य–भामह–विचरित काव्यलङ्कार भाष्यकार देवेन्द्रनाथ शर्मा (बिहार–राष्ट्रभाषा–परिषद ., पटना , 1962), p. 139.
5. दण्डिकृतांव्यादर्शापराभिधम काव्यालक्षणम् रत्नश्रीज्ञानकर्ता रत्नश्रिया टीकया समलंकृतम , संस्कर्तारौ : अनन्तलाल ठक्कुर and उपेन्द्र झा (मिथिला–विद्यापीठ–प्रकाशन, दरभङ्गा, 1957), p. 5.
6. 6केशवमिश्रकृतः अलङ्कारशोखरः संशोधकः अनन्तराम शास्त्री वेताल (चौखम्बा संस्कृत सीरीज ऑफिस, बनारस सिटी, 1927) , p.14.
7. भामह–विरचित काव्यालङ्कार, cited above, p. 6.
8. कविश्रीराजशेखरकृता काव्यमीमांसा ed. C.D. Dalal and R.A. Sastry (Oriental Institute, Baroda, 1934), p. 21.
9. Graham Hough, *Style and Stylistics* (Routledge and Kegan Paul, London, 1972), p. 28.
10. G.H. Vallins, *The Best English* (Andre Deutsch, London, 1960), p. 17.
11. Chadburn, Style: 'The Art and Craft of Self-expression', *Good English How to Speak and Write it* (Odhams Press Limited, London, 1949), p. 219.
12. Marjorie Boulton, *The Anatomy of Prose* (Routledge and Kegan Paul Ltd, London, 1962), p. 84.
13. काव्यमीमांसा cited above, p. 52
14. Ibid.
15. Pearl Hogrefe, *The Process of Creative Writing* (Harper and Brothers, New York, 1956), p. 275.
16. काव्यमीमांसा cited above, p. 52.
17. पाण्डितवरवामनविरचितानि काव्यालंकारसूत्राणि संशोधक नारायण राम आचार्य (निर्णयसागर प्रेस, मुंबई, 1953) p. 11
18. S. Ives, *A New Handbook for Writers* (Alfred A. Knopf, New York, 1960), p. 275.
19. Marjorie Boulton, *The Anatomy of Poetry* (Routledge and Kegan Paul Ltd, London, 1968), p. 153.
20. C. Brooks and R.P. Warren, *Fundamentals of Good Writing* (A Handbook of Modern Rhetoric), (Dennis Dobson, London, 1968), p. 319.
21. *A New Handbook For Writers*, cited above, p. 58.

22. Reproduced by Bonamy Dobree in *Modern Prose Style* (The Clarendon Press, Oxford, 1956), pp. 217.18.
23. काव्यमीमांसा cited above, p. 52.
24. *Fundamentals of Good Writing*, cited above, p. 319.
25. *The Process of Creative Writing*, cited above, p. 276.
26. *The Anatomy of Poetry*, cited above, pp. 152-53.
27. काव्यमीमांसा cited above, p. 52.
28. *The Process of Creative Writing*, cited above, p. 20.
29. काव्यामीमांसा cited above, p. 19.
30. Herbert Read, *English Prose Style* (Lyall Book Depot Ludhiana, 1968), p. 59.
31. *Style and Stylistics* , cited above, p. 11.
32. काव्यमीमांसा cited above, p. 52.
33. All these दोष are quoted from भोजविरचतम्‌ सरस्वतीकण्ठाभरणम्‌ Edited by Anundoram Barooah (Publication Board, Assam, Gauhati-3, 1969), pp. 2-4, 7-9, and 12-14.
34. भामह–विरचित काव्यालङ्कार, cited above, p. 141.
35. सरस्वतीकण्ठाभरणम्‌, cited above, pp. 4, 9, 12 & 14.
36. महाकविक्षेमेन्द्रकृत कविकण्ठाभरण, संपादक वामन केशव लेले (मोतीलाल बनारसीदास, दिल्ली–पटना–वाराणसी, 1967)pp. 98 & 72.
37. सरस्वतीकण्ठाभरणम्‌, cited above, pp. 1-4, 6-12 and 13-17.
38. काव्यमीमांसा, cited above, p. 21.
39. कविकण्ठाभरणम, cited above, p. 72.
40. श्रीहेमचन्द्रविरचितं काव्यानुशासनम्‌ सटीकम्‌, संशोधक – शिवदत्तशर्मा का. पा. परब ' वा. ल. पणशीकर (निर्णयसागर प्रेस, मुंबई, 1934), pp. 13-18.
41. श्रीरुद्रटप्रणीतः काव्यालंकारः नमिसाधुकृतया टिप्पण्या समेतः, संशोधक दुर्गाप्रसाद ' वा. ल. पणशीकर (निर्णयसागर प्रेस, मुंबई, 1928), p. 35.
42. सःस्वतीकण्ठाभरणम्‌, cited above, pp. 7, 14.
43. Fundamentals of Good Writing, cited above, p. 327.
44. The Process of *Creative Writing*, cited above, p. 20.
45. *A New Handbook For Writers*, cited above, p. 58-59.
46. Ibid, p. 275.
47. *The Anatomy of Poetry*, cited above, pp. 152-53.
48. Ibid, p. 155.
49. काव्यालंकारसूत्राणि, cited above, p. 11.
50. *The Anatomy of Poetry*, cited above, p. 153.

51. काव्यमीमांसा, cited above, pp. 20-21.
52. कविकण्ठाभरणम्, cited above, p. 72.
53. Ibid, p. 68.
54. श्रीमद्वामनाचार्यविरचिता काव्यालङ्कारसूत्रवृत्तिः, व्याख्याकार केदारनाथ शर्मा (चौखम्बा अमरभारती प्रकाशन, वाराणसी, 1979), p. 37.
55. *Fundamentals of Good Writing*, cited above, p. 327.
56. W.S. Morgan, *Writing And Revising* (The Macmillan Company, New York, 1957), p. 45.
57. *A New Handbook For Writers*, cited above, p. 275.
58. B.B. Cohen, *Writing About Literature*, (Scott, Foresman and Company, Chicago, 1963), p. 102.
59. *Style And Stylistics* , cited above, p. 11.
60. *The Process of Creative Writing*, cited above, p. 20.
61. Ibid, p. 276.
62. E.J. Steichen, 'The Living Joy of Pictures' in *Studies in Prose Writing*, ed. J.R. Kreuzer and L. Cogam (Holt, Rinehart and Winston, New York, 1961), p. 148.

Author-Reader Relationship in Literature

Dhirendra Nath Tarafdar

What are you reading my Lord?
Words words words.
—*Hamlet.*

In this paper I would like to discuss:

"The relationship between author and reader in literature". But before doing so it is necessary to define the meaning of the terms 'Author' and 'Reader'.

In Sanskrit literary criticism, generally the term '*Kavi*' is used to stand for what can be paraphrased in English as 'Author' and the term 'Reader' can be compared with the term '*Sahṛdaya*', which may be paraphrased in English as 'Connoiseur'. In these very two senses I have used the terms author and reader in this paper.

An author (*Kavi*) is first and foremost a seer (*draṣṭā*). His creative genius (*Pratibhā*) penetrates into all directions and he starts seeing in and through the nature of each and every object. But mere vision is not enough. It must be co-ordinated by the creative faculty which enables the poet to translate into words, the numberless things that his imagination pictures. He brings objectivity to subjective world of his creation through his words. Consequently, the creation of the author is mainly intended for others, though he too does incidentally share it with readers. On the other hand, the reader recreates the author's world all for himself. So, for the communication between author and reader and also to exchange their views words are the only source or constitutional materials. Because, words are the vehicle of thought. According to S.H.

Burton: "Words mean something to us because they are associated with the ideas that already exist in our minds. When we use words we do not transmit thoughts directly. We transmit symbols which, we hope, will have for our readers association closely corresponding to the association that the words have for us".[1] And he also held that, "The associations which, for the speaker or writer, are clustered round the symbol that he transmits with hardly ever be identical with the associations that the received symbol arouses in the mind of the hearer or reader".[2]

The words are the means whereby an author seeks to arouse in the reader thoughts or emotions as nearly as possible identical with those of his own. They are the symbols of the things and ideas and the reader understands the mind of the author only by allowing thoses symbols to re-create in his mind the appropriate things and ideas conveyed to him. There is a double responsibility here. The author chooses the right words and the reader opens his mind to the influence of those words and expression with the author. Author should not use such a word which can spoil the whole expression. According to S.H. Burton, "One false word may destroy the whole effect that he was aiming at just as the employment of the wrong chemical might explode an unstable mixture in a laboratory."[3]

Poetry is not merely an intellectual pursuit. Its original value lies more in the aesthetic pleasure it creates in the mind of the reader. This naturally implies that the poet's genius (*Pratibhā*) is concerned with the emotional and imaginative aspects of things.

Almost all the Sanskrit rhetoricians and also western critics both ancient as well as modern have described the characteristics of the author (*kavi*) and reader (*Sahṛdaya*) in their treatises. Most of them agree on one point that the poetic imagination or genius (*Pratibhā*) is the principal cause or requirement of the author (*Kavi*). According to Bhāmaha, *Pratibhā* (genius) is the sine qua non (indispensable) for the author. He says, "Even a dull headed (untalented) person is able to study the *Śāstra* with the help of the instruction of the teacher, but he is unable to create poetry. It is possible only on the part of that person who possesses *Pratibhā* (genius), ("*Gurūpadeśādadhyetuṁ Śāstraṁ Jaḍadhiyo'pyalam / Kāvyaṁ tu jāyate jātu kasyacitpratibhāvataḥ*" //).[4]

But that is not all for an author: "An aspirant for poetic fame sets himself with the knowledge of Grammar, metre, lexicography, epic stories, worldly affairs, logic and fine arts".[5] He says, "The poet should be acquainted with the knowledge of sound and meaning by reading different essays from various authors before writing a poetic composition.[6]

Daṇdin, an ancient rhetorician, too echoed the same tune in his '*Kāvyādarśā*: but he is more explicit than Bhāmaha. He says, "An inborn genius has knowledge free from doubts and constant training or practice are the cause of this excellence in poetry" - *("Naisargikī ca Pratibhā Śrutam ca bahu nirmalam / amandaścābhiyogo'Syāḥ Kāranaṁ Kāvya Sampadaḥ//*" — K.D.I. 103, p. 78). According to him, '*Pratibhā*' or genius is the impression of previous birth which is carried by him in this birth. Nevertheless, "Though in some case there may be lack of that wondrous genius, the product of preceding births, yet the goddess of speech, when worshipped by learning and application, is sure to grant some boon of poetry to him".

> *("Na Vidyate Yadyapi pūrvavāsanāguṇānubandhi Pratibhānamadbhutam / Śrutena Yatnena ca vāgupāsitā dhruvaṁ Karotyeva Kamapyanugrahaṁ //*
>
> — K.D. 1. 104, p. 78).

The matter is treated much more elaborately by Ācārya Vāmana. He mentions in his '*Kāvyālaṁkārasūtrā*, "There are two types of poet, namely: (I) *Arocakin*— having discriminating faculty, who possesses fastidious taste, and (II) *Satṛṇābhyavahārin* (non-discriminating) - who possesses indiscriminate taste".[7] In the *Vṛtti* Vāmana himself paraphrases them as *Vivekin* (discriminate) and *Avivekin* (indiscriminate). According to Vāmana *Vivekins* are worth introducing because they are endowed with the ability of discrimination ("*Purveśiṣyāḥ Vivekitvāt //*" K.A.S. — 1.2.2), while the latter i.e., *Avivekin* should not be introduced because they cannot discriminate ("Netare tadviparyayāt" — K.A.S. 1.2.3). An *Avivekin* is not capable of discriminating any thing and so he is not fit for to be introduced to any systematic learning ("*Na śāstraṁ adravyeṣu arthavat//*" - K.A.S. 1.2.4). He mentioned: The genius (*Pratibhā*) is the cause of poetic creation

("*Kavitva bījaṁ Pratibhānam*" // - K.A.S. 1.3.16). In *Vṛtti* he explained the term '*Pratibhā*': "*Kavitvasya bījaṁ Kavitvabījaṁ Janmāntarāgatasaṁskāraviśeṣaḥ Kaścit/ Yasmādbījaṁ Vinā Kāvyaṁ na niṣpadyate/ Niṣpannaṁ Vā'vahāsyāyatanaṁ syāt//*"[8]

Ācarya Mammaṭa also accepts the view of Vāmana. He says, "Poetic genius may be called the germ of poetry. This is a peculiar faculty, without which there could either be no poetical expression or, if there were, would be ridiculous" ("*Śaktiḥ Kavitva bījarūpaḥ Saṁskāraviśeṣaḥ yaṁ Vinā Kāvyaṁ na Prasaret Prasṛtaṁ Vā Upahasanīyaṁ syāt*").

Rudraṭa, the rhetorician, next to Vāmana, accepts the threefold requirement of poet or author (*Kavi*) laid down by the earlier writers. According to him *Śakti* (genius), *Vyutpatti* (culture) and *Abhyāsa* (Practice) are the cause of *Kāvya* ("*Tritayaṁ idaṁ Vyāpriyate Śaktirvyutpattirabhyāsaḥ*").[10] He says, "*Śakti* and *Pratibhā* are synonymous. Words and meanings flash on the minds of the poet as a result of genius, *Vyutpatti* or learning assists him in adopting the essential and avoiding the non-essential and practice will lend excellence to genius".[11] So, these three elements are indispensable for poetic composition.

Kuntaka, another ancient rhetorician, held the idea that it is an extraordinary mode of expression which can produce the *Rasa* (Sentiment) in the mind of connoiseurs (*Sahṛdayas*) and to have aesthetic enjoyment. This is called, in his language, '*Vaidagdhyabhaṅgibhaṇiti*', where he says that it is nothing but the skill of the poet, which is called '*Kavikauśala*'. This '*Kavikauśala*' (Poetic mode of expression) is inseparable from the poet or author (*Kavi*) and this is nothing but genius (*Pratibhā*), by which a poetic expression can be possible with the help of *Vyutpatti* (culture) and *Abhyāsa* (Practice). According to Kuntaka, "*Pratibhā* (genius) is the key-stone of the poetic device" (*Kavipratibhā prauḍhireva pradhānyenāvatiṣṭhate*).[12] Whatever charm there may be in poetry all that is attributable only to *Pratibhā* (genius) ("*Yatkiñcanāpi Saundaryam tatsarvaṁ Pratibhānaṁ*"— (V.J., 1.28, p. 28). Because, if the poet is so poor in imagination and so weak in skilled speech that he shows, there is not even a jot of beauty in the context" ("*Pratibhādaridryadainyādatisvalpasubhāṣitena Kavinā*

Varṇasāvarṇyaramyatāmātramatroditam, na punarvācyavaicitrya Kaṇikā Kācidapyasti').[13] Words worth held the idea:

"While describing things in language really used by man the poets throw over them a certain colouring of imagination, whereby things shall be presented to the mind in an unusual aspect".[14]

The poet attaches significance to things around him to which others are insensible. However, he can make common things interesting and people can see them in the light of new and unsuspected meanings and enjoy an aesthetic pleasure. Bhaṭṭatauta[15] says, "Poetic imagination or *Pratibhā* is the gift of mind by whose aid one can Visualize myriad things anew". In his language: "*Prajñā navanavonmeṣaśālinī Pratibhā matā / Tadanuprāṇanājīvadvarṇanānipuṇaḥ Kaviḥ // Tasya Karma Smṛtam Kāvyaṁ* / (— Dhvanyālokalocana).

In the later times Rājaśekhara, the author of *Kāvyamīmāṁsā*, has clarified the matter in details in his treatise. According to him *Pratibhā* (genius) is the primary requirement of a poet. Without this *Pratibhā* no poetic composition is possible. Neverthless, *Vyutpatti* (culture) and *Abhyāsa* (Practice) are also the necessary requirements of the poetic creation. He defines *Pratibhā* as "By which the words, meanings, embelishments and charming expressions become manifest in poetic composition". ("*Yā śabdagrāmamarthasārthamalaṁkāratantramuktimārgamanyadapitathāvidhamadhihṛdayaṁ Pratibhāsayati sā Pratibhā*").[16] He says, "*Pratibhā* and *Vyutpatti* can create a good piece of poetry when both of them are involved in it" (*Pratibhā Vyutpattī mithaḥ Samavete śreyasyau*').[17] However, strictly speaking, "*Pratibhā* and *Vyutpatti* both are equally essential for a poet". (*Pratibhā vyutpattimānśca Kaviḥ kavirityucyate*").[18]

Rājaśekhara has also given equal importance to *Abhyāsa* (practice) besides *Pratibhā* and *Vyutpatti*. He defines *Abhyāsa* (practice) as "It is nothing but the continuous process of exercise and is applicable for all the purposes and by *abhyāsa* (Practice) one can become perfect" (*Aviccehedena Śīlanamabhyāsaḥ/ sa hi sarvagāmī sarvatra niratiśayam kauśalamādhatte //*).[19] He further adds another required element for a creative composition. He says, "A self absorbed meditation (*Samādhi*) is very much essential to create a piece of poetic composition"

(*Kāvyakarmaṇi Kaveḥ Samādhi Paraṁ Vyāpriyate*).[20] According to him, "*Samādhi* is the concentration of mind". ("*Manasaḥ ekāgratā Samādhi*").[21] *Samādhi* is the internal effort where as *Abhyāsa* is the external ("*Samādhirāntaraḥ prayatnobāhyastvabhyāsaḥ*").[22] Rājaśekhara's concept of the nature of poetry is that:

> "Poetry will be characterized on the basis of the temparament of the poet" ("*Sa Yatsvabhāvaḥ Kaviḥ tadanurūpaṁ Kāvyaṁ*").[23].

Denis Donoghue, a western critic of the modern age, says the following about creative imagination, "We think imagination a wonderful power, unpredictable and diverse, and we are satisfied to call it divine ..... A promethean says of it that it is the most precious part of man, perhaps the only precious part, the only respect in which man's claim to superior character is tenable".[24]

Ānandavardhana, the exponent of *Dhvani* theory, observes that: "A poet writing a whole work should be entirely bound by the demands made by sentiment (*Rasa*)" (*Kavinā Kāvyamupanibadhnatā Sarvātmanā rasaparatantreṇa bhavitavyam |*").[25] According to him: "In the vast universe of poetry, the poet alone is the creator and this world (Poetic world) would be created according to the choice of the poet" (*Apāre Kāvyasaṁsāre Kavirekaḥprajāpatiḥ / Yathā'smai rocate Viśvaṁ tathedaṁ parivartate ||*").[26] Ānandavardhana also accepts the utility of *Pratibhā* in the composition of literary work. He says, "If the poetic composition is endowed with the poetic genius (*Pratibhā*) then it would be permanent" (*Na Kāvyārtha Virāmo'sti yadi syātpratibhāguṇaḥ*").[27] He holds the idea about the relative importance of *Śakti* and *Vyutpatti* in poetry that, "The poet's imagination could work such as magic that shortcomings in taste and want of learning might remain unnoticed in particular contexts while the deficiency of his genius would at once and invariably catch attention of readers" ("*Avyutpattikṛto doṣaḥ Śaktyā Saṁvṛiyate Kaveḥ / Yastvaśaktikṛtastasya sa jhaṭityavabhāsate*").[28]

Abhinavaguptapāda, the commentator of *Dhvanyāloka*, defined *Pratibhā* in his *Locana* He says: "The poetic imagination or genius (*Pratibhā*) is a wisdom which can create an unprecedented thing. The peculiarity of *Pratibhā* is conducive to the composition of poetry suffused with *Rasa* (Sentiment) and aesthetic beauty". (*Pratibhā apūrvavastunirmāṇakṣamā Prajñā| Tasyā Viśeṣaḥ Rasāveśavaiśadyasaundaryakāvyanirmāṇakṣamatvaṁ*".[29]

From all these we can conclude that the unique gift of a poet, which cannot be acquired, is the creative imagination or *Pratibhā* (genius). But reader too must have *Pratibhā* (imagination), without which they cannot respond to the poetic composition. According to Abhinavagupta: "He is the *Sahṛdaya*, whose heart has been made transparent (receptive) like a mirror by constant practicing of poetry and who is, therefore, able to become immediately a person with the emotion of portrayed". In his Language:

> "*Yeṣāṁ Kāvyānusilanābhyāsavaśād Viśadībhūte manomukure Varananīyatanmayībhavanayogyatā te svahṛdayasaṁvādabhājaḥ Sahṛdayāḥ*".[30]

Ānandavardhana says, "It is not understood by a mere learning in grammar and in lexicons. It is understood only by those who have an insight into the true significance of poetry". ("*Śabdārthaśasanajñānamātreṇaiva na vedyate| Vedyate sa tu kāvyārtha tattvajñaireva kevalam||*"— Dhv. 1.7, p. 94). Hemachandra says, "One who composes a poem or one who is a critic of poetry only he can be a perfect man to understand the poetry, and he is a *poet* and *Sahṛdaya* respectively. ("*Kāvyaṁ kartuṁ Jānanti Vicārayanti Vā ye te kāvyavidaḥ kavisahṛdayāḥ*).[31] According to Bhaṭṭanāyaka, author and reader are equal in imagination. He says, "*Nāyakasya kaveḥ śrotuḥ Samāno'nubhavastataḥ*").[32]

According to Rajaśekhara, there are two types of *Pratibhā*, namely; (1) *Kārayitrī Pratibhā* (creative genius) — which helps the author create a piece of composition, and (2) *Bhāvayitri Pratibhā* (discriminative genius)—which helps the reader grasp the intended meaning of the author and have aesthetic enjoyment. He again divides and redivides these two *Pratibhās* and explained them elaborately.[33] The classification of *Pratibhā* made by him is given in the next page.

He also has described the nature of each and every type of *Pratibhā* in his *K.M.*[34] From this analysis we may conclude that the literary work has two poles, which we might call the artistic and the aesthetic, the artistic pole is the author's expression and the aesthetic is the realization

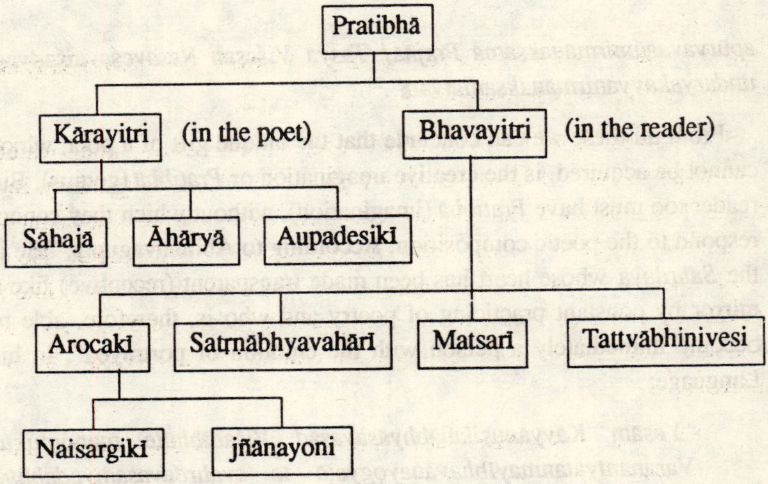

accomplished by the reader. Regarding this two-pole theory (i.e. artistic and aesthetic) I would like to show how Horst, Ruthrof, a western critic, has shown the reader's responses as appropriate or inappropriate to the author's intention. H. Ruthrof says, "If the intended reader reception is not coded in the text itself, the system of frames within which we experience literary works, just as the social situations pertaining to pragmatic statements, supplies the cues for an aesthetic response. Neverthless, we are always free to allow or disregard coded meaning intention, so that there are the appropriate and inappropriate modes of response, as shown in figure[35] below:

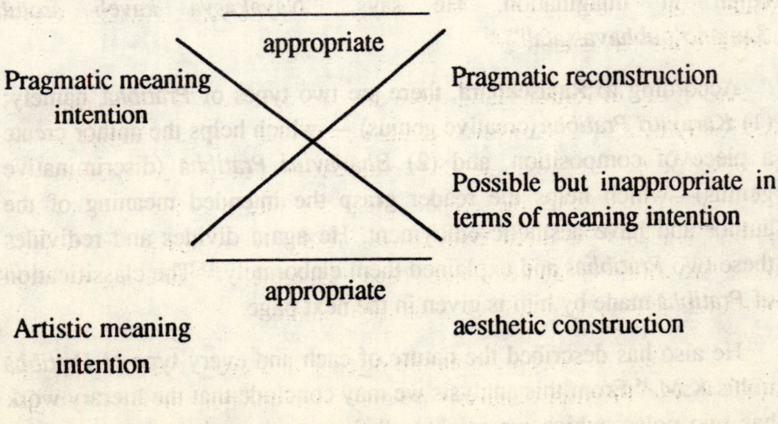

Here, in this figure, it has been shown how a reader responds to the author's intention; how the pragmatic meaning intention and artistic meaning intention of the poet are appropriate to the pragmatic reconstruction and aesthetic construction of the reader respectively; on the other hand how pragmatic and artistic meaning intentions are possible but inappropriate to aesthetic construction and pragmatic reconstruction respectively.

In *Vakroktijīvita* of Kuntaka we find this type of expression, where Kuntaka says, "Poetry is that word and meaning together enshrouded with a style revealing the artistic creativity of the poet on the one hand and giving aesthetic enjoyment to the connoisseurs (*Sahṛdayas*) on the other" ("*Śabdārthau Sahitau Vakrakavivyāpāraśalini / Bandhe* Vyavasthitau Kāvyaṁ tadvidāhladakāriṇi//").[36]

It is further conceived in poetics that an ideal reader too must possess those three elements, namely; *Pratibhā*, *Vyutpatti* and *Abhyāsa* so that he can grasp the intended meaning of a piece of poetic composition of an author. While the *Pratibhā* in the author is of creative nature, in the reader it is of grasping nature.

Frank J.D. Angelo has shown how the author's purpose is related to the desired response in the reader.[37] Here I have shown that scheme in the following manner:

Writer's Purpose	*Reader's response*
To inform or instruct.	Understanding.
To convince or persuade.	Belief or action.
To entertain or please.	Aesthetic pleasure.
To express strong feeling and emotions.	Conduct or thought governed by emotion.

Northrop Frye once wrote: "It is said of Boehme that his books are like picnic to which the author brings the words and the readers the meanings".[38]

There seems to exist a peculiar relationship between the stratification of a piece of composition and the reader's stock of knowledge: The improvement at any given moment in the reader's process from audio-visual sign to interpritative abstraction at a high level, a moment which has been shown to be bound up with the essential nature of literary works, appears to be parallaled by increasing complexity in the typified extrinsic knowledge of which the reader must avail himself.

On the contrary, the reader must first discover for himself the code underlying the composition, and this is tantamount to bringing out the meaning. The process of discovering is itself a linguistic action in so far as it constitutes the means by which the reader may communicate with the composition.

According to Roman Ingarden: "The literary work is a purely intentional construct with its ontological source in the creative acts of the author's consciousness and its physical foundation in the printed text or any other physical tool or reproduction (e.g., tape). Owing to the stratification of its language, the literary work of art is inter-subjectively accessible as well as reproduceable, it is therefore an inter–subjective, intentional object linked to a community of readers. As such, the literary work is nothing physical and transcends all acts of consciousness of author and reader alike".[39]

The style of an author is also an important factor of poetic expression. This style or stylistic device helps the reader grasp the intended meanings and motivate them. According to Harbert Read, "A personal style may be clear and concrete, but it is not ordered. The images, though hard and distinct, are haphazard. They form picturesque ruin, not a symmetrical structure. The details of this order we may call the idiom of the writer. An idiom is, literally, what a man makes his own, just as an idiom in language is what a particular language makes its own. And just as the idiom of one language cannot be translated into the idiom of another without giving an impression of falsity, so a writer's idiom is personal to himself, and cannot be copied or assimilated by other writers".[40]

Nils Erik Enkvist[41] has made a clear cut conception about the relationship between the author and the reader by a diagram. In this diagram he has tried to show how the author and reader grasp the same idea from a given context.

In the diagram, the speaker/writer and listener/reader are both part of a given context A. By Extralinguistic motivation the speaker wants to convey a message to listener. This message is to begin with encoded grammatically: only grammatical items pass through the first screen, non-grammatical items being caught. Next, the grammatical items are screened, stylistically by criteria determined by context A. This second screen passes all stylistically neutral items as well as style markers bound to context A, but retains all style markers that cannot occur in context A. Only items screened grammatically and stylistically are thus capable of entering into the speaker's style.[41]

In this diagram it has been shown only one view of style as choice in the author; in the case of the reader the matter will be the same. In the extreme case of expression of ideas the relationship between author, piece of composition and reader is just one as between an ideologist, his idiology and disciple. Ruthrof says, "The relation between narrator, world and implied reader is thus one between an idiologist, his idiology and disciple".[42]

Finally, it is noticed that the author and the reader are fundamentally one. Because the author is basically a reader. According to Ruthrof' an author acts as a player in the game of story telling, inviting the reader to join him as a partner. He says, "The relationship between narrator, presented world, and implied reader as player, game, and playmate is one of reduced dependency and control".[43]

The Sanskrit term for 'Reader' namely, '*Sahṛdaya*' itself suggests that a reader should have the similar faculties of an author, namely, the imagination, culture, education, emotions, etc., etc..

This further indicates to the relationship which is intended between an 'Author' and a 'Reader' which is nothing but being collocated in similar context, i.e. being brought to an identical context intended by the author. So, there is no doubt that they are inter-related and also inter-dependent.

REFERENCES AND NOTES

1. S.H. Burton: 'The criticism of Prose', p. 26.
2. Ibid.
3. S.H. Burton: 'The criticism of Poetry', p. 78.
4. *Kāvyālaṁkāra*of Bhāmaha - 1.5, p. 3.
5. Ibid., p. 1.9, p. 5.
   "*Śabdacchandobhidhānārthā itihāsāśrayāḥ kathāḥ/*
   Loko Yoktiḥ Kalāśceti mantavyā Kāvyagairhyamī//"
6. Ibid., 1.10., p. 5.
   "*Sabdābhidheya Vijñāya Kṛtvā tadvidupāsanām/*
   Vilokyānyanibandhāṁśca Kāryaḥ Kāvyakriyādaraḥ//"
7. Kāvyālamkāra sūtra of Vāmana,- 1.2.1.
   "*Arocakinaḥ Satṛnābhyavahāriṇaśca Kavayaḥ//*"
8. Ibid., *Vṛtti* of *Kārika* 1.3.16.
   Translation: "It is nothing but *Saṁskāra* or impression of previous birth. Without this faculty poetry cannot be composed. If composed at all, it will be nothing but ridiculous".
9. *Kāvyaprakāśa*of Mammaṭa - 1.3; *Vṛitti*.
10. *Kāvyalaṁkāra*of Rudraṭa - 1.14, p. 9.
11. Ibid., *Vṛtti*, p. 10.
    "*Tatra Śaktyā Sabdarthau manasi saṁnidhīyete/*
    Tayoḥ Sārāsāragrahaṇanirāsau Vyutpattyā Kriyete/
    Abhyāsena Śakterutkarasa ādhīyata iti Śaktyādivyāparaḥ//"
12. *Vakroktijivita* of Kuntaka - 1.7, *Vṛtti*; p. 12.
13. Ibid., 1.7. *Vṛtti*, p. 7.
14. K. Krishnamoorty - 'Essays in Sanskrit Criticism':- 'Observations of Sanskrit Literary Criticism on Poetic Imagination; p. 197.
15. The work of Bhaṭṭatauta is '*Kavyakautukā*' which is not yet available. This quotation is from the *locana* on *Dhvanyāloka* where it is mentioned as the statement of Bhaṭṭatauta.
16. *Kāvyamīmāṁsā* of Rajaśekhara - ch. 4.27.
17. Ibid., ch. 5., p. 40.
18. Ibid., p. 41.
19. Ibid., ch. 4. 27.

20. Ibid.,
21. Ibid.,
22. Ibid.,
23. Ibid., ch. 10, p. 123.
24. Denis Donoghu: Thieves of Fine; p. 62 (Faber and Faber/London/ 1973). T.S. Eliot Memorial Lectures., 1972.
25. *Dhvanyāloka* of Ānandavardhana - ch. 3; *Vṛtti*; p. 796.
26. Ibid., ch. 3; p. 1229.
27. Ibid., 4.6, p. 1363.
28. Ibid., ch. 3; p. 738.
29. *Dhvonyālokalocana* - He has quoted the verse from Bhaṭṭatauta's *Kāvyakautuka*
30. Ibid., I., I, Locan PP. 39-40.
31. *Kāvyānuśāsana* of Hemachandra - 1.9 - *Viveka*, p. 13.
32. *Hṛdayadarpaṇa* by Bhaṭṭanāyaka is not available.But Abhinavagupta has quoted him in his *Locane*
33. *K.M.* Raj. — ch. 4., PP. 29-34.
34. Ibid.
35. Horst Ruthrof: The reader's construction of narrative, PP. 53-54.
36. *V.J.* of Kuntaka - 1.7, p. 6.
37. Frank J.D. 'Angelo: 'Process and thought in composition', p. 26.
38. Wolfgang Iser - 'The act of Reader,' p. 27.
39. Horst Ruthrof: 'The reader's construction of narrative': p. 56.
40. Herbert Read: 'English Prose Style': 'Personality': p. 178.
41. Nils Erik Enkvist — 'On defining Style' : An Essay in Applied linguistics", ('Linguistic and Style' ed. by John Spencer): p. 128.
42. H.Ruthrof: 'The reader's constructions of narrative,' p. 128.
43. Ibid., p. 132.

Indian Poetics as a New Dimension of Comparative Literature: Its Potentials, Possibilities, and Pitfalls

Suresh V. Dhayagude

"An artificial demarcation of subject matter and methodology, a mechanistic concept of sources and influences, a motivation by cultural nationalism, however generous - these seem to me the symptoms of the long-drawn-out crisis of comparative Literature."

- *Rene Wellek*

Comparison is a fundamental method of getting knowledge common to all forms of higher studies. But its application in Comparative Literature is rather hesitant and shaky. This is apparent from the different controversies raging among comparatists even about such a basic question as the nature, range and scope of the subject. How serious this state of affairs is, is put very explicitly by Rene Wellek in the followng words - "The most serious of the precarious state of our study is the fact that it has not been able to establish a distinct subject-matter and a specific methodology."[1]

The present crisis of Comparative Literature springs from this confusion. It springs mainly from a lack of boldness, from hesitation, from a narrow conception of its nature and function. It also springs from obsession with non-literary considerations. It springs also from the unnecessary confusion between 'general literature' and 'comparative literature'.

In order to throw more light on this confusion, it is necessary to take a historical retrospect. Comparative Literature was first conceived in the nineteenth century as a study of oral literature, especially as a study of folk-tale themes and their migration from country to country, and their eventual incorporation into 'higher' and 'artistic' literature. It began as a reaction against the narrow nationalism of much of the nineteenth century literary scholarship, as a protest against the isolationism of many historians of English, French, German, Italian and other literatures. It was cultivated often by men who stood at crossroads of nations. But with the passage of time this came to be completely reversed. The conception of Comparative Literature as a study of sources and influences establishing causal relationships led to an unfortunate consequence. It produced, what Rene Wellek calls, "a strange system of cultural book-keeping, a desire to accumulate credits for one's nation by proving as many influences on other nations or, more subtly by proving that my nation has assimilated and "understood" a foreign master more fully than any other".[2] What began as a protest against narrow nationalism has ended thus as a voice of narrow nationalism. No wonder that Comparative Literature has fallen into disrepute with impartial students of literature.

But this is not all. There is even a greater confusion regarding the subject-matter and methodology of Comparative Literature. According to Van Tieghem, for example, Comparative Literature is the study of interrelationships between *two* literatures and it is to be distinguished from 'general' literature which is concerned with movements and fashions which sweep through *more than two* literatures. According to Baldensparger the proper subject-matter of Comparative Literature is interested more in the background. Carre and Guyard widen the scope of this subject by incorporating into it non-literary subjects like a study of national illusions of fixed ideas which nations have each other - subjects like England and the English in the French novel", "the Italian in Elizabethan drama", etc. This is nothing but dissolving national scholarship into national psychology. It is narrow nationalism in a different garb.

The unwillingness of comparatists to discuss problems of literary theory is another besetting difficulty. They distinguish between 'Comparative Literature' and 'General Literature' which is taken to mean theory and principles of literature, poetics, in other words. But this is an artificial distinction. Very fortunately it has often been ignored or set aside by competent comparitists. We can here mention, by way of example, Spingarn's study of literary criticism in the Renaissance, and that of Hathaway's of the same subject in comparatively recent years but in greater depth and detail, and Lilian Furst's *Romanticism in Perspective*, Eric Auerbach's classical study of realism in his monumental work *Mimesis*, to name only a few works. To bring discussion of literary ideas within the purview of Comparative Literature is completely logical since one of its primary concerns is relationships between two or more literatures as shown by sources and influences. These are nothing but ideas leading in many instances ultimately to literary theory. This shows that the distinction between 'comparative' and 'general' literature is unnecessary and that these two have the tendency to merge inevitably. Therefore, poetics is legitimately a part of Comparative Literature.

But so far the study of poetics as part of Comparative Literature is confined only to Western poetics. The argument in support of this is that Western literature forms a unity, a whole and that there is continuity in it from ancient Greek and Latin literatures down to modern European and American literatures, including Latin American literatures. This tradition has continued from the ancient times through the Middle Ages and the Renaissance. There is much truth in this argument, but even this conception of Comparative Literature is narrow to the extent that it ignores some important literary traditions in the world - the Chinese, the Japanese and the Indian tradition, for example. In this paper I propose to show how inclusion of these can give new dimensions to Comparative Literature. I propose to do so by concentrating on that literary tradition with which I have some acquaintance, namely, Indian tradition, and there also on Indian poetics.

There are still people, in fact plenty of people, who raise their eyebrows in exasperation at the mention of a comparative study of Western and Indian poetics. What is there to compare between these two? - they ask. They are like those Europeans in the eighteenth and early nineteenth centuries who scoffed at the European Sanskritists comparing the Sanskrit language with Greek and Latin. But the eventual entry of Sanskrit in the intellectual life of Europe proved to be a turning point with far reaching consequences. It very significantly modified the ideas of European scholars in the fields of linguistics, religion, folklore, and philosophy. It established firmly a relationship between India and Europe. So much so that Max Muller declared:

"The concept of the European man has been changed and widely extended by our acquaintance with India and we know now that we are something different from what we thought we were."[3]

"India is not, as you may imagine, a distant, strange, or at the very utmost, a curious country. India for the future belongs to Europe; it has its place in the Indo-European world; it has its place in our history, and what is the very life of history, the history of the human mind."[4]

It is as a part of the history of the human mind that I stress the inclusion of Indian poetics in Comparative literature. I am not thinking here of any sources and influences; the thought of establishing any kind of derivation - such as "A is derived from B" - is far from my mind in this present context. My stress is on juxtaposing literary ideas purely as literary ideas apart from sources and influences and on studying them in a comparative light.

In short, my stress is on the possibilities and potentials of Indian poetics as part of Comparative Literature. The first difficulty that confronts us here is that of definition. What exactly do we mean by Indian Poetics? The term 'Indian' here is very wide; it includes a large number of languages and literatures both ancient and modern. Accordingly, 'Indian Poetics' must mean theories of literature, literary ideas, principles and doctrines in all these. Theoretically, there is nothing wrong in this position. Practically, however, this all is an unwieldy mass and, therefore, a line of demarcation must be drawn somewhere to bring the subject within manageable limits. For my purpose I have done this by restricting the scope of Indian Poetics to Sanskrit Poetics for the following reasons:-

(i) Sanskrit Poetics eminently qualifies for the designation 'Indian Poetics' because it is widely known to the students of poetics all over India. Its theories of *riti, alankara, dhvani aucitya, rasa* etc. are studied and discussed all over india even by those who are not students of Sanskrit, but who are students of literature and literary thoery.

(ii) Sanskrit Poetics contains India's most important contribution to poetics so far.

(iii) It represents the genuine Indian point of view un-influenced by foreign theories. Its literary theories are not restatements or modifications (or both) of Western theories of literature as many theories in modern Indian languages are.

With this definition of Indian Poetics in mind, I proceed to expatiate on its potentials and possibilities, as a new dimension of Comparative Literature.

Let us begin with the problem of poetic language, a basic question common to all schools of poetics. That poetry uses words in a way altogether different from the way we use it in everyday life is a fact acknowledged on all hands. Poetry gives words a haunting quality and a power which they do not possess in everyday usage. How this happens is worth investigating. It is a problem of semantics or semasiology, a science of the future, as I.A. Richards puts it.[5] Indian poetics has done a lot of valuable spade work in this field in the form of the *Dhvani* theory. Some comparative study of this theory has been attempted but much more remains to be done. It is a challenging field to both semanicists and poeticians. It is a great potential of Indian Poetics with vast possibilities for Comparative Literature.

Another subject of abiding interest in poetics is the question of decorum, the rule which, Cicero maintained, governs art and life alike. It is the principle of selection which underlies all art; it is at the same time the moral principle that connects literature with life. Now the question is - What is decorum? To what extent is it a moral concept and to what extent is it aesthetic? Can it be aesthetic without being moral ? Is it possible to afford aesthetic experience without observing decorum? When and why is it violated in art? Can it really be violated? What is decorum in a larger sense and what is it in a narrower sense? How can we distinguish these? These are some of the basic questions which the problem of decorum raises. Indian poetics also deals with this question at length in its concept of *aucitya* A comparative study of this area in another potential of Indian Poetics with many possibilities.

Style and stylistics have attracted the attention of many students of literature in recent years. The *alaṅkāra* and *Rīti* schools of Indian Poetics are an abundant field for him to browse through. Here also there are plenty of theoretical questions for him to study in a comparative light. Questions such as - What is poetic style? Is it always measurable quantitatively? Is it quantitative at all? Is style nothing but decorum of language? How does style help a writer project different levels of meaning and experience at once? What are the observations of Indian poeticians on these and in what way do they add to or modify the Western theories of style? All such questions are worth probing into in a comparative light. This is one more potential of Indian Poetics as a new dimension of Comparative Literature.

The theory of *Rasa* is considered to be the apex of India's contribution to poetics. It is a basic concept like the concept of *dharma* in ethics and that of the cipher in mathematics - both great contributions to the world of knowledge by India. *Rasa* is not just one theory but a complex of very subtle interrelated literary doctrines trying to unravel the mystery of aesthetic experience in its totality. It is doubtful whether Western Poetics or any other system of poetics in the world for the matter of that has such a comprehensive theory of literature. It is wrong to suppose, as some critics suppose, that all implications of this theory have been exhausted and that it has nothing more to offer. It is possible to study it intensively from unconventional and fresh angles, i.e., from the comparative point of view. I may suggest here a few questions for such a study of the *rasa* theory. Is aesthetic experience purely emotional? Has it also an intellectual content? Anandavardhana speaks of the *santarasa*, it is the aesthetic feeling of philosophical quiescence. Is this kind of feeling possible without some kind of ratiocination? What is the nature of aesthetic joy? Is catharsis a kind of *rasa*? What is the Sublime from the point of view of the *rasa* theory? Is it the same thing as *adbhuta* rasa? One can think of scores of such questions.' I mention here only a few to exemplify some of the potentials and possibilities of Indian Poetics as a new dimension of Comparative Literature.

In addition, there are broad general questions of poetics. Take for example the question of the nature and function of the imagination, or the question of literature as knowledge; or the perennial ontological questions like What is art? Is it a kind of make-believe or is it a truth higher than everyday reality? It is ideality or an escape? Does it enervate and weaken man or does it fit him to live as a civilised being? One can think of many more such questions. I do not intend to give here an exhaustive list of them. Further, I do not at all mean to say or suggest that these questions have been discussed in this very wording and in this very form and that the contexts in which they are discussed are the same as in Western Poetics. But I do mean that though the formulation and the mode of discussion are different, the questions are basically the same. But the answers and the rationale of arriving at them are not the same. That is exactly the point where comparative study becomes relevant and is called for. Indian Poetics abounds in valuable theoretical speculations on such basic questions. They are a challenging field to any truly disinterested student of Comparative Literature.

With this, I suppose, I have given a fairly detailed account of the potentials and possibilities of Indian Poetics as a new dimension of Comparative Literature. Many more possibilities will come into sight with an intensive study of this subject. Now with this much about the potentials and possibilities, I turn to the next part of my paper, namely, pitfalls.

In my opening remarks I referred to narrow nationalism as going against the spirit of Comparative Literature. For fear of repetition I do not dwell on it again. I also referred to hesitation, to a lack of boldness, and to a narrow conception of the nature and function of Comparative Literature as the besetting difficulties of this nascent intellectual discipline. How these handicap the subject under discussion is worth examining. Narrow nationalism, however, is not the problem here; rather its opposite is the problem; and its opposite is not wider nationalism; it is absence of the national feeling. We Indians are often unnecessarily apologetic about ourselves and about our national heritage. We unnecessarily feel guilty of jingoism, of cultural expansionism in such matters. This peculiar feeling has its roots in respect of some students of literature not in the thorough knowledge of our heritage, but in its opposite, namely, complete ignorance of our heritage. And in respect of those who have a good understanding of our heritage, it springs, in most cases, from hesitation, from a lack of boldness to put our heritage under a comparative light. In either case the result is the same; it is narrowness of outlook. Without going into any further details of this point, I would like to sum up this discussion with the following well known aphorism -

> He knows not England
> Who only England knows.

The only way to rise above narrow nationalism in literary studies is to cultivate internationalism; the only way to cultivate internationalism in literary studies is to develop Comparative Literature. If we cultivate this study dispassionately, in the truly scientific spirit, impartially, only to satisfy our curiosity, there is nothing to fear from jingoism and there is no scope for cultural expansionism. If we collect and sift all available evidence in this field with utmost honesty, care and logical rigour, avoiding the extremes of overstatement and understatement, there is nothing to fear from these pitfalls.

The proviso of rigorous scientific study is essential to prevent our subject from falling into another pitfall, namely, hasty, improvised researches. These will lead nowhere. This danger has particularly become apparent in recent years. Many research students with merely a nodding acquaintance with Indian Poetics or with Western Poetics have been fascinated by the possibilities of this new dimension of Comparative Literature. There is nothing wrong in the fascination; it must be welcomed. But it is essential to temper fascination with scientific rigour.

If cultivated thus avoiding these pitfalls, Indian Poetics will prove, I hope, to be a great boon to Comparative Literature as the entry of Sanskrit did a century ago to linguistics, comparative religion, culture and allied disciplines. It is a science of the future, and students of Comparative Literature will inevitably turn their attention increasingly to it for its great potentials. Max Muller predicted this possibility long ago while speaking in connection with other parts of our heritage; but his words are equally applicable to Indian Poetics as a new dimension of Comparative Literature. I deem it fit therefore to conclude this paper with his words:-

"Whatever sphere of the human mind you may select for your special study, whether it be language, or religion, or mythology, or philosophy whether it be laws or customs, primitive art or primitive science, everywhere you have to go to India, whether you like it or not, because some of the most valuable or most instructive materials in the history of man are treasured up in India and in India only."[6]

NOTES

1. International Comparative Literature Association - Proceedings of the Second Congress, North Carolina, Vol. I.
2. Ibid.
3. India - What Can It Teach Us? (1883, Lond. : Longmans), p. 29.
4. Ibid, p. 14.
5. *Coleridge on Imagination* p. 1.
6. *India - What Can It Teach Us*, p. 15.

Implications of the Concept of '*Aucitya*' for Criticism

V.N. Dhavale

Among the many hard and fast principles of criticism that ancient Sanskrit and Prakrit rhetoricians propounded, '*Aucitya*' is probably the last important contribution. *Aucitya* was primarily sponsored by the versatile and prolific writer Kṣemendra in the 11th century. The Sanskrit word *Aucitya* is generally translated as 'fitness', 'propriety', 'aptness', 'suitability', 'decorum' etc. This apparent latecomer in the field of Sanskrit poetics has usually been neglected, or casually noted, by writers dealing with ancient Indian poetic theory. Dr. S.K. De, for example, in his *History of Sanskrit Poetics* remarks:

> "There is hardly anything original in the theory औचित्य itself; for though it rightly insists upon a standard of propriety in poetic expression, it ultimately resolves itself into assuming a more or less variable criterion of taste or personal appreciation which आनंदवर्धन and others admit as *sahṛdayatva*..."

There seem to be many reasons for this comparative neglect. The chief reason perhaps is, that by the end of the 11th century innumerable aspects of poetic or literary greatness had been exhaustively described and analysed in great detail by several learned authors and commentators. Hardly anything that could appear original, revolutionary or seminal awaited discovery. The last great work in the long list of works, an aesthetic theory appeared in the 17th century the रसगंगाधर of the learned poet जगन्नाथ who also had to rely heavily on earlier works. औचित्य is, in a sense, the last important school of criticism. It must be admitted, however, that the significance of औचित्य in literary theory had been recognized by many aestheticians long before क्षेमेन्द्र emphasized it in his औचित्यविचारचर्या.

Certain well-known features appear to characterize all the basic theories of poetry in India —रस, रीति, अलंकार, ध्वनि, वक्रोकिन्त etc. The propounder makes the theory appear not only the best theory by and large, but also seems to regard it on some occasions as entirely self-sufficient. He barely notices the limitations of the theory. And since in most cases the illustrations are only short stanzas, many times only मुक्तकंठ (a detached stanza, the meaning of which is complete in itself), or stray verses from the great epics, plays or 'longer' poems. The theory appears to be convincing in that particular context. It need not, however, be so in all contexts. The description of various figures of speech (अलंकार) which engaged the attention of several rhetoricians naturally depends on short passages for illustration. But even more general theories such as रीति, वक्रग्रविम or औचित्य frequently rely on verses of two or four lines. It is time that some writers also take note of 'negative' examples in order to establish the importance of their point of view. क्षेमेन्द्र himself, for example, invariably cites negative instances also - that is those which are really characterized by the absence of औचित्य, according to him. It is also true that occasionally Sanskrit writers considered a long poem as a whole, as when *Ramayana* was described as an example of करुण रस. But the method followed by many writers often creates the impression that they are unable to see the wood for the trees. They concern themselves with very short passages. The unit for purposes of criticism is a particular detail. Each leader of a rhetorical school also makes emphatic statements which, taken out of context, appear to be uncompromising and dogmatic. For example, रीतिरात्मा काव्यस्य (वामन) काव्य स्यात्मा ध्वनिः (आनंदवर्धन), सैषा सदैव वक्रोकिन्त (भामह), अ चित्यं रससिद्धस्य स्थिरं काव्यस्य जीविनम् (क्षेमेन्द्र).

But in the course of discussion many of these authors recognize the relevance of other approaches also, and seem to take note of other theories. क्षेमेन्द्र himself admits the importance of *Rasa* for poetry in the statement cited above.

Ancient Indian rhetoricians looked for exactness in their theories. They define all the key terms used in their works, divide and subdivide the topics of discussion, and frequently indulge in detailed classification which, on the face of it, appears almost scintific and exhaustive. But the criteria used for classification are not always satisfactory, for sometimes they depend on grammatical details peculiar to Sanskrit. A good deal of discussion in the fields of अलंकार, रीति, ध्वनि etc. rests on certain peculiar features of the language. Thus the common use of सन्धि and समास, the absolute freedom in the field of syntax, in word-formation and sentence construction, are peculiarities which very few languages share - even Indian languages derived mainly from Sanskrit have given up many of these special features. No theory dependent on the exceptional characteristics of a particular language can be of univessal use or validity. This is naturally true of many concepts used in the discussion of अलंकार, रीति,, or even वक्रोकिन्त. The three concepts which appear to have wider application or utility are ध्वनि, औचित्य and of course the old theory of रस.

Before we take up the question of how for औचित्य is an 'apt' theory of poetry or literature, or of some aspects of literature, we must consider the general outline presented by क्षेमेन्द्र. At the outset, like many other writers on poetics, he offers a definition of the key term औचित्य :

उचितं प्राहुराचार्यः सहशं किर्या यस्य तत् ।
उचितस्य च यो भावस्त दौ चित्यं प्रचक्षते ।।
अलंकारा ए स्त्वलंकाराः गुणा एंव गुणाः सदा ।
औ चित्यं रससिदन्ध स्थिर्रे काव्यस्त्य जीवितम् ।

The second verse proves that क्षेमेन्द्र does not altogether ignore other aspects of poetry such as रस and अलंकार but merely insists on the all-pervasive importance of his own point of view. His definition, however, only tells us something which every school boy knows - viz., that औ चित्य is derived from उचित , and that whatever is सहिया (fit, becoming, suitable) in a given case is उचित .

How far is this concept new? And how far, whether old or new, is it really useful in practical criticism? That the theory is not really new or original can be easily proved. The great आनंदवर्धन had already commented on the significance of औचित्य in his ध्वन्यालोक and had summed up the matter in his well-known verse -

अनौचित्यद्ते नान्यद् रसभङ्गस्य कारणम् ।
प्रसिद्धौचित्यबन्धस्तु रसस्यो पनिषत् परा ।।

Dr. De has translated this verse as "There is no other circumstance which leads to the violation of *Rasa* than impropriety; The supreme secret of *Rasa* consists in observing the established rules of propriety." Several other authors also had considered the concept of औ चित्य in their discussion of गुण दोष etc. महिमभट्ट another well-known writer of the 11th century, described काव्यदोष as illustrations of अनौचित्य. Dr. Raghavan has given us the history of this concept (औचित्य) in detail in his *Same Concepts of the Alamkāra Śnstrā*.

क्षेमेन्द्र's special contribution to aesthetic theory is his ubiquitous insistence on औचित्य . He follows the usual practice of Sanskrit writers of making every theory as exact as possible and specifically mentions twenty-seven places or cases of application of his theory and concludes that other possible applications can, of course, he discovered by the reader on his own. The twenty-seven cases, however, prove that he does not care to discriminate between what is really general and what is only particular, between a matter of general utility and a matter of local detail. He mentions, for example, the importance of aptness or fitness in connection with many grammatical details such as verb, adjective, prefixes, gender, number etc., aptness in connection with general concepts such as रस, गुण etc. and also the very important aspect of all writing — aptness in the choice of words, in characterization and in the relation of some of these details to the work as a whole (प्रबन्ध) . There are also miscellaneous aspects of Sanskrit poetry which have very little significance for the modern reader — the use of the concluding stanzas in a long poem or critical work (आशीर्वचन) , or the significance of 'names' (नामौ चित्य). क्षेमेन्द्र 's comment on नामौ चित्य reminds us of the famous verse in प्रसन्नराघव :

गुणग्रामविसंवादि नामापि हि महात्मनाम् ।
यथा सुवर्ण श्रीखंड रत्नाकर सुरधाकराः ।।

Even a cussory glance at the list of twenty-seven points considered by क्षेमेन्द्र reveals no doubt the author's desire to be exact and exhaustive. But a modern reader cannot regard all the points equally relevant in a discussion of literature, especially modern literature. But ignoring for a while the traditional distinctions and classifications, our main concern should be with the propriety and utility of the concept of औचित्य itself. Does it help us in determining the greatness of literature? Is it a significant contribution to literary theory?

It is necessary, therefore, to examine the concept more critically. औ चित्य 's definition of औ चित्य is merely an etymological explanation. The abstract noun from the adjective उचित is औचित्य . It is the quality or state of being उचित . And उचित, according to scholars, is whatever is becoming, fit, right, suitable etc. in any particular case. Whenever we speak of fitness or suitability, two or more entities must be involved. औ चित्य can only be a relation between two ideas, entities, etc. It is not a self-sufficient, independent ultimate like goodness, beauty, happiness or pleasure. It is not an intrinsic value, but an instrumental value. Even in क्षेमेन्द्र's discussion the chief objective is रस not औचित्य for its own sake, whatever that might mean. औचित्य must always depend on several extraneous factors. Nothing, standing by itself, is eithr उचित or otherwise unless we place it in some situation and relate it to something else, that is, unless we provide a particular context.

Aptness (propriety, suitability) is one of those qualities or characteristics which are generally not noticed unless they are absent. Aptness, we may say, is conspicuous only by its absence. For example, when a man's speech, dress, manners and general behaviour are what we expect in a certain situation, we hardly notice these things and no comment is called for. It is only the absence of what we consider proper that invites unfavourable criticism. The concept of propriety presupposes a certain norm in any definite context. Since we are here concerned only with the concept of propriety in relation to poetry or literature, we must consider it in the light of various factors that influence our enjoyment of literature. Do we really expect or admire every kind of औचित्य in a literary piece? औचित्य may be regarded as a kind of *logical* relation. As Samuel Alexander pointed out long ago, "when a relation relates certain terms it makes a connected whole of those terms. The relation may be described as the whole situation into which its terms enter in virtue of that relation." Thus 'relation' must imply the togetherness of two or more entities in one situation, or one whole, whose parts fit in with each other. क्षेमेन्द्र is very much concerned with verbal, syntactic and structural propriety in poetry. In his long list of twenty-seven possibilities he even includes 'impropriety' in relation to space and time — particularly grammatical irregularities in the use of tense etc. Curiously enough he does not refer to anachronisms or anatopisms, though as factual errors they are examples of अनौचित्य My contention now is that in many cases we regard अनौचित्य as a mark of originality and greatness in literature. Shakespeare's innumerable grammatical irregularities create '*A Shakespearian Grammar*'. He tells us about gulio Romano in *The Winter's Tale,* and also about the sea-coast in Bohemia. And in *King lear* we are assured that

"This prophecy Merlin will make for I live before his time."

If the function of 'propriety' is to contribute to the total effect of poetry, the sentiment of रस which it generates, even factual errors are obviously improper. But our experience is that they sometimes add to our enjoyment, as malapropisims, for example, certainly do. They may better reveal 'character' or make a passage humorous, witty or even pathetic. 'Aptness' is not thus an absolute good. It can only claim instrumental value on certain occasions.

The praise of औचित्य is no doubt based on common sense and experience, especially in social life. But nothing in itself in either good or bad, but thinking makes it so. And nothing in itself is either proper or improper but the context, the situation makes it so. औचित्य therefore, is an *external* relation or a relational property. The relation is not necessarily dyadic or dual but may even be multiple, as when we try to judge propriety with reference to several entities. It may be possible to give our reasons why a certain phrase or situation, or a whole speech is inappropriate. But when we try to give our reasons we are mostly guided by our knowledge of several facts, perhaps relevant, but not necessarily based on the words we read: They are external facts. For examle, when क्षेमेन्द्र criticizes Kalidasa for using the word भव as a synonym for शिव in the well-known staza —

क्रोधं प्रभो संहर संहरेति
यावदि्‌न्गः खेमरूतां चरन्ति ।

तावत्स वन्हिर्भवनेम जन्मा
भस्मावशेषं मदनं चकार ।।

his knowledge of other synonyms for शिव, their literary suggestions and legendery associations are what guide him. The associations of the word भव are for him 'inappropriate'. क्षेमेन्द्र ignores the obvious possibility that perhaps Kalidasa's choice was determined by metrical fitness. क्षेमेन्द्र's comment on the stanza is a nice illustration of what literary criticism, may amount to, especially in the discussion of a writer's diction. It frequently expresses only a subjective preference, an instinctive response to a certain verbal arangement: and the critic's remarks we not necessairly convincing.

I feel there are far too many difficulties in accepting traditional औचित्य as the invariable concomitant of good writing. Though on the face of it we cannot assert that propriety is not a merit. The real problem for the critic who wants to use this yardstick for judging any literary piece will be, 'Is there any infallible criterion of propriety?' The concept is no doubt valuable in non-literary, situations, though even in social life, we know, there are the eccentrics and the rebels. Unconventional behaviour attracts the attention of all much more easily than normal or accepted behaviour. This is true of literature also. During the last five hundred years or more, unconventional details have been praised as the special merit of 'modern' literature. The history of western literature goes to show that literary greatness has generally been associated with novelty, with the avoidance of the expected and the familier. Every period in the history of any literature seems to have two types of writers — traditional writers who choose whatever is proper in diction, sentiment, structure, literary form, and even social and moral codes; and there are the rebels and experimenters, who violate the accepted sense of propriety in every possible way. Shakespeare here also seems to lead the way by announcing, like his own King Lear,

"No, they cannot touch me for coining; I am the King himself."

Since Shakespeare's experiments in grammar, syntax, verse-structure etc. are quite familiar to all I shall not cite any illustrations. Even the unconventional mixture of 'tragedy' and 'comedy', criticised by many contemporaries and even later critics, is an instance of the search which every great writer has to make to discover an 'appropriate' form. But at the time it is discovered, it is new and not appropriate for many. The inclusion of humour in great tragedy, the inclusion of sad and serious situations even in Romantic Comedy, the scant respect for the three unities, etc. are now regarded as the poet's great achievement. But was Shakespeare's method proper when it was first introduced?

It seems that originality must always violate the norms of propriety. We admire the 'conceits' of Metaphysical writers, and of their modern followers like T.S. Eliot. We want new companions, new imagery, new symbols: but for some critics they must appear 'improper'. Donne's reference to the 'two souls of lovers' as

'It they he two, they are two so
As stiff twin compasses are two..."

is a familiar illustration. Eliot supplies many more. Is Eliot's adaptation of various passages from English, French and other languages proper or improper? When we read Wallace Stevens's line 'The only emperor is the emperor of ice-cream' or Day dewis's phrase 'pasteurize mother's milk', can we apply the canon of propriety? What is 'charming and original' for some readers must appear 'shocking' to some others. There is no doubt that conventional propriety has been disregarded by many old and new writers. In the field of poetry, fiction, drama, we now admire the experimenters. But an experiment generally always involves a deliberate and more or less bold violation of simple propriety. Metaphysical poetry, the poetry of Eliot, Pound or the Surrealists, the fiction of steme, Games Joyce, goha Barth, the plays of Becket and Brecht, for one reason or another, attract us. But the reason cannot be that everything is 'apt', or expected. It is the unexpected word, scene, situation, imagery, structure, point of view, that really appeal to us.

Even Western critics, old and new, do off and on mention the relevance of propriety. But they do not turn it into a *sine qua non* of all good writing. It is present in many of Aristotle's well-known pronouncements, and also in some passages from other distinguished critics. One or two instances should suffice. Dr. Johnson, the great champion of rational and common sense criticism, naturally blames authors who suddenly lapse into impropriety. In his classic attack on Shakespeare's faults, he tells us:

> "He (Shakespeare) is not long soft and pathetic without some idle conceit or contemptible equivocation. He no sooner begins to more than he counteracts himself..."

And in his downright condemnation of Shakespeare's quibbles, he naturally invokes the canon of propriety:

> "A quibble, poor and bassen as it is, gave him such delight that he was content to purchase it by the sacrifice of reason, propriety and truth. A quibble was to him the fatal Cleopatra for which he lost the world and was content to lose it."

To cite a somewhat modern instance, the famous philosopher George Santayana, in his *Poehy and Religion* tells us that 'The poet is a rebuilder of the imagination' and adds:

> "For his (poet's) complete equipment, then, it is necessary, in the first place, that he sing: That his voice be pure and well pitched, and that his numbers flow; then, at a higher stage, his images must fit with one another..."

But we also know that the theory of the Imagination in the hands of its greatest exponents, Wordsworth and Colendge, indirectly challenges this very view of propriety, Coleridge, in his famous description of the Imagination in *Biographia Literaria* and elsewhere, insists on 'the balance or reconciliation of opposite or discordant qualities.' Are opposites normally compatible with each other? Coleridges' insistence on organic unity, or Aristotle's concept of 'probability', of course suggest's the importance of compatibility in every word or situation used in a poem or play. The parts must properly contribute to the total effect. But the theory of the Imagination (or प्रतिभा which is नवनवोन्मेषशालिनी प्रज्ञा) cannot be very happy with the theory of propriety. औचित्य in a way justifies the 18th century view of literature — that the writer should be guided more by 'Reason' than by anything else.

Moreover, the criteria for औचित्य will not necessarily be 'internal' or literary - they can frequently be extra-literary criteria. We consider any literary work in a specific spatial and temporal context. It is necessary, therefore, for the critic to collect information about social, linguistic, political, historical and other details before he can apply the touchstone of propriety to any literary piece. The judgment of literature must be guided by extra-literary factors. The claim that literature provides its own internal criteria for the critic is thus easily challenged. Even 'internal necessity' or 'organic unity' must be subjected to extra-literary considerations. It is obvious that the changes in language, in modes of thought, in social and political atmosphere, will affect our concept of propriety. The concept will be interpreted on the strength of the critic's own knowledge, his experience, and his expectations from literature. Propriety can also include the norms of morality. A critic who wants to examine propriety everywhere can end by becoming a moral critic. It is true that क्षेमेन्द्र does not fight shy of verses that may appear 'immoral' even to a modern reader. But he is certainly shocked by कालिदास's description of the romantic - physical love of gods and Kings. A critic may legislate for gods: but can he legislate against human behaviour?

My main contention is that the criterion of औचित्य will mititate against the modern preference for originality, novelty and individuality. In discussing 'aptness' in characterization, for example, क्षेमेन्द्र assumes that the characters in poems and plays are already known to the reader: that is, from sources other than the poem or play being criticised. This was possible because only historical or legendary characters were chosen as heroes and heroines. But what about later literature in which 'invention' is regarded as a great achievement? When we discuss even semi-historical characters like Lear, or Caesar, or Antory, we have to remember that the characters exist only in Shakespeare's plays. We know them only through Shakespeare's language — that is, it is the language and situations used by the poet that create his characters. How can we first form a judgment about these characters and then criticize the propriety of this or that phrase, this or that situation? The characters are created by the cumulative effect of Shakespeare's words. It is necessary, of course, that there should be internal consistency in a play or a poem. That every detail should satisfy the canon of probability, as Aristotle pointed out long ago. But even here, if we believe in modern psychological theories, especially some of the psychoanalytical schools, or general concepts in Abnormal psychology, we must think twice before invoking the uliquitous principle of औचित्य . Our entire attitude towards the use of language in literature has changed. So has our concept of structure in all fiction. This is true not only of English literature, but of several others. Language is being subjected to every kind of experiment in France and elsewhere — from the strict rule of the law to extreme lawlessness. In modern criticism, the law breaker is more respected than the one who is timid enough to follow the law. As in real life, in literary theory also, respect for the law is even theoretically condemned, and the law-breaker is, *ipso facto*, more respectable.

This is not to suggest that औचित्य is altogether a lost cause. It will have its champions in every age and country. But the concept is sometimes so vague and elusive that unless one wants to be condemned as old-fashioned and orthodox, no one will venture to use it. We like to enjoy jolts and shocks in literature, though not, of course, in real life.

Adbhuta in the Dénouement of Drama

Saroj Deshpande

Bharata, in the Nāṭyaśāstra (Nś), enjoins that "in all poetic works, literary artists should invariably employ *aḍbhutarasa* (the marvellous sentiment) in the *nirvahaṇa saṁdhi* (dénouement)."[1] As Bharataś concern is drama, this refers to dramatic works principally. The specific mention of *adbhuta* in denouement begs the question: what motive could there be behind this precept, or, in other words, why does Bharata regard *adbhuta* as essential in the dénouement? A clear or direct aswer to this is not provided either by Bharata or by later theoreticians who reiterate the precept. Perhaps Bharata had known such plays and gave scientific sanction to the common dramatic practice. Although it is claimed now that dramatic performances did take place in days prior to Bharata, yet no written plays of this early period are available to us. We cannot, therefore, say with certainty that Bharata gave scientific sanction to an already existing common dramatic practice; nor can we say that he found in *adbhuta* a convenient tool to wind up intriguing situations in the theme. The NŚ reveals such care and perception about detail concerning stage that it appears an untenable proposition. Bharata speaks at length and in minute detail about acoustics, gait, costumes, symbolical acting, stylised representation etc.[2] Unfortunately, however, historical evidence is lacking, and we can, at the best, postulate a working hypothesis that Bharata had thought *adbhuta* to be a structural, aesthetical and philosophical necessity. An absolute bifurcation of structure from aesthetics is not intended here. It is true that an inevitably developing structural pattern, in its necessary completeness, contributes substantially to its aesthetic quality. Yet the two are different in some respects and so the distinction. A careful analysis of the role *adbhuta* has to play in the dénouement, as Bharata intended it, reveals in the first place how *adbhuta* is a structural necessity, and in the second place, how the meaning and scope of *adbhuta* is restricted to allow only the joyous aspects, thus leading to a happy ending. A happy ending is a crucial factor in the design of drama since Sanskrit drama was devoid of formal tragedy.

Structurally, Sanskrit drama needs have *adbhuta* in the dénouement. The structure of drama, according to Sanskrit dramatic theory, is the scheme of *avasthās* (Stages) and *saṁdhis* (juncture) and *saṁdhyaṅgas* (parts of junctures). These form the infrastructure of the drama. "The main theme of drama covers the entire stretch of action of the principal character, the hero, who reaps the fruits of his own labour as well as of the endeavours of all those who support him. It must necessarily have a beginning and an end. As these two stages cannot sustain the interest in the action, they must be intervened by obstacles, efforts for their removal, success of such efforts and finally the ultimate success of the undertaking. In view of this psychological phenomenon, the entire dramatic action is divided into five stages."[3]

Drama is broadly classified by Bharata into ten types.[4] Each type has different objectives, span and magnitude. The member of *saṁdhis* in any type differs accordingly. Each type has as many *saṁdhis* as are suitable to the total design it has. Logically, however, it remains a structural necessity that all types should have two *saṁdhis*, *mukha* (beginning), and *nirvahaṇa* (dénouement). Adding Bharata's precept of *adbhuta* in the dénouement leads one to expect *adbhuta* in the dénouement of every play. By *adbhuta* Bharata means only those extra ordinary things which would arouse joyous wonder. Those which arouse fearful wonder do not become the determinants of the marvellous sentiment. A demon, a superhuman being arouses wonder. In Bharata's theory, a harmless demon like Ghaṭotkaca in the Madhyama-vyāyoga is a determinant of the marvellous sentiment, while a fearful one like Rāvaṇa arouses the terrible and a disgusting one like the demon-couple in Veṇīsaṁhāra arouses the hideous sentiment. Not all extra ordinary things are conducive to the marvellous sentiment, but only the agreeable and pleasant among the extra ordinary. The general mood of the *nirvahaṇa* is gay as is indicated by its various parts.[5] Bharata's insistence on the avoidance of other aspects of *adbhuta* and admission to the joyous wonderful alone in the dénouement rules out the possibility of tragedy. *Adbhuta*, by itself, is wide and comprehensive. It encompasses all aspects of the appalling including the sublime. But the sublime which derives its impact from a painful realisation of the smallness of human existence does not form a *vibhāva* (determinant) of the marvellous sentiment. Sanskrit dramatic theory does not admit the crushing, devastating, uprooting *adbhuta* in the province of *rasa*. Even as pitted against *adbhuta*, human existence is not conceived as petty or insignificant. It thus differs fundamentally from the sublime. This also lies at the root of the absence of formal tragedy. It deserves a reference in passing to the only tragedy worth the name. Bhāsa's *ūrubhaṅga*, a one-act play, is a formal tragedy. Bhāsa has set aside many directives of the NŚ and the explanation of this fact lies outside the scope of the present essay.

Stages and junctures form the infrastructure of drama. A juncture contains the dramatic content which is helpful to its corresponding stage. It gives a coherent picture of the stage with which it overlaps. The unit of *saṁdhi* is *saṁdhyaṅga* and it is manifest through dialogues in drama. Dialogues are necessarily interlinked, ensuring a smooth integration of the story. The scheme of pure action (*avasthās*) finds its projection in actual multiple action through *saṁdhis*.

To understand why *adbhuta* is essential in the dénouement it would do better to trace the development of the theme from the penultimate stage, *vimaraś*[6] (deliberation). The goal which appeared almost within reach is herein endangered due to fresh calamities. The effort and will of the hero and the obstacles and odds against him are matched. Suspense with an element of despair dominate this stage. This dénouement sees the hero pulled out to the final achievement of goal. *vimaraś* witnesses deadlock and stalemate, almost a hopelessness.[7] The way out of the jammed situation is *adbhuta*. It leads to the unexpected and hence more enjoyable attainment of the goal. Structurally, thus, *adbhuta* becomes essential. It must be noted here, that in Sanskrit plays, more often than not, the structure or design of a play is not an inevitably developing totality. The characters do not grow through situations.[8] They are stereotypes. The *Adbhuta* in the end looks like a perfect device in a weak and deliberate design, something resembling a "deus —ex machina" of the Greek theatre. Nevertheless, in the given framework of sanskrit drama with all its limitations, it must be admitted that *adbhuta* is structurally necessary in the dénouement.

Treating drama as an audio-visual medium, as a form, aesthetically, *adbhuta* becomes necessary. In the analysis of drama, audience is a very important factor. Sanskrit drama was a production for large audiences.[9] They were not drawing-room plays. This nature of the performances would explain the need for the portrayal of broad emotion. *Adbhuta* has easy mass-appeal. It ensures favourable audience response. As a form, drama has limitations of time and space. Notwithstanding these, a dramatist endeavours to keep the audience in the grip of interest throughout. He therefore employs the technique of tension and release of tension. He juxtaposes *hāsya* (laughter) to *karuṇa* (grief) and *adbhuta* to intrigue. The mounting tension and suspense in the *vimarśa-saṁdhi* followed by *adbhuta* in the *nirvahaṇa* serves both as a release of tension and a retainer of interest. This is why, as a form, drama needs have *adbhuta* in the final stage. If it comes through supernatural agencies, it magnifies the hero's greatness and helps the ennobling of the audience as intended by Bharata. It fruitfully serves the purpose of a desired happy ending. The NŚ categorically disallows formal tragedy. Bharata unequivocally says that death, except when there is a possibility of the revival of the hero,[10] and disaster should not be staged. Fall of a King, abdiction and the like[11] should also be avoided. A play is so structured as to avoid tragedy although the way to the happy ending be paved with tragic suffering.[12] The end should not be catastrophic. Bharata has excluded catastrophe both explicitly and implicitly, explicitly by giving a directive not to stage catastrophic events and implicitly by fixing the mood of the dénouement as gay. The insistence on avoiding tragedy seems to have two possible explanations. It can, firstly, be an adjustment to the medium. The epics Mahābhārata and Rāmāyaṇa being partly history and not only literature, were realistic. We find in them an acceptance of stark reality and life as it actually confronts persons. But the plays based on these very epics shun realism. They have an escapist approach to the themes which are handled and hence even facts are remoulded so as to suit the happy endings. The most glaring example is that of the Uttara-Rāma-Carita. The literary notion of poetic justice which was absent in the historical epics is dominant in the plays based on them.

The other explanation is based on the philosophical implications of the success or fall of the hero. Bharata's cryptic aphorisms do not lead us much further but Abhinavagupta's explanations of Bharata are a good guideline. Abhinava feels that unless a drama served some one of the *puruṣārthas* (goals of human life), through a relevant sentiment, its function would not be fulfilled.[13] The correlation of drama and sentiments to *puruṣārthas* ennobles the audience. Bharata wants drama not only to entertain, but to teach and ennoble.[14] The fruit which the hero desires being difficult to attain, the final success of the hero is an inspiration and an exhortation to the spectators. The task being extra ordinary, marvellous is used. *Adbhuta* in the context of an ordinary goal would be meaningless. The worthiness of the hero, the nobility of the goal, the magnificence of the entire action should lead to a joyous wonder and subsequent ennobling of the audience.[15] The hero has to emerge triumphant. He cannot be defeated. In a formal tragedy the fall of the hero is conceivable because he is too small for the forces which he fights, may those be external or internal. The fight and the final defeat are both conceived on a grand scale. According to Indian theory, the fall of the hero is inconceivable. It is incompatible with the philosophical concept of *puruṣārthas* The real aim in any field of activity is *mokṣa* (deliverance). Deliverance presupposes that human existence is a continuum. The hero might even be released through his apparent fall and death. The tragedy would then be absolutely superficial.[16] The idea of greatness in defeat is a commoplace in the Mahābhārata. In the later plays, greatness and defeat seem incongruent. Intrinsic worth has to be rewarded with material triumph. The great epics are both grand tragedies. The Mahābhārata is a saga of collossal waste, disaster and death. Fate plays a menacing role. It is not just realistic, but surrealistic. As a sharp contrast, the plays based on them are happy-ending escapist plays. They show the triumph of the good and the defeat of the evil - an idealistic moral value. Literature is supposed to produce idealistic models if it is to be an exhortation to people. The joyous *adbhuta* and happy ending are thus justified.

Adbhuta in the dénouement thus seems necessary from three points of view, structural, aesthetical and philosophical. The interpretation has two drawbacks although it is the only interpretation plausible. Firstly, perhaps we are reading too much in Bharata's words and secondly, it remains purely on the theoretical level, as is easily seen from the sanskrit plays. Abhinava speaks of a noble goal whereas in the plays the goal is no more than the search of a new beloved, fairer, lovelier and more youthful. The exhortation and ennobling remains only a theoretical standard. In practice, *adbhuta* becomes a technical aid, a situation which may, perhaps, explain the defeat of sanskrit drama.

NOTES

1. सर्वेषां काव्यानां नानारसभावयुक्तियुक्तानाम् ।
   निर्वहने कर्तव्यो नित्यं हि रसोऽद्भुतस्तज्ज्ञैः ।। NŚ 18.38
2. NŚ 2.19, 2.80, 81, 82, 2.100 etc.
3. S.N. Shastri - 'Laws and Practice of Sanskrit Drama' Delhi, pp 81
4. NŚ 18. 7, 8
5. NŚ 19. 61-63 and 19.90 to 96 along with the Abhinavabhārati on it.
6. NŚ 19.39.
7. Abhinavabhārati on NŚ 19.39
   तुल्यबलविरोधक विधीयमानवैधुर्य व्याधुनन संधीयमान स्फार फलावलधकनाया च पुरुषकारः सुत्तरामुद्धुरकन्धरमभिवतीति......
   .... स्थाहि पुरुषकार इ।।लिन एव श्राध्यन्ते .... प्राणसंदेहादपि अनेनात्मा समुत्तारितः ....
8. The hero in Bhāsa's Avimāraka serves as an illustration.
9. The open air theaters discovered near Sitabenga and Joginara in Madhya Pradesh.
10. Abhinavabhārati on NŚ 18.33
    किन्च यत्न प्रत्यापत्तिशून्यं मरणं तत्प्रक्रियाविहधत्वान्न अयधज्यम् ।
11. NŚ 18.33-35
12. Uttara-Rāma-Carita.
13. Abhinavabhārati on NŚ 6.
    तत्र पुरुषार्थनिष्ठाः काश्चित्संविदः इति आधान्यम - तधयारतिः कामत्तदनुषङ्गिधर्मार्थनिष्ठा, क्रधधस्ततत्श्रधानेत्वर्थनिष्ठ, कामधर्मपर्यवासितधऽपि उत्साहः, समस्तधर्मादिपर्यवसितः तत्वज्ञानजनितनिर्वेदत्रायध ज्ञमश्च मधक्षधपाय इति तावदेषां श्राधान्यम् ।
14. NŚ 1.14, 1.114, 115 etc.
15. Abhinavabhārati on NŚ 19.39
16. Duryodhana's death in ūrubhanga of Bhāsa.

Poetics of Hindi Prose A Study of an Essay in Method and Principles

Suresh Kumar

An experimental study of an essay by Hazari Prasad Dwivedi is presented to demonstrate the contribution, however modest, it can make to the intended aim of construction of the structuralist theory of Hindi essay as a part of theory construction for Hindi literature in terms of linguistic, literary, and cultural ethos of its own. It is proposed that the general theory of text semiotics, as being developed in the present times on a global basis, not only holds promise for fulfilling the objective but also, in all probability, for contributing to clarifying the issue as to how far we are able to hold our own in the wake of the pressures generated by the traditional Indian (i.e. Sanskrit) and western systems of poetics.

Perspective

The paper has a notional orientation to a certain extent with a certain aim. The intended aim is to provide for starting a dialogue for an immanent theory of literature for Hindi, or, for that matter, Marathi or any other Indian Language. The notion behind this aim is the feeling that we have yet to evolve a theoretical and methodological framework for literary texts of Hindi in a way as to be able to reflect the identity of the literary- creative tradition of Hindi language (despite) in keeping with its multifamous (its eclectic) character. Excessive dependence on canons of Sanskrit and Western poetics for constructing the foundation of Hindi literary theory is an oft-repeated observation. While the same could be validated for the initial stages of development of Hindi poetics, the same can hardly be justified in–the present times. There is a growing awareness to have something that may also look our own in addition to being our own in reality — reality of relatedness to the variety of text types of Hindi creative writing, especially of the present century.

It is proposed that the answer to this problem, in the present state of our knowledge, is the general theory of text semiotics. The theory of text semiotics is no doubt western in origin, but it is the language-based and generalized nature of this theory which accounts for the theoretical justification of the proposal by providing the heuristic basis for constructing the literary theory. The position adopted in this paper is that while the eclectic view of the problem is the right course, text-linguistically oriented study of literary writings of Hindi should form the central part of our theoretical framework. The eclecticism leaves us enough scope for maintaining the inheritance from Sanskrit poetics and assimilating the influence from Western poetics. What is important is that we have a strong consciousness of the basic commitment reflecting itself adequately in the critical practice.

It is in this sense that the term 'Indian Poetics and Literary Stylistics', one of the themes of this seminar, is understood in the present context. Accordingly, a poetics of Hindi prose would be developed in keeping with the linguistic, literary, and cultural ethos of Hindi prose writings. Developing a poetics of Hindi prose would require extensive work in descriptive stylistic analysis of a wide range of prose types within the theoretical framework of the general theory of text semiotics.

Speaking briefly, text semiotics is a multi-disciplinary system for the multi-dimensional and therefore multi-functional character of the text in which the study of 'language use' plays a central role. It is a three-tier system comprising text thematics, text stylistics, and text pragmatics which take care of the interactive and mutually dependent levels of content, language use, and situational dimension respectively. The term 'thematics' and 'pragmatics' are understood here in a somewhat extended and modified sense. As such, thematics covers the entire area of content, and pragmatics refers to the factors of the author's attitude towards the text and his readership.

The essay text by Dwivedi chosen for this study is नाखून क्यों बढते हैं 'why do the nails grow' — one of his much-discussed and much-admired essayistic writings, generally included in the anthologies of Hindi essay meant to serve as a reference volume or as a textbook for university students. Essay being the weakest of all the literary forms in the sense that it is the least convention ridden vis-a-vis poetry, fiction, and drama, is, for the same reason, the strongest candidate for such an experimental study as taken up here. Besides, the half-way house position it occupies between the extreme points of the literary and the non-literary, an essay is the happy hunting ground for a student of text semiotics. It is in the essay that the various dimensions of a literary text are revealed with moderate sophistication and therefore amenable to analysis and interpretation more convincingly and communicatively.

Analysis

We present below our analysis in the comprehensive framework set up above. The text is dealt with at thematic, stylistic, and pragmatic levels, followed by statements on the literary dimension and the specific character of the text, and general theoretical implications for poetics of Hindi prose.

Thematics of the Text

The main issues considered are: summary paraphrase; structure, and design.

Thematic summary paraphrase of the text

We cut the nails at regular intervals but they grow again. Why? They remind us of the many uses to which they have been put by man in course of the history of mankind. They have been used as weapons on one hand and cosmetic tools on the other. Besides, they remind us of the beastly instinct in the man which accounts for the use of nails as a weapon, not only in the past but even now also. However, man has always striven for progress, for elevation of his instinct, for turning a weaponlike thing into a cosmetic tool, for self-control — all symbolised in his cutting of nails at regular intervals. His drive for self-control is evinced from language as well where we have such words as स्वाधीनता, स्वतंत्रता and स्वराज्य wherein स्व signifies 'self'. In fact, self-control is the essence of the universal human religion. Though history is replete with instances of violence repeated at every stage, it also shows that man has always tried to exercise self-control. Speaking alternatively, nails have been growing ever since and man has been cutting them right thence.

Thematic Structure of the Text

The dialectic of 'growing of nails vs cutting of nails'[1] emerges as the superordinate thematic component of the text. This is the main proposition. It is reinforced by a series of dialectics of equivalent sub-propositions occurring variously in the text at irregular intervals:

Nature vs Man[2]
Beastliness vs Humaneness[3]
Impertinence vs Self-control[4]
Instinctiveness vs Restraint[5]

Supporting role is played by the factors of evidence and quote which may be identified as props. Evidence has been collected from such diverse fields as history, erotics, life sciences, and language to prove the main point. History of man[6], erotics[7], and life sciences[8] have something to tell us about the functions of the nails, while language has evidence to prove as to how man reacted to the tendency of nails growing again signifying his will to control himself[9]. The solitary quote is from Mahabharata to lend support to the implications of evidence from language[10]. While evidence from history and life sciences relates to the debit column of the series, it is the evidence from erotics and language together with the quote from Mahabharata which adds up to the credit column of the series.

Thematic Structural design of the Text

Vertically, the text appears to be a three-tier structure arranged in the hierarchy as given below:

Main proposition

Sub-propositions

Propping elements

Horizontally, it is repetition with variation of the main proposition along which are juxtaposed the sub-propositions and propping elements, cutting across the vertical column at different points to build up the texture of the text.

Stylistics of the Text

Language used in the text realises the thematic content in a way so as the text is received by the reader in a special manner. The 'special' in the manner not only affects the thematic dimension but also refers to the personal authority of the essayist together with the set of literary conventions of the specific genre to which the text belongs.

Syntactically, the variety of sentence patterns employed is dominated by statement sentences, interspersed with interrogatives with well-marked function. While the former are appropriate to the exposition of the thematic content by performing cognitive language function, the latter type underlines the proximity between the author and the reader by performing the phatic language function.[11] Series of imperatives in indirect mode of narration account obliquely for the element of pontification that the text appears to be communicating.[12]

Sentences employed are rather short and simple accounting for the higher level of communicability. In many a case, chains of short independent clauses are used which contribute to intensify the effect of the message in the micro-context.[13] Then there are antitheses,[14] almost restricted to the main proposition and the sub-propositions, to drive the point home carried by these categories.

Clarity and communicability are the main semantic features blended harmoniously with the special effect of contrast centered on antitheses as stated earlier. Lexical consistency achieved through by and large nativized lexicon, correlates directly with the above-mentioned semantic features. Even the special features of registral vocabulary — the technical terms — relating to distinct branches of knowledge, such as history, erotics, religion, and life sciences may be stated as coming from a rather familiar level of the stock of words, and thus pose no serious intelligibility gaps. However, there are a few expressions of Sanskrit origin accounting for *tatsamization*[15] in the otherwise nativized word stock, which nevertheless coexist with items from other layers of vocabulary within the sentence[16] as well as beyond the sentence within a given text fragment.

As for discoursal features, the text under study calls for special comments. It is right here that one is struck by the off beat behaviour of those features which are felt to be working against the norms of textual organization built up in the reader's mind by formal written prose of discursive type. Speaking in a general way, it is the texual incoherence that greets the reader and forces his attention on the intended meaning. The text fragments which go to build up larger units are rather loose-knit. As for surface level realisation, cohesive ties are used rather sparingly and in a deviant fashion. For example, use of ततः किम् in the beginning of the paragraph is a case of deviant cohesive tie.

Similarly, ties between larger organizing notions are also rather loose. The text boundary of the propping element of evidence from language (भारतीय भाषाओं नें प्रायः.....etc.) begins rather abruptly and shows no logical connection whatsoever with the textual representation of the preceding notion. Taken as a whole, it is heterogeneity rather than homogeneity that marks the discourse structure of the text.

Pragmatics of the Text

As for the pragmatic dimension of the text, we are impressed by the author's close involvement with the theme of the text signalled primarily through the first person personal pronoun मैं and its oblique forms.[17] We also take notice of the marginally informal and hence close relationship with the reader that the author seeks to enter into, and as such selects expressions dominated by the first person personal pronoun and other categories.[18]

Literary Dimension

The text analysed in the foregoing sections represents an exercise in the text-structural analysis of the creativity of language used in the genre of essay in the domain of Hindi literature by a specific author — Hazari Prasad Dwivedi. It has a quasi-logical character and an element of the author's personal involvement with the discourse theme as also his effort to establish close rapport with the reader. He draws heavily on the cultural heritage of the mankind in general and Indian society in particular for developing the central theme of his essay. He uses language in a way that is his own on the one hand and contributes to evolving the norm of language use in the genre of essay in Hindi literature on the other.

The Specific Character

It may be recalled at this point that we had emphasized the relative uniqueness of the linguistic, literary, and cultural ethos of a particular literature. How true it is, is proved by critical remarks on this very essay, bearing out the non-native view of Hindi literature, by a German student of my institute Hans-Jorg Paulenz who holds a Master's degree in Indology from Bonn in West Germany. His remarks read as follows:

"Dvivedi (D) on the one hand failed to discuss the various aspects of the function of nails, and on the other hand he presented a rather boring sermon on man's belligerent nature and human behaviour which should not have been discussed."

"Ideas presented by D lack originality and drive, and furthermore that his choice of words is poor and that his style of writing is neither brilliant nor interesting. Instead of being creative, D poroduced an essay of dubious literary worth, if it may be called literature at all."[19]

While Paulenz is entitled to his views, he appears to be oblivious of specific nature of norms of language use, literary appreciation, and cultural background relating to Hindi literature. Culturally, we are not averse to sermonizing in creative writings. Examined critically, the essay as a creative form, as compared with other literary forms, is a quasi-logical piece of writing. If a westerner reacts disapprovingly as regards originality and drive in Dwivedi's ideas, it is chiefly his sophisticated background which conditions his behaviour — a situation not necessarily shared by the Indian readers in general. His remarks on Dwivedi's choice of words will have to be taken with a pinch of salt, as is well known that the ability to appreciate norms of language use, that too in a foreign/second language, takes a long time to mature. On the whole, Paulenz's remarks are of great theoretical interest inasmuch as they represent the concept of interference in understanding and appreciating the non-native literature.

Conclusion

Generalisations of a limited nature are in order, at least for the limited purpose of the present paper. These relate to the essayistic writing in Hindi until stated otherwise.

Creativity of Hindi essay is defined by the following features: (a) Theme selection — There is no restriction on range. A mundane subject is treated in a serious manner and vice-versa producing a blend of the ordinary and the extra-ordinary. (b) Stylistic choices — Subjectivity in language use, establishing personal authority of the essayist, is sought to be matched by the communicativeness, thus establishing rapport with the readership. Equally important is the fact of textual incoherence, realising the quasi-logical character of the essay. (c) Pragmatic dimension — Author is closely involved with the text as well as with the addressee, which is evident from the choice of subjective and communicative language forms. We would like to conclude, on the strength of the above, that the structuralist view of the text and the correlating structural method of analysis should be the guiding principle for a poetics of Hindi prose.

NOTES

1. 'नाखून का बढना मनुष्य के भीतर की पशुता की निशानी है और उसे नही बढने देना मनुष्य की अपनी इच्छा है , अपना आदर्श है।
2. लेकिन प्रकृति है कि यह अब भी नाखून कध जिलाए जा रही है और मनुष्य है कि वह अब भी काटे जा रहा है।"
3. "........ उसके भीतर नख बढा लेने की जो सहजात वृत्ति है, वह उसके पशुत्व का प्रमाण है, काटने की जो प्रवृत्ति है वह उसकी मनुष्यता की निशानी है।"
4. "उच्छृंखलता पशु की प्रवृत्ति है, "स्व" का बंधन मनुष्य का स्वभाव है।"
5. "मनुष्य में जो घृणा है, जो अनायास – बिना सिखाए आ जाती है, वह पशुत्व का द्योतक है और अपने कध संयम रखना ...... मनुष्य का स्वधर्म है ।"
6. "कुछ लाख ही वर्ष की बात है, जब मनुष्य जंगली था, वनमानुष जैसाः उसे नाखुन की जरुरत थी । ..... वही उसके अस्त्र थे ।"
7. "कुछ हजार साल पहले मनुष्य ने नाखुन को सुकुमार विनोदों के लिए उपयद्यग में लाना शुरु किया था ।"
8. "मानव शरीर का अध्ययन करने वाले प्राणिविज्ञानिर्यी का निश्चित मत है कि मानव – चित्र की भांति मानव–शरीर में भी बहुत सी अभ्यास जन्य सहज वृत्तियाँ रह गयी हैं ।..... नाखुन का बढना उनमें से एक है ।"
9. "उसने अपनी आजादी के जितने भी नामकरण किये – स्वतंत्रता, स्वराज्य, स्वाधीनता – उन सब में "स्व" का बंधन अवश्य रखा ।"
10. "एतद्धि त्रितयं श्रेष्ठं सर्वभूतेषु भारत ।
11. "मेरा मन पूछता है– किस अधर ? मनुष्य किस अधर बढ रहा है ? मनुष्यता की अधर या पशुता की अधर ?"
12. "एक बूढा । उसने कहा था– बाहर नहीं, भीतर की ओर देखो, हिंसा को मन से दूर करो, मिथ्या कध हटाओ ......।"
13. "नाग हारे, सुपर्ण हारे, यक्ष हारे, गंधर्व हारे, असुर हारे, राक्षस हारे ;" बडे–बडे नेता कहते हैं, वस्तुओं की कमी है, और मशीन बैठाअध, और उत्पादन बढाओ, और धन की वृद्धि करो, और बाह्य उपकरणीं की ताकत बढाओ ।"
14. Sentenees in notes 1—S.
15. "तुम वही लाख वर्ष पहले के नखदंतावलम्बी जीव हो ।" "ततः किम्" । "सिक्थक और अलकतक"। "लेकिन समस्त उधहोगामिनी वृत्तिर्यी को ....."। "अंगरेजी की अनुवर्तिता ....."। "....नयी अनुसंधित्सा.."।
16. '..... चक्कर में डाल देने वाले प्रश्न "(but not विभ्रमकारी प्रश्न) ।" "अस्त्र बढाने की प्रवृत्ति ..." (but not अस्त्रवृद्धि की प्रवृत्ति) ।" "पशुता की निशानी" (but not पशुता का चिन्ह)" असल में, सहजात वृत्तियाँ ..." (but not वस्तुतः, सहजात वृत्तियाँ) ।
17. "मेरा मन पूच्छता है ....": "मेरी निबर्धध बालिका ने ...": "मैं पूछता हूँ...": "मैं ऐसा नहीं मान्ता ....": "मुझे आश्चर्य होता है...."।

18. "बच्चे कभी–कभी चक्कर में डाल देने वाले प्रश्न कर बैठते हैं । "..इस बात से बच्चीं को परिचित करा देना वांहनीय जान पडता है कि ..." । "बच्चे यह जाने तो अच्द्धा हद्य कि ...." ।

19. समन्वय (27), 1986: केंद्रीय हिन्दी संस्थान, आगरा ।

REFERENCES

De Beaugrande, R.A. and Dressler, W.U. 1981. *Introduction to Textlinguistics*. London: Longman

Borbe, T. (ed.) 1983. *Semiotics Unfolding Vol. II*: Semiotics in Text and Literature; Linguistics and Semiotics.

Berlin-New York-Amsterdam: Mouton Publishers.

Chatman, S. (ed.) 1971. *Literary Style : A Symposium*. Oxford: The University Press.

Dolezel, L. 1971. Toward a structural theory of content in prose fiction. In: Chatman (ed.), 95-110

Dressler, W.U. 1977. *Current Trends in Textlinguistics*. Berlin m New York: de Gruyyer.

Eco, U. 1979. *The Role of the Reader*. Bloomington and London: Indiana University Press.

Grabe, w. 1984. Written discourse analysis. *Annual Review of Applied Linguistics* 5, 101-23.

Hawkes, T. 1977. *Structuralism and Semiotics*. London: Methuen.

Kelkar, Ashok R. 1969. The being of a poem. *Foundations of Language* 5, 17-33.

------- 1970. Some notes on language and literature. *Indian Linguistics* 31.3, 1-11.

गेंद्र 1985. भारतीय समीक्षा और आचार्य शुक्ल की काव्यदृष्टि । दिल्लीः राजपाल एण्ड सन्स ।

Scholes, R. and Klaus, Carl H. 1969. *Elements of the Essay*. Oxford: The University Press.

Suresh Kumar 1977. Discourse structure and literary interpretation. *Indian Linguistics* 38, 145-50.

------- 1981. Discourse structure in a Hindi short story.*Studies in Linguistic Sciences* 11.2, 51-66.

Zydatiss, W. 1983. Text typologies and translation. *The Incorporated Linguist* 20.4, 212 ff.